by land or by sea

Cuisine of the United States Power Squadrons®

by land or by sea

First Printing   October, 2004   3,000 copies

ISBN 1-891148-41-9

Copies of **by land or by sea** may be obtained by sending $25.00 plus $6.95 shipping to the address below.

United States Power Squadrons
P.O. Box 30423
Raleigh, NC 27622

Order froms are located in the back of the cookbook.

WIMMER
COOKBOOKS

A CONSOLIDATED GRAPHICS COMPANY

800.548.2537   wimmerco.com

Table of Contents

Denotes—Recipes Kids Can Make

Denotes—Recipes Good For The Boat

*Denotes—Recipes from the Current Chief Commander,
Past Chief Commanders and their wives*

The Ladies Auxiliaries of USPS – A Brief History

When USPS was formed in 1914 by a group of men, it was founded on the customs of the current times, which believed strongly that men had their clubs and women had theirs and the twain should never mix. This premise held sway for 28 years but started to crack in Seattle, Washington. The Seattle Power Squadron received its charter in the spring of 1941 and held their first Seamanship class. Several of the members' wives took this course receiving a "Certificate of Accomplishment" upon completion. These same women along with a few others realized they could be of great use to their new squadron, and in 1942 proceeded to form the Women's Auxiliary of the Seattle Power Squadron a.k.a., the WASP's. Their commander contacted National who told them there were no other auxiliaries in USPS, but he saw no reason why they shouldn't have one. That was good enough for the WASP's who were off and running, writing their by-laws and electing officers, teaching themselves boating skills and enjoying each others companionship. The ladies soon became well established raising money for squadron, attending social functions and doing all sorts of volunteer chores for the squadron. The ladies wrote, published and sold a cookbook, *Galley Grub,* which proved very profitable for them. The ladies sold them by the hundreds even at the Seattle Boat Show where they put on cooking demonstrations. Through their efforts in founding the first auxiliary, many other auxiliaries were encouraged to start as the Seattle PS helped their neighbors to establish squadrons in Bellevue, Everett, Possession Sound and Poverty Bay, Washington.

In 1954 as auxiliaries spread among the squadrons of USPS, the members of the National Bridge decided that a committee should be formed to handle requests from and to answer questions for these new auxiliaries. The first committee had no official title or home. It was only in 1958 that the Auxiliary Advisory Committee was created as a new committee within the Administrative Dept. Since women were not members of USPS at this time, the committee had all male members. This changed, however, with the vote to offer membership to women in 1982. In 1983 the first women joined the committee and women have made up the majority of the committee members since then. The first woman chairman of the committee was P/R/C Priscilla B. Clarke, AP. Several more ladies have filled this role since then. Today the committee is charged with the responsibility to provide support and to aid the auxiliaries of USPS. They review by-laws, produce a directory of auxiliary officers, provide an on-line newsletter, and have a meeting at each Governing Board where auxiliary members can share ideas for fund raising, interesting programs and ways to gain and retain members. Up to date information concerning the Auxiliary Advisory Committee can be found on the USPS web site under the Administrative Dept. The committee members are always willing to lend a helping hand to the auxiliaries of USPS.

As with all good ideas, word of the Western auxiliaries started to spread throughout USPS and auxiliaries started to organize in many parts of the country. Following the lead of their Western sisters, auxiliaries became the usual and not an exception in the Mid-West and the Southern squadrons. In 1987 there were 125 auxiliaries officially listed by the Ladies Auxiliary Advisory Committee. These auxiliaries purchased most of the office equipment needed as well as many of the projectors, overhead projectors, screen, speaker system, etc. This in addition to organizing parties, cooking, serving refreshments at meetings and boating classes, and teaching safe boating classes to youngsters. The New York State's text, *Make Safe Make Shore,* was used by many of the auxiliaries over the years to make youngsters safer around the water.

In 1982 USPS after 68 years as a male only organization, the members voted to open membership to women. This gesture, embraced by many women, was the first step in the gradual disbandment of many of the auxiliaries. Other reasons consisted of the all too common problem of filling the officer slots and the busy schedules of many working women in today's world. The WASP's, our first auxiliary was no exception and in 1992 voted to disband. However, there are still bright spots among the auxiliaries. The Daytona Beach Auxiliary voted to disband several years ago for the usual reasons. The ladies who enjoyed each other's company and who were still hard at work for the squadron voted to reorganize last year and are going great guns. Some of the auxiliaries have been showing some growth and their efforts are recognized by the Auxiliary Advisory Committee each year at a Governing Board with an appropriate plaque which they are proud to display. Today only 35 auxiliaries remain of the 125, however, most are still active in supporting their squadrons and making the squadrons social functions run smoothly.

This cookbook, a compilation of many recipes from past and present auxiliary members as well as our past chief commanders, is a good testament of the hard work and dedication of the women of USPS. Read it, use the recipes (all of which have been tested) and enjoy.

Acknowledgments

The Auxiliary Advisory Committee is grateful for the combined efforts of a great number of USPS members who contributed to the success of this book not only with their recipes and testing of recipes, but their time and support of this undertaking.

Special recognition is offered to P/C/C Richard W. Miner, SN and Nancy Miner. They collected recipes and tested recipes but their encouragement and enthusiasm was priceless. P/C/C Miner sold books and sold the idea of a national cookbook.

The Operating Committee for 2002-2004 was especially helpful with the logistics of such a project as this book. Special recognition is due P/C/C Theodore H. Smith, SN, for taking the message out to the Squadrons with his Chief's message. The Chief's representatives invited members to participate and see their recipes in print. V/C Ernest G. Marshburn, SN, was the catalyst in beginning a National Cook Book and his help was of great importance in the book's birth.

P/R/C Kenneth D. Link, JN, prepared the break pages that are so important in telling the UNITED STATES POWER SQUADRONS story and mission for serving the boating public through education. P/D/C Mary Jane Schnoor, SN, researched the history of the Squadron Auxiliaries.

The Law Committee, Flag and Etiquette Committee, and Marketing Committee are to be recognized for their contributions.

The members of the Auxiliary Advisory Committee are grateful for all the efforts extended to them which aided in the completion of the first national cookbook. A special thanks goes to Editor Donna M. Selden. Without her work and dedication there would be no BY LAND OR BY SEA, CUISINE OF THE UNITED STATES POWER SQUADRONS. Her vision of a great book and her organizational skills were very necessary to this edition. She brought the ideas to reality. We of the Committee are indebted to her and her vision.

The members of the Auxiliary Advisory Committee are Assistant Chairman, Stf/C Lois Neef, S, the main typist and record keeper for the data base, P/R/C Patricia C. Armstrong, JN, Joyce Bruner, D/Lt Marion Cartwright, P/R/C Priscilla B. Clarke, AP, D/Lt Reyna Henry, SN, D/Lt/C Judy Holmes, AP, Sally Lemus, D/Lt/C Gloria Schulke, AP, Editor Donna Selden, S, D/Lt Jane Keil, P/R/C Franklin P. Wright, SN, and Chairman, R/C Carmen Adame, AP.

Power Boats Save The Day!

This might have been the newspaper heading in 1912 when a small group of power boating enthusiasts from the Boston Yacht Club aided a flotilla of sailors caught in a sudden storm. This story has repeated itself, but in different ways over the 90 year history of the United States Power Squadrons (USPS).

Charles Chapman, associate editor of Motor Boating Magazine gave the idea of a power squadron full-page coverage and in 1913, thirty delegates from several yachting clubs in the New York area joined together to begin discussions about a new organization called the United States Power Squadrons.

From that meager beginning came what is today an organization of nearly 60 thousand dedicated family boating enthusiasts who serve their communities and our nation. As partners with government agencies and other non-profit groups, USPS provides safe boating education, reliable waterway charts, vessel examinations, environmental support, homeland security and are a resource for boating course materials for partners like the American Canoe Association.

Elsewhere in this cookbook are short items about the work of the members of USPS. We hope you find the information interesting and will consider becoming a member of the largest and greatest fraternity of family boating enthusiasts, educators and civic service providers.

Won't you join us? For more information call 1-888-367-8777

Thanks for listening!

USPS Cookbook –
Motorboats To The Rescue – 1912

Artist Demers, depicts The Great Rescue!

The picture on the cover of this cookbook represents the efforts of Donald Demers, a renowned marine artist. His works are considered masterpieces. In the early years of motor boating in the United States, many were used as tenders for sailors who needed transport if their sail boats were becalmed. Mr. Demers delved into the archives of the New York Yacht Club library and other repositories of data relating to early nautical history to research information on an incident which occurred during July of 1912.

Many yacht clubs like the Boston Yacht Club had sailors with motor tenders used for transport. These yachtsmen would bond together on weekends, and in the case of the Boston Yacht Club would perform drills to increase their skills and knowledge in small boat handling, deck work, performance and safety.

During July of 1912, on a weekend sail by members of the Boston Yacht Club a sudden storm arose placing many of the sail boats in distress, ripping sails from masts and dismasting several. Roger Upton, one of the founders of the United States Power Squadrons and other power boat owners, risk life and limb, some in the middle of then night, to come to the aid of the sailors. An article on the rescue was prepared by George Story in the September issue of *Motorboat Magazine*.

Mr. Demers has captured the spirit of the rescue in this outstanding painting, presented to the United States Power Squadrons on the occasion of their 90th Anniversary as an organization. Enjoy the detail, feel the spray in your face and the sense of excitement and anxiety as these early motor boaters worked to rescue their friends from possible disaster.

If you have more interest in the history of the United States Power Squadrons, call 1-888-367-8777.

Won't you join us?

appetizers
& beverages

power squadron auxiliary

Hi Cheryl, what are you doing for lunch?

This call and many like it have been the genesis of an organization which is the backbone of support for many of the USPS squadrons. We hope you have read, in this cookbook, about the wonderful work of the United States Power Squadrons by its many units spread across the country.

If you have an interest in boating safety education, helping plan social events and arranging for guest speakers, working on activities for young boaters and the many other activities of the local squadrons then this group is for you.

Begun in Seattle, Washington in 1941, the USPS Auxiliaries organization has a long heritage of working shoulder to shoulder with squadron members on boating education and civic service projects including the environment, vessel safety, cooperative chart work, youth activities and many other squadron functions.

The auxiliaries provides speakers for local civic groups on the work of USPS and boating safety education. Would you consider looking into the United States Power Squadrons Auxiliary organization?

For more information call 1-888-367-8777. Thanks for listening!

D/5 Mainline Mainstays, Miles River
   The Half-Miles, Sue Island Wasips

D/6 Rochester Squadronettes

D/7 Rocky River Riverbelles

D/8 Homestead Haps, Pompano Beach
   Power Squadron Auxiliary,
   Vero Beach Shipmates

D/9 Flint Power Squadron Auxiliary,
   Wyandotte Wyandottes

D/13 Covina Squadronettes,
   San Fernando Valley Squadronettes,
   Santana White Caps, Valley Ho Sea Gals

D/15 Fort Walton Ahoy, Mobile Maps,
   New Orleans Ladies Auxiliary

D/16 Bellevue Sea Belles

D/17 Atlanta Sail & Power
   Squadron Auxiliary

D/20 Decatur Anc-Hers

D-22 Anclote Key Tarps, Anna Maria
   Island Helpmates, Cape Coral Cape
   Mates, Clearwater Caps, Fort Meyers
   "C" Belles

D/23 Banana River "Peels", Cocoa
   Beach Coco-Nauts, Daytona Beach
   Sea Siters

D/24 Wabash Valley Firstmates

D/26 Lake Hartwell Power & Sail
   Squadron Auxiliary

D/29 Columbus Seagals

D/32 Fort Vancouver Lady Skippers

Shrimp Mold

1 (10¾-ounce) can cream
    of shrimp or chicken
    soup
1 (8-ounce) package cream
    cheese, softened
1 cup mayonnaise
1 tablespoon water
1 (¼-ounce) envelope
    unflavored gelatin

1 cup chopped celery
2 bunches green onion,
    chopped
1 pound small shrimp,
    cooked, peeled and
    deveined
   Chopped lettuce leaves
    and assorted crackers

DID YOU KNOW?

*If the sky is red in
the evening, the weather
will probably be pleasant
the next day? Don't forget
to check the weather each
day before boating.*

Cook and stir soup and cream cheese until smooth. Stir in mayonnaise.
Remove from heat. Combine water and gelatin. Add to soup mixture.
Add celery, onion, and shrimp and mix thoroughly. Pour mixture
into a greased mold. Refrigerate overnight. Unmold onto a bed of
chopped lettuce. Serve with crackers.

Yield: 6 to 8 servings

Priscilla Leathers • San Diego Power Squadron • California

Layered Crab

3 (4-ounce) packages
    cream cheese, softened
2 tablespoons
    Worcestershire sauce
1 tablespoon lemon juice
2 tablespoons mayonnaise
1 small onion, minced
   Garlic salt to taste

1 (6-ounce) bottle chili
    sauce
1 cup shredded crabmeat
½ cup shredded mozzarella,
    Cheddar, or Monterey
    Jack cheese
   Chopped black olives
   Wheat or assorted crackers

Combine cream cheese, Worcestershire sauce, juice, mayonnaise,
onion and garlic salt. Press mixture into a plastic wrap lined 9-inch
pie pan. Cover and refrigerate. When ready to serve, invert onto a
platter. Remove plastic wrap. Top with a layer of chili sauce, crabmeat,
cheese and olives. Serve with wheat or assorted crackers.

Yield: 10 to 12 servings

Robert C. Flint • Seminole Power Squadron • Florida

DID YOU KNOW?

"Warming up" the engine is best done by cruising at half speed. Idling for long periods of time is bad for mechanical components. Be sure the engine is sufficiently warmed to prevent stalling when power is applied.

Crab Cheese Pâté

½	pound crabmeat	¼	teaspoon pepper
1	tablespoon lemon juice	1	(8-ounce) package cream
1	tablespoon minced onion		cheese, softened
1	tablespoon prepared	¼	cup pecans
	horseradish	2	teaspoons snipped parsley
			Assorted crackers

Combine crabmeat, juice, onion, horseradish, pepper and cream cheese. Mix until well blended. Stir in pecans and refrigerate until firm. Form mixture into a fish shape on a serving board or platter. Garnish with parsley. Serve with crackers.

Yield: 6 to 8 servings

Ernie Marshburn • Tar River Sail & Power Squadron • North Carolina

Crab Stuffed Baby Portobellos

24	(1-inch) baby portobello mushrooms		Dash of pepper
1	(8-ounce) package cream cheese, softened	1	pound crabmeat, finely chopped
½	cup finely chopped green onion	1	cup finely chopped tomatoes
¼	cup mayonnaise	½	cup finely shredded mozzarella cheese
1	teaspoon lemon juice	½	cup finely crushed herb stuffing mix
½	teaspoon Old Bay seasoning	12	grape tomatoes, halved

Preheat oven to 425 degrees. Remove stems and scoop out inside of mushrooms. Discard stems and inside pieces. Set caps aside. Beat cream cheese until smooth. Add green onion, mayonnaise, juice, seasoning and pepper. Mix well. Stir in crabmeat, tomatoes and cheese. Spoon mixture evenly into mushroom caps. Sprinkle each with 1 teaspoon bread crumbs. Place on a baking sheet. Bake at 425 degrees 10 minutes or until tops are lightly browned. Garnish with a tomato half.

Yield: 6 to 8 servings

Charlotte Ward • Hilton Head Power Squadron • South Carolina

Hot Crab Dip

3   (6½-ounce) cans crabmeat
3   (8-ounce) packages
      cream cheese, softened
2   tablespoons prepared
      mustard
1   tablespoon powdered
      sugar
½   cup mayonnaise
½   cup white wine
1   tablespoon onion juice
1   tablespoon lemon juice
    Assorted crackers

Combine crabmeat, cream cheese, mustard, powdered sugar, mayonnaise, wine, onion juice and lemon juice in the top of a double boiler. Cook and stir over low heat until smooth and bubbly. Serve with assorted crackers.

Yield: 10 to 12 servings

Priscilla B. Clarke   •   Swiftwater Power Squadron   •   New York

Salmon Ball

2   (7½-ounce) cans salmon,
      drained, remove bones
      and skin, flaked
1   (8-ounce) package cream
      cheese, softened
1   tablespoon lemon juice
2   teaspoons minced onion
1   teaspoon horseradish
½   teaspoon salt
¼   teaspoon liquid smoke
½   cup chopped pecans
3   tablespoons snipped
      parsley
    Assorted crackers

Combine salmon, cream cheese, juice, onion, horseradish, salt and liquid smoke. Mix well. Shape into desired size balls. Wrap in plastic wrap and refrigerate several hours. Combine pecans and parsley. Roll balls in pecan mixture until well coated. Refrigerate until ready to serve with crackers.

Yield: 6 to 8 servings

Tammie Tartar   •   Seattle Power Squadron   •   Washington State

Salmon Log

2 (7½-ounce) cans salmon,
   drained, remove bones
   and skin
1 (8-ounce) package cream
   cheese, softened
2 tablespoons minced
   onion

1 teaspoon horseradish
¼ teaspoon salt
1 teaspoon liquid smoke
½ cup chopped walnuts
3 tablespoons snipped
   parsley
   Assorted crackers

Combine salmon, cream cheese, onion, horseradish, salt and liquid smoke. Mix thoroughly. Shape mixture into a log and wrap in foil. Refrigerate 2 hours. Combine walnuts and parsley. Roll log in nut mixture. Serve with crackers.

Yield: 6 to 8 servings

Gerry Desmarais • Winooski Valley Sail and Power Squadron • Vermont

Ruby Salmon Spread

1 (7-ounce) can red
   salmon, drained
1 (8-ounce) package cream
   cheese, softened
1 teaspoon lemon juice

5 green onions, finely
   chopped
   Salt, pepper and garlic
   powder to taste
   Crackers, toasted bagel
   chips or pita chips

Combine salmon, cream cheese, juice, green onion, salt, pepper and garlic powder. Mix thoroughly with a fork. Cover and refrigerate 2 to 24 hours. Serve with crackers, bagel chips or pita chips.

Yield: 20 servings (2 cups)

Nancy Miller • Marathon Power Squadron • Florida

Pickled Oysters

3 dozen medium oysters, shucked
1 medium red onion, thinly sliced
2 red chili peppers, slivered
½ tablespoon peppercorns

1 bay leaf
½ cup cider vinegar
½ teaspoon salt
Dash of Tabasco sauce
Round buttery crackers

Plunge oysters into 4 cups boiling water. Remove from heat and let stand 5 minutes. Drain well. Layer oyster, onion, pepper, and peppercorn in a pint jar. Place bay leaf halfway up jar. Whisk together vinegar, salt and Tabasco. Pour into jar. Seal and refrigerate at least 3 days. Use small cocktail forks and serve with round buttery crackers.

Yield: 8 to 10 servings

Lynn Wythe • Lake Murray Power Squadron • South Carolina

DID YOU KNOW?

A vessel less than 7 meters (about 21 feet) is not required to show an anchor light if anchored in an area not normally navigated by other vessels? Its wise to know the navigation rules.

Spicy Cheese Wrapped Pigs

2¼ cups all-purpose flour
1 cup cornmeal
1½ teaspoons baking powder
¼ teaspoon baking soda
½ teaspoon salt
⅔ cup vegetable shortening

1 cup shredded sharp Cheddar cheese
1¼ cups buttermilk
1 pound mini smoked sausages
Assorted dipping mustards

Sift together flour, cornmeal, baking powder, baking soda and salt. Cut in shortening. Add cheese. Stir in buttermilk until dough forms into a ball. Turn out onto a floured surface. Knead 5 to 7 times. Divide into 6 balls. Roll each ball into a 6-inch diameter circle. Cut into 8 wedges with a pizza cutter. Place a sausage on the wide edge and roll up. Place seam-side down on a greased baking sheet. Bake at 500 degrees 8 to 10 minutes. Serve warm with assorted dipping mustards.

Yield: 12 servings

Carolyn Black • Everett Power Squadron • Washington State

Char Siu (BBQ Pork)

2-3 pounds pork loin or butt,
   cut into chunks
1   tablespoon salt
1   tablespoon hoisin
   (sweet Chinese sauce)
1   tablespoon soy sauce
¾   cup sugar

½   teaspoon Chinese five
   spice seasoning
2   teaspoons red food
   coloring
1   tablespoon sherry
   Sesame seeds and hot
   mustard for garnish

Place pork in a 1-gallon zip-top plastic bag. Combine salt, hoisin, soy sauce, sugar, five-spice seasoning, food coloring and sherry. Pour mixture into bag, turning to coat meat. Marinate in the refrigerator overnight. Bake pork at 250 degrees 45 to 50 minutes, basting with marinade. Thinly slice pork then sprinkle with sesame seeds and serve with hot mustard.

Yield: 6 to 8 servings

Jeanette Myers • Agate Pass Power Squadron • Washington State

JEZEBEL SAUCE

1 (18-ounce) jar
pineapple preserves
1 (18-ounce) jar apple
jelly
1 (5-ounce) jar
horseradish
1 (1-ounce) can dry
mustard
Cream cheese, softened
and crackers

Combine preserves, jelly, horseradish and mustard. Mix well. Refrigerate 2 to 3 days. Pour over cream cheese and serve with crackers.

Yield: 3 cups

Carol Stidger
Berkshire Power Squadron
Massachusetts

Ham Ring

2   (8-ounce) packages
   refrigerated crescent
   rolls
¾   cup shredded Swiss
   cheese
¼   cup diced cooked ham
2   cups chopped broccoli

1   small onion, chopped
2   tablespoons Dijon
   mustard
1   teaspoon lemon juice
¼   cup chopped parsley

Unroll dough. Place triangles on a 12-inch pizza pan forming a ring with the pointed ends facing outer edge of pan, wide ends overlapping. Press wide ends together. Combine cheese, ham, broccoli, onion, mustard, juice and parsley. Spoon mixture over wide ends of triangles. Fold points over filling and tuck under the wide ends. Bake at 375 degrees 20 to 25 minutes.

Yield: 8 to 10 servings

Rosemary Halligan Enoch • Quad City Power Squadron • Iowa

Deviled Ham Dip

½ cup sour cream
1 (4½-ounce) can deviled
    ham
2 tablespoons pickle relish

¼ teaspoon Worcestershire
    sauce
   Dash of salt and garlic salt
   Crunchy crackers or chips

Combine sour cream, ham, relish, Worcestershire sauce, salt and garlic salt. Mix well. Serve with crackers or chips

Yield: 4 servings

Rosemary Hurley • Cape Cod Power Squadron • Massachusetts

Ham and Asparagus Cheesecake

1 sleeve round buttery
    crackers, crushed
6 tablespoons butter, melted
1 (8-ounce) package cream
    cheese, softened
3 large eggs
1 (8-ounce) container sour
    cream
¼ cup all-purpose flour
¼ teaspoon pepper

1 cup shredded Swiss cheese
1¼ cups diced cooked ham
1 pound asparagus,
    trimmed and cut into
    1-inch pieces or
    2 (10½-ounce) cans,
    drained
4 green onions, minced
   Chopped green onion
    and cooked asparagus
    tips for garnish

Combine cracker crumbs and butter. Press into the bottom of a 9-inch springform pan. Bake at 350 degrees 10 minutes. Cool on a wire rack. Reduce oven to 300 degrees. Beat cream cheese 2 to 3 minutes until light and fluffy. Add eggs, one at a time, beating well after each addition. Add sour cream, flour, and pepper and beat until well blended. Stir in cheese. Pour one-third cheese mixture into pan. Layer with ham. Pour one-third cheese mixture over ham. Layer asparagus and onion. Top with remaining cheese mixture.

Bake at 300 degrees 1 hour or until center is set. Turn off oven, with door ajar and leave cake in oven 1 hour. Cover and refrigerate. Garnish with green onion and asparagus tips.

Yield: 12 to 15 servings

Norma Martin • Huntsville Power Squadron • Alabama

DID YOU KNOW?

*Sometimes an anchor
line becomes a mass of
kinks when used or stored.
To remove kinks, you may
trail a line astern of a
moving boat. Take care
to avoid tangles in the
propeller and with
other vessels.*

Reuben Bundles

1   (8-ounce) can sauerkraut,
    drained and snipped
¼   teaspoon caraway seed
1   cup diced corned beef
½   cup shredded Swiss
    cheese
1   tablespoon parsley

½   cup mayonnaise
1   tablespoon chopped
    green onion
1   tablespoon chili sauce
2   (8-ounce) packages
    refrigerated crescent
    rolls

Combine sauerkraut and caraway seed. Set aside. Mix corned beef,
Swiss cheese and parsley. Whisk together mayonnaise, onion and chili
sauce. Unroll crescent rolls. Press two triangles together to make a
square. Spread mayonnaise mixture over each square. Spoon corned
beef mixture on one-half of square. Top with sauerkraut mixture.
Roll up dough and seal edges. Bake at 425 degrees 10 minutes.

Yield: 8 servings

Millie Steffe   •   St. Louis Power Squadron   •   Missouri

Sauerkraut Balls

¼   pound bulk sausage
¼   pound canned ground ham
1   (4-ounce) can corned beef
¼   cup chopped onion
½   teaspoon parsley
½   teaspoon salt
1   cup all-purpose flour
½   teaspoon dry mustard

1   cup milk
3   cups sauerkraut, drained
    well
2   eggs
⅔   cup water
    Bread crumbs
    Hot mustard sauce for
    dipping

Brown sausage, ham and corned beef in a skillet. Add onion, parsley
and salt and cook until bubbly. Stir in flour and mustard. Cook until
flour is incorporated. Add milk and cook until thickened. Stir in
sauerkraut and mix well. Place in a bowl and refrigerate until cold.
Shape mixture into balls. Whisk together eggs and water. Dip balls in
egg mixture and dredge in bread crumbs. Deep fry until golden
browned. Serve with hot mustard sauce.

Yield: 8 to 10 servings

Donita Jenkins   •   Missouri Ozarks Power Squadron   •   Missouri

English Sausage Balls

2	pounds bulk sausage		Bread crumbs
12	hard-cooked eggs, peeled		Salt and pepper to taste

Press sausage around eggs to form a ball. Roll ball in bread crumbs. Heat oil in a deep fryer to 300 to 400 degrees. Fry sausage balls 2 to 3 minutes until browned. Cut into quarters and season with salt and pepper. Serve hot or cold with steak sauce.

Yield: 12 servings

Jayne Robinson • Port Huron Power Squadron • Michigan

Sweet and Sour Chicken Wings

¼	cup vinegar		1	tablespoon soy sauce
½	teaspoon garlic powder		1	teaspoon Worcestershire sauce
½	cup packed brown sugar		1	tablespoon chopped onion
1	tablespoon lemon juice		½	teaspoon ground ginger
1	tablespoon wine (optional)		1	teaspoon poultry seasoning
2	tablespoons ketchup		15-20	chicken wings
1	tablespoon mustard			

Combine vinegar, garlic, brown sugar, juice, wine, ketchup, mustard, soy sauce, Worcestershire sauce, onion, ginger and poultry seasoning in a 13 x 9 x 2-inch baking dish. Mix well. Add wings and stir to coat. Refrigerate overnight. Bake, stirring often, at 400 degrees about 1 hour or until sauce caramelizes and sticks to wings.

Yield: 6 servings

Nancy Harvey • Cambridge Sail & Power Squadron • Maryland

Chicken Curry Cheese Spread

1⅓ cups finely chopped
    cooked chicken
1 (8-ounce) package cream
    cheese, softened
¼ cup raisins
⅔ cup chopped celery

2 green onions, chopped
1 teaspoon curry powder
1 teaspoon grated ginger
    Almonds or peanuts and
    coconut for garnish
    Assorted crackers

Combine chicken, cream cheese, raisins, celery, onion, curry and ginger. Mix until well blended. Top with nuts and coconut. Serve with crackers.

Yield: 8 to 10 servings

Irene Freeman • Cape Fear Power Squadron • North Carolina

Chafing Dish Meatballs

1½ pounds ground chuck
½ cup dry bread crumbs,
    sifted
1 teaspoon salt
¼ teaspoon pepper
1 egg, slightly beaten
½ cup milk
¼ cup vegetable shortening

2 cups canned tomato juice
2 tablespoons all-purpose
    flour
¾ cup barbecue sauce
¼ cup water
1 (20-ounce) can pineapple
    chunks, drained
    Stuffed olives, drained

Mix together ground chuck, bread crumbs, salt, pepper, egg and milk with two forks until well blended. Shape mixture into ½-¾-inch balls. Place meatballs in a 13 x 9 x 2-inch baking dish with shortening. Refrigerate. Combine tomato juice and flour in a saucepan. Cook and stir until smooth. Blend in barbecue sauce and water. Refrigerate sauce.

Thirty minutes prior to serving, bake meatballs at 350 degrees 30 minutes. Drain excess fat from browned meatballs. Pour in tomato sauce and bake an additional 45 minutes. Spoon meatballs into a chafing dish. Place pineapple and olives around meatballs. Spoon sauce over all.

Yield: 70 meatballs

Shirley Nordquist • Nobscot Power Squadron • Massachusetts

Beef Roll Up Mini-Sandwiches

1   (8-ounce) package cream
    cheese, softened
1   teaspoon crushed garlic
1   tablespoon milk
    Creamed style
    horseradish to taste
1   (14-ounce) package flour
    tortillas
1   pound thinly sliced deli
    roast beef
1   pound thinly sliced
    Cheddar cheese
    Spinach leaves, rinsed
    and dried
1   red onion, very thinly
    sliced

Combine cream cheese, garlic, milk and horseradish. Lay tortilla on a
cutting board. Trim edges on both sides to make a straight edge.
Spread a layer of cream cheese mixture on tortilla. Layer roast beef,
cheese, spinach and onion. All ingredients are placed all the way out
to the straight edge. Tightly roll up tortilla, starting at curved edge.
Secure four toothpicks down the length of tortilla. Slice between
toothpicks. Repeat with remaining tortillas and ingredients. May be
prepared a day in advance.

Yield: 15 to 20 servings

Cindy Kenney • Ann Arbor Power Squadron • Michigan

⚓ Pepperoni Dip

3-4 ounces pepperoni,
    chopped small
4   ounces cream cheese,
    softened
½   cup sour cream
1   teaspoon finely chopped
    onion
2   tablespoons mayonnaise
1   tablespoon ketchup
    Assorted crackers

Combine pepperoni, cream cheese, sour cream, onion, mayonnaise
and ketchup. Mix until well blended. Cover and refrigerate. Serve
with crackers.

Yield: 4 to 6 servings

Micky McNelis • Dundalk Power Squadron • Maryland

DID YOU KNOW?

When docking in a strong wind, current or tight quarters, it is smart to let the docklines do the work to minimize stress and embarrassment. A boating course can help you understand how.

Dock Party BBQ Tarts

1	stick butter, softened	½	cup barbecue sauce
1	(3-ounce) package cream cheese, softened	¼	cup chopped onion
1	cup all-purpose flour	2	tablespoons packed brown sugar
1	pound ground beef		Shredded Cheddar cheese

Cream butter and cream cheese. Stir in flour to form a soft dough. Refrigerate at least 1 hour or overnight. Shape dough into 24 walnut-size balls. Place each ball in a mini-muffin pan. Press dough against sides to form a tart.

Brown beef and drain well. Stir in sauce, onion and brown sugar. Cook over medium heat until hot and bubbly. Divide evenly among unbaked tart shells. Bake at 350 degrees 25 minutes. Sprinkle with cheese the last 5 minutes of baking.

Yield: 10 to 12 servings

Carolyn Lebo • Ventura Power Squadron • California

Beer Balls

1	pound ground chuck	4	teaspoons vinegar
1	cup ketchup	4	teaspoons Worcestershire sauce
1	cup beer		
4	teaspoons sugar		Salt and pepper to taste

Shape meat into 18 balls. Brown on a baking sheet in the oven at 350 degrees 10 to 15 minutes. Combine ketchup, beer, sugar, vinegar, Worcestershire sauce, salt and pepper in a saucepan. Bring to boil. Add meatballs. Simmer 3 hours.

Yield: 18 meatballs

Linda Peoples • Banana River Power Squadron • Florida

Olive and Dried Beef Casserole

2 teaspoons dehydrated onion

2 teaspoons sherry

2 (8-ounce) packages cream cheese, softened

¼ cup minced black olives, drained

¼ cup minced green olives, drained

1 (2-ounce) jar dried beef, rinsed and minced

Assorted crackers

Reconstitute onion in sherry. Combine onion and sherry with cream cheese, black and green olives and beef. Refrigerate 30 minutes. Shape mixture into a ball. Serve with crackers.

Yield: 6 to 8 servings

Judy Howard • Rome Sail & Power Squadron • Georgia

Chislets (Spicy Beef Morsels)

3 pounds boneless beef sirloin or top round, cut into bite size cubes

½ cup beer

⅔ cup soy sauce

¼ cup extra virgin olive oil

6 garlic cloves, minced

1 tablespoon grated fresh ginger

3 long green onions, cut ⅛-inch rounds

2 tablespoons crushed red pepper

½ teaspoon salt

Combine beef, beer, soy sauce, oil, garlic, ginger, green onion, red pepper and salt. Marinate in the refrigerator at least 24 hours or up to 3 days. This marinade will cook the meat or you can microwave, broil or fry the drained cubes until browned. The inside will be medium rare.

Yield: 10 to 12 servings

Cliff Anthes • Beaverton Power Squadron • Oregon

Mock Boursin

2	garlic cloves, crushed	½	teaspoon dried marjoram
2	(8-ounce) packages cream cheese, softened	½	teaspoon dried chives
2	sticks butter, softened	¼	teaspoon ground thyme
½	teaspoon salt	¼	teaspoon pepper
½	teaspoon dried basil	1	teaspoon dried dill
			Assorted crackers

Combine garlic, cream cheese and butter in a food processor. Blend until smooth. Add salt, basil, marjoram, chives, thyme, pepper and dill. Blend well. Serve with crackers. Store in the refrigerator for 1 month.

Yield: 6 to 8 servings

Jean Maassel • Annapolis Sail & Power Squadron • Maryland

Marinated Cheese

½	cup olive oil	1	teaspoon sugar
½	cup seasoned rice vinegar	½	teaspoon salt
1	(2-ounce) jar diced pimentos, drained	½	teaspoon pepper
3	tablespoons chopped parsley	1	(8-ounce) block sharp Cheddar cheese
3	tablespoons minced green onion	1	(8-ounce) package cream cheese, chilled
¾	teaspoon dried basil		Parsley sprigs for garnish
3	garlic cloves, minced		Assorted crackers

Combine oil, vinegar, pimento, parsley, green onion, basil, garlic, sugar, salt and pepper in a jar. Seal lid tightly and shake vigorously. Cut cheese in half lengthwise and then into ¼-inch slices. Repeat with cream cheese. Arrange cheese slices alternately in a shallow dish, standing slices on edge. Pour marinade over cheese. Cover and refrigerate at least 8 hours.

Transfer cheese slices to a serving platter preserving pattern. Spoon marinade over cheese. Garnish with parsley sprigs. Serve with crackers.

Yield: 15 servings

Robert Small • Jacksonville Power Squadron • Florida

Garlic Cheese Ball

2   (8-ounce) packages
    cream cheese, softened
2   garlic cloves, minced
2   tablespoons dry sherry

Sliced green olives for
    garnish
Assorted crackers

Combine cream cheese, garlic and sherry. Shape mixture into a ball. Garnish with olives and refrigerate. Serve with crackers.

Yield: 6 to 8 servings

Sherry Goldman • Housatonic River Power Squadron • Connecticut

Blue Cheese Shortbread
with Cream Cheese and Chutney

½   cup blue cheese, room
    temperature
3   tablespoons unsalted
    butter, softened
½   cup all-purpose flour
¼   cup cornstarch
¼   teaspoon pepper

¼   teaspoon kosher salt
⅓   cup chopped walnuts
3   tablespoons cream
    cheese, softened
3   tablespoons chutney
½   cup toasted walnut halves
    for garnish

Blend blue cheese and butter in a food processor until smooth. Combine flour, cornstarch, pepper and salt in a bowl. Add to blue cheese and pulse to blend. Add walnuts and pulse just until incorporated. Do not overmix. Shape mixture into a ball and wrap in plastic wrap. Refrigerate at least 1 hour.

Place ball on plastic wrap and cover with another piece of plastic wrap. Roll out dough to ⅛-inch thickness. Remove wrap and cut with a 1-inch fluted round cookie cutter. Place on a parchment-lined paper baking sheet. Repeat until all dough is used. Bake at 325 degrees 25 minutes. Let cool. Spread ¼ teaspoon cream cheese on each shortbread. Top each with chutney and a walnut half.

Yield: 8 to 10 servings

Donna Selden • Richmond Sail & Power Squadron • Virginia

Zucchini Appetizers

3	cups thinly sliced zucchini	½	teaspoon seasoned salt
1	cup biscuit baking mix		Dash of pepper
½	cup finely chopped onion	½	teaspoon dried oregano
½	cup grated Parmesan cheese	1	garlic clove, finely chopped
1	tablespoon snipped parsley	½	cup vegetable oil
		4	eggs, slightly beaten

Combine zucchini, baking mix, onion, cheese, parsley, salt, pepper, oregano, garlic, oil and eggs. Mix thoroughly. Spread mixture into a greased 13 x 9 x 2-inch baking dish. Bake at 350 degrees 25 to 30 minutes or until golden browned. Cut into 2 x 1-inch squares. Serve warm.

Yield: 4 dozen squares

Patricia Diane Allison • Tres Rios Power Squadron • California

Roasted Red Pepper and Artichoke Tapenade

1	(7-ounce) jar roasted red peppers, drained and coarsely chopped	3	tablespoons olive oil
1	(14-ounce) can artichoke hearts, drained and coarsely chopped	¼	cup capers, drained
		2	garlic cloves
⅓	cup fresh parsley, stems removed	1½	tablespoons fresh lemon juice
½	cup freshly grated Parmesan cheese		Salt and pepper to taste
			French bread rounds or crackers

Combine peppers, artichokes, parsley, cheese, oil, capers, garlic and juice in a food processor. Pulse until well blended and finely chopped. Do not purée. Season with salt and pepper. Serve on French bread rounds or crackers. Best made a day in advance. Cover and refrigerate.

Yield: 6 to 8 servings

Leftover Tapenade is delicious on hot pasta.

Chris Puckett • Greensboro Power Squadron • North Carolina

Artichoke Nibbles

2   (6-ounce) jars marinated
    artichoke hearts
1   small onion, finely
    chopped
1   garlic clove, minced
4   eggs
¼   cup fine bread crumbs

¼   teaspoon salt
⅛   teaspoon Tabasco sauce
⅛   teaspoon dried oregano
⅛   teaspoon pepper
1   cup shredded sharp
    Cheddar cheese
1   tablespoon minced parsley

Drain liquid from one jar of artichoke hearts into a skillet. Drain and discard liquid from other jar. Chop artichokes and set aside. Sauté onion and garlic about 5 minutes until tender. Set aside. Combine eggs, bread crumbs, salt, Tabasco, oregano and pepper. Add cheese, parsley, onion and garlic mixture and artichokes. Mix well. Pour mixture into a greased 11 x 7 x 2-inch baking dish. Bake at 325 degrees 30 minutes or until set. Cool in pan. Cut into 1-inch squares.

Yield: 8 to 10 servings

Loretta Bierschenk   •   Palm Beach Power Squadron   •   Florida

Crunchy Cranberry-Stuffed Mushrooms

1   (6-ounce) package
    chicken or pork
    stuffing mix
¾   cup coarsely chopped
    fresh cranberries

½-¾ cup chopped pecans
2   pounds mushrooms
1   stick butter (Do not use
    margarine)

Prepare stuffing according to package directions except use ¼ cup less water. Add cranberries and pecans. Remove mushroom stems and chop a few to add to stuffing. Scoop out inside of mushroom. Melt butter in microwave until hot. Dip each mushroom in butter and place in a shallow microwave dish. Stuff mushroom caps with stuffing mix. Top each with a piece of cranberry. May be refrigerated at this point. Cook in microwave 4 minutes. Serve hot.

Yield: 8 to 10 servings

Lena Parsons   •   Coral Ridge Sail & Power Squadron   •   Florida

Mushroom Pâté

1 (8-ounce) package mushrooms, chopped	1 roasted garlic clove
½ small sweet onion, chopped	Salt and pepper to taste
1 (8-ounce) package cream cheese, softened	Chopped rosemary for garnish
1 tablespoon chopped fresh rosemary	Toast points or assorted crackers

Sauté mushroom and onion until tender. Combine mushroom mixture, cream cheese, rosemary, garlic, salt and pepper in a food processor. Process until well blended. Spoon mixture into a serving bowl. Cover and refrigerate at least 24 hours. Garnish with fresh rosemary. Serve with toast points or assorted crackers.

Yield: 12 to 16 servings

Nigel Hargreaves • Sebastian Inlet Power Squadron • Florida

Black Bean and Corn Salsa

4 ears of corn or 2 (15-ounce) cans	½ cup chopped parsley
2 tablespoon butter	¼ cup chopped red onion
1-2 jalapeño peppers	¼ cup chopped tomatoes
1 sweet red pepper	¾ teaspoon minced garlic
Juice of two limes	1 tablespoon olive oil
1 (15-ounce) black beans, rinsed and drained	¼ teaspoon cayenne pepper
	½ teaspoon pepper

Grill corn, basting with butter, or sauté in 2 tablespoons butter until golden. Cut kernels from cob. Grill jalapeño peppers 5 to 10 minutes and red pepper 10 to 15 minutes until charred. Allow to cool. Peel skin and chop. Discard seeds. Place in a large bowl with corn, juice, black beans, parsley, onion, tomatoes, garlic, oil cayenne and pepper. Toss until well mixed.

Yield: 8 to 10 servings

Henry Spradlin • Western N.C. Sail & Power Squadron • North Carolina

Black Bean Salsa

2　(15-ounce) cans black beans, drained
1　(15-ounce) can shoe peg corn, drained
2　large ripe tomatoes, chopped
1　red onion, finely chopped

　　Juice of one lime
3-4　tablespoons chopped cilantro
1　ripe avocado, chopped
1　tablespoon olive oil
　　Salt and pepper to taste
　　Tortilla chips

Combine black beans, corn, tomatoes, onion, juice, cilantro, avocado, oil, salt and pepper. Mix well and serve with tortilla chips.

Yield: 8 servings

Margo McGilvrey • Seneca Power Squadron • New York

Tamale Bites

2　cups crumbled corn bread
1　(10-ounce) can mild enchilada sauce, divided
½　teaspoon salt

1½　pounds ground beef, crumbled
1　(8-ounce) can tomato sauce
½　cup shredded Monterey Jack cheese

Combine crumbs, ½ cup enchilada sauce and salt. Add crumbled ground beef. Shape into 1-inch balls. Place in a shallow baking dish. Bake, uncovered, at 350 degrees 18 to 20 minutes or until meat is cooked. In a saucepan, combine tomato sauce and remaining enchilada sauce. Place cooked meatballs in a chafing dish. Pour sauce over meat. Top with cheese. Keep warm.

Yield: 90 bites

Rosemary Halligan Enoch • Quad City Power Squadron • Iowa

STRAWBERRY AND PEPPER SALSA

2 cups chopped strawberries
¾ cup chopped bell pepper
¼ cup chopped sweet onion
2 teaspoons minced cilantro
1 tablespoon minced parsley
¼ cup French style dressing
Dash of salt
Dash of pepper (optional)
3 drops Louisiana hot sauce (optional)
Tortilla chips

Combine strawberries, bell pepper, onion, cilantro and parsley in a bowl. Whisk together dressing, salt, pepper and hot sauce. Pour dressing over mixture and toss to coat. Refrigerate 1 hour. Serve with tortilla chips.

Yield: 3 cups

Dortha Lang

Bellevue
Sail & Power Squadron

Washington State

Sweet Pumpkin Dip

2	(8-ounce) packages cream cheese, softened	2	cups sifted powdered sugar
1	(15-ounce) can pumpkin	1	teaspoon cinnamon
		1	teaspoon ground ginger

Beat cream cheese and pumpkin until smooth. Add powdered sugar, cinnamon and ginger. Beat until well blended. Cover and refrigerate at least 1 hour. Serve as a dip or spread with fruit, graham crackers, toasted mini-bagels, fruit muffins or English muffins.

Yield: 5½ cups

Donna Dunlap • Pamlico Power Squadron • North Carolina

Garlic Pretzels

1	(20-ounce) package mini pretzels	1	tablespoon garlic salt
1	(1-ounce) package dry ranch dressing mix	¼	teaspoon dried dill
		1	cup vegetable oil

Combine pretzels, dressing mix, salt, dill and oil in a large bowl. Marinate 24 hours, stirring occasionally. Store in an airtight container.

Yield: 6 to 8 servings

Janet Williams • Mohawk Hudson Power Squadron • New York

Herb Butter Spread

8	sticks butter, softened	1	teaspoon crushed red pepper
2	cups sour cream	½	teaspoon salt
2	cups finely chopped chives		Assorted crackers or tortilla chips
5	garlic cloves, minced		

Cream butter, sour cream, chives, garlic, red pepper and salt. Mix until well blended. Refrigerate until ready to serve. Serve with crackers or tortillas.

Yield: 20 to 30 servings

Jeanne Hauser • Southern Tier Power Squadron • New York

Pecan Morsels

4	cups pecans or walnuts	1	teaspoon salt
2	egg whites	1	stick butter
1	cup sugar		

Roast pecans on a baking sheet at 250 degrees 30 minutes. Cool. Beat egg whites until soft peaks form. Add sugar and salt and beat until very stiff. Melt butter on baking sheet. Fold pecans into meringue. Spoon mounds of mixture onto baking sheet. Bake at 250 degrees 45 minutes, turning every 15 minutes with a spatula. Increase temperature to 300 degrees and bake 15 minutes more. Cool on sheet. Break apart before storing in an airtight container.

Yield: 15 servings

Agnes Hudson • Watertown Sail & Power Squadron • New York

DID YOU KNOW?

When anchoring for the night, it is important to show an anchor light on certain boats. Do you know which size boat must show an anchor light? Do Sail boats have the same requirements? The Power Squadron Boating Course can help you know when an anchor light is required.

Stuffed Eggs

6	hard-cooked eggs, peeled	1	tablespoon salad dressing or mayonnaise
2	tablespoons chopped green olives	1	tablespoon plain yogurt
2	tablespoons chopped capers		Dash of white pepper
2	tablespoons chopped radish	1	tablespoon chopped parsley or thin radish slices for garnish
1	teaspoon anchovy paste		

Cut eggs in half and remove yolks. Mash egg yolks and add olives, capers, radish and anchovy paste. Mix until well blended. Stir in dressing, yogurt and pepper. Spoon mixture into egg white halves. Refrigerate at least 2 hours. Sprinkle with parsley or radish.

Yield: 12 servings

Carole Tulip • Annapolis Power Squadron • Maryland

Beach Bread

1	(16-ounce) loaf Italian bread, unsliced	1	(4-ounce) jar blue cheese spread
3	tablespoons extra light virgin olive oil	10	(1-ounce) mozzarella cheese slices
¼	cup chopped garlic	10	(¼-inch) tomato slices

Cut bread in half lengthwise. Drizzle oil over each half. Layer garlic evenly over bread. Spread cheese over garlic. Layer cheese and top with tomato slices. Place in a baking dish and loosely tent with foil. Bake at 375 degrees until cheese melts and bread is thoroughly warmed. Remove foil and broil 30 to 45 seconds to toast edges.

Yield: 12 servings

Mitina Schroeder • Newport Power Squadron • Rhode Island

Cheese Stuffed Bread

4	garlic cloves, diced	1	(8-ounce) container sour cream
1	medium onion, diced		
1	(8-ounce) package cream cheese, softened	1	loaf round white bread

Sauté garlic and onion until translucent. Blend garlic, onion, cream cheese and sour cream until smooth. Slice off top of bread. Hollow out bread and tear into pieces. Spoon cheese mixture into hollowed out bread. Cover with foil and bake at 350 degrees 1 hour, 30 minutes. Remove foil and serve with bread pieces for dipping.

Yield: 8 servings

Jean Devane • Pompano Beach Power Squadron • Florida

Quick Cheese Appetizer

1 cup shredded Swiss cheese	2 tablespoons finely minced onion
1 cup mayonnaise	
3-4 tablespoons grated Parmesan cheese	

Combine Swiss cheese, mayonnaise, Parmesan cheese and onion. Spoon mixture into a 1-quart casserole dish. Bake at 350 degrees 20 minutes.

Yield: 4 to 6 servings

Ann Frenz • Patchogue Bay Power Squadron • New York

Cheese Squares

1 (8-ounce) package refrigerator crescent rolls	1 onion, chopped
	2 (8-ounce) packages shredded sharp Cheddar cheese
4 tablespoons butter, melted	
3 eggs, beaten	Dash of cayenne pepper
1 cup chopped stuffed olives	

Unroll rolls and press into the bottom of a 13 x 9 x 2-inch baking dish, pressing seams together. Combine butter, eggs, olives, onion, cheese and cayenne. Spread mixture over dough. Bake at 350 degrees 15 to 20 minutes until set. Cool and cut into squares. May place squares on a baking sheet and freeze. When frozen, place in a plastic bag and return to freezer.

Yield: 20 to 30 servings

Pat Schulz • Rocky River Power Squadron • Ohio

Christmas Snowball

1 (8-ounce) package cream cheese, softened	1 (7-ounce) package chopped coconut
1 (8-ounce) can crushed pineapple, well drained	1 (10-ounce) package fresh spinach leaves
¼ jar chutney, finely chopped	1 (8-ounce) package strawberries
	Assorted crackers

Blend cream cheese, pineapple and chutney. Shape into a ball and roll in coconut. Refrigerate 4 to 6 hours. Place ball in the center of a bed of spinach and garnish strawberries. Serve with crackers.

Yield: 8 to 10 servings

Charlotte G. Ward • Hilton Head Power Squadron • South Carolina

Cheese Ball

4 ounces cream cheese, softened	1 teaspoon onion juice
½ glass Old English cheese	1 garlic clove, minced
½ roll smoky cheese	½ teaspoon Worcestershire sauce
½ cup Roquefort or Blue cheese	Chopped nuts for garnish
	Assorted crackers

Beat together cream cheese, Old English cheese, smoky cheese, juice, garlic and Worcestershire sauce. Shape mixture into a ball and place in refrigerator until firm. Roll in chopped nuts and serve with crackers.

Yield: 6 to 8 servings

Linda Peoples • Banana River Power Squadron • Florida

Tangy Cheese Ball

2   (8-ounce) packages
    shredded sharp Cheddar
    cheese
1   (8-ounce) package blue
    cheese, room
    temperature
1   (8-ounce) package cream
    cheese, softened

Juice of one lemon
2   tablespoons sherry
2   tablespoons
    Worcestershire sauce
1   medium onion, minced
Salt and sugar to taste
    (optional)
Assorted crackers

Combine Cheddar cheese, blue cheese, cream cheese, juice, sherry, Worcestershire sauce, onion, salt and sugar in a food processor. Process until well blended and smooth. Shape mixture into a ball and refrigerate. Serve with crackers.

Yield: 6 to 8 servings

Keith Williams • Wabash Valley Power Squadron • Indiana

DID YOU KNOW?

The numbering system on buoys increases when traveling in from seaward on the Intracoastal Waterway. How about on Western Rivers and the major rivers within the United States? Do they increase, decrease, or are there any numbers at all? How do you know which way you are traveling? The Boat Smart Course offered by USPS can help.

Blue Cheese Ball

1   (8-ounce) package cream
    cheese, softened
1   (8-ounce) packaged blue
    cheese, room
    temperature
1   stick butter, softened

⅓   cup chopped black olives
3   tablespoons finely
    chopped chives
Walnuts, finely chopped
Assorted crackers

Blend cream cheese, blue cheese and butter. Stir in olives and chives. Shape mixture into a ball and roll in walnuts. Serve with crackers.

Yield: 6 to 8 servings

Mary Pickard • Rowayton Sail & Power Squadron • Connecticut

Walnut and Blue Cheese Terrine

1 cup walnuts	Lettuce leaves
1 (8-ounce) package blue or Gorgonzola cheese, room temperature	Fuji or Granny Smith apples, sliced
¼ cup sour cream	Sourdough baguette, sliced

Toast walnuts at 350 degrees 10 minutes until lightly browned and fragrant. Line a 7½ x 3 x 2-inch loaf pan with plastic wrap with generous overhang. Break up cheese into small chunks in a bowl. Add walnuts and sour cream and mix well. Spread mixture evenly into loaf pan. Cover with overlapping wrap. Refrigerate overnight or until very firm.

To serve, unfold plastic wrap and invert onto a platter lined with lettuce. Remove plastic. Arrange apple and baguette slices around terrine.

Yield: 6 to 8 servings

Carole Tulip • Annapolis Power Squadron • Maryland

Artichoke Dip

1 (14-ounce) can artichoke hearts, quartered	1 (8-ounce) package cream cheese, softened
1 cup shredded Parmesan cheese	1 tablespoon lemon juice
1 cup mayonnaise	1 teaspoon dried dill
	Garlic powder and seasoned salt to taste

Combine artichokes, cheese, mayonnaise, cream cheese, juice, dill, garlic powder and salt. Spoon mixture into a 2-quart casserole dish. Bake at 325 degrees 1 hour.

Yield: 8 to 10 servings

Ginger Viers • Richmond Sail & Power Squadron • Virginia

⚓ Dockside Punch

1   quart orange juice
1   quart iced tea
1   quart club soda

½   cup sugar
1   pint vodka
     Orange or lemon slices
     for garnish (optional)

Combine juice, iced tea, club soda and sugar. Mix well. Pour in vodka. Add orange or lemon slices. Eliminate sugar if using sweetened tea.

Yield: 12 to 15 servings

William Maloy • Wawenock Power Squadron • Maine

Hot Damn! Cherries

1 (10-ounce) jar
maraschino cherries,
drained
Hot cinnamon
schnapps

Drain all juice from cherries. Refill jar with schnapps. Marinate cherries. Drain before serving. Great alone, in a drink or on ice cream.

Yield: about 30 cherries

Creighton Maynard
Fort Worth Power Squadron
Texas

Watermelon Lemonade

8   cups (1-inch) seedless
     watermelon pieces
1   cup fresh lemon juice
3½ cups water

1   cup sugar
     Ice cubes and lemon
     wedges

Blend watermelon and juice in two batches in a blender until smooth. Transfer to a pitcher. Bring water and sugar to boil, stirring until sugar melts. Add hot syrup to watermelon mixture and stir well. Refrigerate 2 hours until cold. Fill tall glasses with ice cubes. Pour in lemonade and garnish with wedges.

Yield: 9 cups

Lynn Tweet • Santana Power Squadron • California

DID YOU KNOW?

Those of us who travel, frequently encounter locks on the waterways. Do you know which is the best side on which to moor when in the lock? The windward side is best, it keeps the vessel off the wall. A boating class might help with such simple tips.

Mollie Hogan

2	(6-ounce) cans frozen orange juice concentrate, thawed	6	eggs, well beaten
	Juice of six lemons	1	cup sugar
		1	(750 ml) bottle dry gin

Combine orange juice, lemon juice, sugar and gin. Mix well. May be served or stored in refrigerator. To serve, pour 1 jigger of mixture in an 8-ounce high ball glass over ice.

Yield: 30 servings

Marti Katterhenry • Anna Maria Island Power Squadron • Florida

Bloody Marys Aboard Fruition

1	(32-ounce) can clamato juice	⅓	cup lemon juice
1	(32-ounce) can tomato-vegetable cocktail	1	tablespoon course ground pepper
1	tablespoon Tabasco sauce	1	tablespoon Old Bay seasoning
¼	cup Worcestershire sauce	1	tablespoon steak sauce
1	tablespoon celery salt		Vodka to taste
2	tablespoons horseradish		

Combine clamato juice, tomato juice, Tabasco, Worcestershire sauce, celery salt, horseradish, lemon juice, pepper, Old Bay seasoning and steak sauce in a shaker container. Shake well. Fill a glass with ice and a shot of vodka. Fill with tomato mixture and stir.

Yield: 12 servings

Donna Selden • Richmond Sail & Power Squadron • Virginia

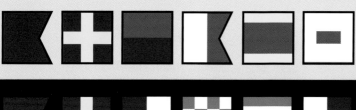

breads
& brunch

community service

how may we be of service?

Everyone wants to feel that they have been a contributor or has been of service to others. USPS has a simple mission, focused on boating, the environment, homeland security and our waterways critical to safety.

USPS members serve their communities in many ways, some related to boating, others relating to services needed by the community where volunteers serve best. Our principle mission in the area of service is boater education. USPS teaches some 1400 classes annually to approximately 35,000 beginner and experienced boaters from border to border and sea to sea.

Beside this all important service to boating education USPS also serves as a partner with the boater providing free vessel safety checks to insure boats have the required safety equipment and that the boat itself is seaworthy. USPS works with the chart division of the National Ocean Service to provide valuable chart information and verification of data related to navigational aids, depths, clearances, currents, weather and other critical information relating to coastal navigation and aeronautical charts.

USPS is partnering with the U.S. Coast Guard and the Army Corps of Engineers on protecting our homeland and has recently created a new environmental department to aid in monitoring and protecting the valuable waterways and wetlands of the US.

One of our country's most important resources is its youth. USPS is partnering with the Sea Scouts Venture group and other young boater organizations to help educate and train young leaders in boating safety and education. Computer games and training programs for young America continue under development.

USPS is a service organization. Won't you join us?

For more information call 1-888-367-8777. Thanks for listening!

Refrigerator Rolls

2	cups warm water (115 to 120 degrees)	1	egg, beaten
½	cup sugar	1	stick butter, softened
1½	teaspoons salt	6½-7	cups sifted all-purpose flour
2	packages active dry yeast		

Mix together water, sugar and salt. Sprinkle yeast on top. Let stand 5 minutes. Stir until dissolved. Add egg and butter. Mix thoroughly. Slowly add flour in two batches until dough is easy to handle. Place dough in a greased bowl, turning to coat top. Cover tightly with waxed paper and a damp cloth. Refrigerate overnight. Shape dough into desired size rolls. Place in a baking dish. Cover with a damp cloth. Let rise until touch leaves an impression. Bake at 400 degrees 12 to 15 minutes.

Yield: 3½ dozen

Makes wonderful cinnamon rolls or donuts and maple bars in deep fryer.

Lois Neef   •   Anclote Key Sail & Power Squadron   •   Florida

Bisquick Cinnamon Rolls

2¼	cups baking biscuit mix	2	tablespoons sugar
2	tablespoons sugar	¼	cup packed brown sugar
⅔	cup milk	½	teaspoon cinnamon
4	tablespoons butter, melted	½	cup raisins

Combine baking mix, sugar and milk until soft dough forms. Knead dough on a floured surface and roll into a rectangle ⅛-inch thick. Spread butter over dough. Sprinkle with sugar, brown sugar and cinnamon. Dot with raisins and roll up. Cut into ½-inch thick slices. Lay flat on a greased baking sheet and bake at 400 degrees 8 to 10 minutes.

Yield: 6 servings

Margaret McConnell   •   Fort Vancouver Power Squadron   •   Washington State

Sour Cream Blueberry Muffins

2	cups biscuit baking mix	1	(8-ounce) container sour cream
¾	cup plus 2 tablespoons sugar, divided	1	cup fresh or frozen blueberries
2	eggs		

Combine baking mix and ¾ cup sugar. Stir in eggs and sour cream just until combined. Fold in blueberries. Pour batter into greased muffin cups filling three-fourths full. Sprinkle with remaining 2 tablespoons sugar. Bake at 375 degrees 20 to 25 minutes.

Yield: 1 dozen

Jean Moseley   •   Charles River Sail & Power Squadron   •   Massachusetts

Jordan Marsh Blueberry Muffins

1	stick butter, softened	½	teaspoon salt
1	cup sugar	½	cup milk
2	eggs	1	teaspoon vanilla
2	cups all-purpose flour	2½	cups blueberries, divided
2	teaspoons baking powder	2	teaspoons sugar

Cream butter and sugar until fluffy with an electric mixer. Add eggs, one at a time, beating well after each addition. Sift together flour, baking powder and salt. Add dry ingredients, alternately with milk to creamed mixture. Stir in vanilla. Mash ½-cup blueberries and stir in by hand. Fold in remaining whole blueberries. Pour batter into greased muffins cups, filling three-fourths full. Sprinkle tops with sugar. Bake at 375 degrees 30 minutes. Cool in pan.

Yield: 1 dozen large muffins

Sally and Charles Perkins   •   Attleboro Sail & Power Squadron
Massachusetts

★ Zesty Corn Muffins

¾ cup all-purpose flour
¼ cup soy flour
1 cup yellow cornmeal
2 tablespoons sugar
4 teaspoons baking powder
1 teaspoon salt

1 cup buttermilk
¼ cup soy oil
2 eggs, slightly beaten
½ cup shredded Cheddar
cheese
¼ cup chopped green chilies

Preheat oven to 425 degrees. Combine flour, soy flour, cornmeal, sugar, baking powder and salt. Stir together buttermilk, soy oil and eggs. Add to dry ingredients. Gently stir in cheese and green chilies. Pour batter into greased muffin cups. Bake at 425 degrees 22 to 25 minutes.

Yield: 12 muffins

Bruce Steere • Dallas Power Squadron • Texas

Captain Doug's Bran Muffins

1 cup applesauce
¾ cup milk
2 tablespoons butter,
melted
2 cups bran cereal
1 egg, beaten

½ cup packed brown sugar
½ teaspoon cinnamon
1 cup raisins
1½ cups all-purpose flour
2 teaspoons baking powder
½ teaspoon baking soda

Combine applesauce, milk and butter. Pour mixture over bran. Stir in egg and let stand 5 minutes. Add brown sugar, cinnamon and raisins. In a separate bowl, combine flour, baking powder and baking soda. Stir into bran mixture until well blended. Spoon batter into greased muffin cups. Bake at 400 degrees 18 to 20 minutes. Be careful not to overbake.

Yield: 12 muffins

Doug Sewell • Berea Power Squadron • Ohio

Peachy Poppy Seed Muffins

1	stick plus 2 tablespoons butter, softened	1	tablespoon poppy seeds
1	cup sugar	1	teaspoon baking powder
2	eggs	¼	teaspoon salt
½	teaspoon vanilla	1	(6-ounce) jar peach baby food
1¼	cups all-purpose flour		

Cream butter and sugar until smooth. Add eggs and vanilla, mixing well. Combine flour, poppy seeds, baking powder and salt. Add dry ingredients alternately with baby food to creamed mixture. Pour batter into greased muffin cups, filling two-thirds full. Bake at 350 degrees 20 minutes.

Yield: 1 dozen muffins

Judy Roettger • Lima Sail & Power Squadron • Ohio

Six Week Muffin Mix

5	cups all-purpose flour	1	(15-ounce) box raisin bran cereal
5	teaspoons baking soda		
2	teaspoons salt	1	quart buttermilk
1	tablespoon cinnamon	4	eggs, beaten
2	cups sugar	1	cup vegetable oil

Combine flour, baking soda, salt, cinnamon, sugar, cereal and buttermilk in a large bowl. Whisk together eggs and oil. Stir into batter. Cover and refrigerate. Spoon batter into greased muffin cups. Bake at 375 degrees 17 to 20 minutes. May also make as mini muffins.

Yield: several dozen

Batter may be stored covered in the refrigerator for six weeks. Wheat germ may be substituted one for one with flour and may add more raisins.

Andrew E. Bond • Durham Sail & Power Squadron • North Carolina

★ Bobbie's Zucchini Bread

3	eggs	2	zucchini squash, grated
2	cups sugar	2	tablespoons vanilla
1	cup vegetable oil	1	teaspoon baking soda
3	cups all-purpose flour	½	cup chopped nuts
3	teaspoons cinnamon		

Beat eggs until pale yellow. Add sugar, oil, flour, cinnamon, squash, vanilla, baking soda and nuts. Mix thoroughly. Pour batter into two greased and floured 9-inch loaf pans. Bake at 325 degrees 1 hour, 15 minutes.

Yield: 2 loaves

Ray Finley • Lackawanna Power Squadron • New Jersey

DID YOU KNOW?

Fiberglass whips are a good idea to avoid wear and tear on a boat dock for any length of time. Whips hold the boat off the dock and all for some wake, current and tidal fluctuation to occur without allowing the vessel to rub against the dock.

Mango Nut Bread

2	cups all-purpose flour	2	cups coarsely chopped mango
2	teaspoons baking soda	½	cup chopped pecans or walnuts
½	teaspoon salt		
¾	cup sugar	1	tablespoon lime or lemon juice
1	teaspoon cinnamon		
3	large eggs, slightly beaten	½	cup raisins
¾	cup vegetable oil	¼	cup coconut flakes
1	teaspoon vanilla	¼	cup blueberries

Combine flour, baking soda, salt, sugar and cinnamon. Make a well in the center of dry ingredients. Set aside. Combine eggs, oil and vanilla. Add to well and stir just until moistened. Stir in mango, nuts and juice. Add raisins and coconut. Spoon batter into two greased and floured 9 x 5 x 3-inch loaf pans. Top with blueberries and push down into batter. Bake at 350 degrees 1 hour or until tester comes out clean. Cool in pans on wire racks 10 minutes. Remove from pan and cool completely on racks.

Yield: 2 loaves

Dolores Jorgensen • Manatee Sail & Power Squadron • Florida

Spiced Applesauce Bread

1¼ cups applesauce	¼ teaspoon salt
1 cup sugar	1 teaspoon cinnamon, divided
½ cup vegetable oil	
2 eggs	¼ teaspoon ground nutmeg
3 tablespoons milk	¼ teaspoon ground allspice
2 cups sifted all-purpose flour	¾ cup chopped pecans, divided
1 teaspoon baking soda	¼ cup packed brown sugar
½ teaspoon baking powder	

Combine applesauce, sugar, oil, eggs and milk. Sift together flour, baking soda, baking powder, salt, ½ teaspoon cinnamon, nutmeg and allspice. Stir into applesauce mixture and mix well. Add ½ cup pecans. Pour batter into a greased 9 x 5 x 3-inch loaf pan. Combine ¼ cup pecans, brown sugar and ½ teaspoon cinnamon. Sprinkle over batter. Bake at 350 degrees 1 hour or until tester comes out clean.

Yield: 1 loaf

Charlotte Johnson • Grand Lake Sail & Power Squadron • Oklahoma

Chocolate Chip Banana Nut Bread

1 stick butter, softened	1½ cups all-purpose flour
1½ cups sugar	1 teaspoon baking soda
4 bananas, mashed	1 teaspoon salt
½ cup milk	1 (8-ounce) package semi-sweet chocolate chips
2 eggs	
1 teaspoon vanilla	½ cup chopped nuts

Beat butter and sugar until creamy. Combine bananas, milk, eggs and vanilla in a separate bowl. In another bowl, combine flour, baking soda and salt. Add dry ingredients, alternately with banana mixture to creamed mixture. Mix until just blended. Stir in chocolate chips and nuts. Pour batter into two 9 x 5 x 3-inch loaf pans. Bake at 350 degrees 50 to 60 minutes.

Yield: 2 loaves

Jan Greenwood • Miles River Power Squadron • Maryland

Amish Friendship Bread

4¼ cups sugar, divided

4½ cups all-purpose flour, divided

3 cups whole or 2% milk, divided

1 cup vegetable oil

3 eggs

1 teaspoon vanilla

1½ teaspoons baking powder

½ teaspoon salt

3 teaspoons cinnamon, divided

½ teaspoon baking soda

1 (6-ounce) package instant vanilla pudding

1 cup chopped pecans (optional)

Prepare 10 day in advance of serving. Combine ½ cup sugar, ½ cup flour and ½ cup milk in a glass or plastic bowl. Stir with a wooden or plastic spoon. No metal. Bread starter may be stored in the freezer until ready to use. Pour batter into a zip-top plastic bag. Let stand on counter top. Do not refrigerate. **Day 1**-do nothing. **Day 2**-Mush the bag 2 times a day. **Day 3**-through **day 5**-mush the bag 2 times a day.

Day 6-Stir in 1 cup sugar, 1 cup flour and 1 cup milk. Mush together thoroughly. **Day 7**-through **day 9**, mush the bag and let the air out 2 times a day. **Day 10**-Pour and squeeze batter into a large bowl. Add 1 cup sugar, 1 cup flour and 1 cup milk. Stir together and measure four 1 cup starters into large zip-top bags. Give the bags and recipe to friends.

To the remaining batter in the bowl, add oil, ½ cup milk, eggs and vanilla. Mix well. In a separate bowl, combine 2 cups flour, 1 cup sugar, baking powder, salt, 2 teaspoons cinnamon, baking soda, pudding mix and pecans. Stir dry ingredients into batter.

In a small bowl, mix ¾ cup sugar and 1 teaspoon cinnamon. Sprinkle half of the sugar-cinnamon mixture into the bottom of a two greased 9 x 5 x 3-inch loaf pans. Divide batter evenly between two pans. Sprinkle remaining sugar-cinnamon on top. Bake at 325 degrees 1 hour. Cool 10 minutes in pan. Turn out onto plastic wrap. Cool completely. Wrap in plastic wrap.

Yield: 2 loaves

Judy Alter • Raleigh Sail & Power Squadron • North Carolina

1901 Hunter's Corn Bread

1	cup cornmeal	½	teaspoon salt
1	cup all-purpose flour	1	cup milk
4	level teaspoons baking powder	1	egg
2	tablespoons sugar	8-10	slices bacon, diced

Sift together cornmeal, flour, baking powder, sugar and salt. Beat milk and egg together. Add to dry ingredients and mix well. Pour batter into a 9 x 5 x 3-inch loaf pan. Top with bacon. Bake at 350 degrees 20 minutes.

Yield: 1 loaf

Mary Evans • Austin Power Squadron • Texas

Chocolate Chip Coffeecake

1½	cups sugar, divided	2	cups all-purpose flour
1	teaspoon cinnamon	1	teaspoon baking powder
¼	cup chopped pecans	½	teaspoon baking soda
1	stick butter, softened	¼	teaspoon salt
1	(8-ounce) package cream cheese, softened	¼	cup cold milk
2	eggs	1	(6-ounce) package semi-sweet chocolate chips
1	teaspoon vanilla		

Preheat oven to 350 degrees. Combine ¼ cup sugar, cinnamon and pecans. Set topping aside. Beat butter, cream cheese and 1¼ cups sugar until smooth. Add eggs, one at a time, beating well after each addition. Add vanilla, flour, baking powder, baking soda and salt. Mix well. Stir in milk and chocolate chips. Mixture will be thick. Pour batter into a greased 9-inch springform pan. Sprinkle with pecan topping. Bake at 350 degrees 45 to 50 minutes or until tester comes out clean. Cool 15 minutes. Remove sides of pan and cool completely.

Yield: 12 servings

Tippy Cavanagh • Marco Island Sail & Power Squadron • Florida

Apple Nut Coffeecake

Topping

½ cup chopped pecans or walnuts	1 teaspoon cinnamon
½ cup packed brown sugar	2 tablespoons butter, softened

Mix together pecans, brown sugar and cinnamon. Cut in butter. Set aside.

Coffeecake

2 cups all-purpose flour	1 teaspoon baking soda
1 cup sugar	¼ teaspoon salt
1 cup sour cream	1 teaspoon vanilla
1 stick butter, softened	2 cups peeled, chopped apples
2 eggs	
1 teaspoon baking powder	

Combine flour, sugar, sour cream, butter, eggs, baking powder, baking soda, salt and vanilla. Beat at medium speed 2 to 3 minutes until smooth. Fold in apples. Pour batter into a greased 13 x 9 x 2-inch baking dish. Sprinkle topping over batter. Bake at 350 degrees 35 to 40 minutes or until tester comes out clean.

Yield: 12 to 15 servings

Marjorie J. Dorwart • Calumet Power Squadron • Illinois

Captain's French Toast

4 large eggs	Butter for cooking
½ cup whole milk or half & half	8 slices bread, 1-inch thick (egg, challah, brioche or raisin bread)
2 tablespoons sugar	Maple syrup and preserves
¼ teaspoon vanilla	
¼ teaspoon cinnamon	

Whisk together eggs, milk, sugar, vanilla and cinnamon. Melt 1 teaspoon butter in a nonstick skillet over medium heat. Soak 2 slices of bread at a time in egg mixture about 1 minute, pressing down to absorb mixture. Cook in skillet 3 minutes per side until golden browned. Repeat with remaining bread slices. Serve with maple syrup and/or preserves.

Yield: 4 servings

Norm Menchel • Kingsway Power Squadron • New Jersey

Overnight French Toast

1	cup packed brown sugar	1	loaf French bread, cut into ½-inch slices
1	stick butter		
2	tablespoons corn syrup	5	eggs
3	tart apples, peeled and sliced	1½	cups milk
		1	teaspoon vanilla
			Maple syrup and preserves

Cook brown sugar, butter and corn syrup in a skillet until syrupy. Pour syrup into a 13 x 9 x 2-inch baking dish. Arrange apple slices over syrup. Top with bread slices. Whisk together eggs, milk and vanilla. Pour over bread. Cover and refrigerate overnight.

Bake at 350 degrees 40 minutes. Serve with maple syrup and/or preserves. May reheat baked dish.

Yield: 4 to 6 servings

Scott Borzell • Main Line Power Squadron • Pennsylvania

Pear Sundae French Toast

¼	cup plus 3 tablespoons packed brown sugar, divided	3	eggs, slightly beaten
		¾	cup milk
6	tablespoons butter, divided	1	teaspoon vanilla
		¼	teaspoon ground nutmeg
1¼	teaspoons cinnamon, divided	6	slices French bread, 1-inch thick
3	medium ripe pears, peeled and sliced		Vanilla ice cream

Cook ¼ cup brown sugar, 2 tablespoons butter and ¼ teaspoon cinnamon in a skillet until sugar dissolves. Add pears and cook until tender. Set aside. Whisk together eggs, milk, vanilla, nutmeg, 3 tablespoons brown sugar and 1 teaspoon cinnamon. Dip bread in egg mixture, coating each side. Melt remaining 4 tablespoons butter in skillet. Cook bread 2 minutes per side. Top with ice cream and pear mixture.

Yield: 4 to 6 servings

Betty Campanella • Painsville Sail & Power Squadron • Ohio

Anchor Inn French Toast

8-12	ounces cream cheese, softened	12	eggs
16	slices French bread		Milk to taste
¼	cup favorite jelly		Powdered sugar or maple syrup

Spread ½ ounce cream cheese on one side of each bread slice. Spread jelly over cream cheese on 8 slices bread. Top with remaining 8 slices, cheese side inside, to make a sandwich. Whisk together eggs and milk. Dip bread sandwich in egg mixture. Brown in a skillet on both sides. Top with powdered sugar or syrup.

Yield: 4 servings

The Anchor Inn is a fixture in Little Current, Ontario, in the North Channel of Lake Huron. In addition to great local whitefish, we have enjoyed this special French Toast recipe many times and now cook it aboard our boat. Alas, with a new chef, this dish is no longer offered at the Anchor Inn. It is used here with permission of the owner.

Shirley and Thomas Geggie • Birmingham Power Squadron Michigan

French Toast DeCelle

8	slices French bread, cubed	2	cups milk
2	(8-ounce) packages cream cheese, cubed	2	teaspoons vanilla
12	eggs		Ground nutmeg
⅓	cup maple syrup		Maple syrup

Layer bread cubes and cream cheese cubes in an ungreased 13 x 9 x 2-inch baking dish. Whisk together eggs, syrup, milk and vanilla. Slowly pour over bread and cheese. Sprinkle with nutmeg. Cover, place on a tray and refrigerate overnight.

Preheat oven to 375 degrees 1 hour before serving. Place tray with baking dish in oven and bake 45 minutes. Mixture will rise like a soufflé and sink slightly. Serve with warm maple syrup.

Yield: 8 servings

Janice Stevenson • Ocean City Power Squadron • Maryland

Betty Ann's Oatmeal Pancakes

2	cups buttermilk	1	teaspoon baking soda
1½	cups dry old-fashioned oats	¾	teaspoon salt
½	cup all-purpose flour	2	eggs, slightly beaten

Combine buttermilk and oats. Let stand 5 minutes. Stir together flour, baking soda and salt. Add dry ingredients to oatmeal mixture. Stir in eggs. Pour batter onto a hot griddle. Make sure pancakes bubble before turning.

Yield: 4 servings

Elaine Keller   •   Balboa Power Squadron   •   California

Did you know?

Toxic drain cleaners are harmful for the environment. You may unclog drains aboard the boat by flushing it with baking soda followed by boiling water. Environmental concern is everyone's responsibility.

Sybaris Apple Oat Pancakes

2	cups old-fashioned rolled oats	½	teaspoon cinnamon
½	cup stone ground whole wheat flour	½	teaspoon ground nutmeg
3	tablespoons sugar	2	cups buttermilk
1	teaspoon baking soda	2	eggs
1	teaspoon baking powder	2	tablespoons canola oil
½	teaspoon salt	1	teaspoon vanilla
			Thin-sliced apples

Combine oats, flour, sugar, baking soda, baking powder, salt, cinnamon, nutmeg, buttermilk, eggs, oil and vanilla. Mix thoroughly. Let batter sit at least 2 hours or overnight before cooking. If batter is too thick, add more buttermilk. Pour batter onto a hot griddle. Add apple slices to pancakes before flipping.

Yield: 4 to 6 servings

Rich Stidger   •   Berkshire Power Squadron   •   Massachusetts

Potato Pancakes with Clams

2	pounds potatoes, peeled and grated
½	medium onion, grated
2	large eggs
¼-⅜	pound chopped fresh clams or canned, drained
1	teaspoon dried parsley
¼	teaspoon pepper
2-3	tablespoons all-purpose flour
	Olive oil for cooking
	Applesauce and sour cream for garnish

Combine potato, onion, eggs, clams, parsley and pepper. Mix well. Add flour, one tablespoon at a time, to reach a non-liquid consistency. Place 1 tablespoon batter onto a hot oiled skillet. Cook potato until both sides are browned. Serve with applesauce and sour cream.

Yield: 2 to 4 servings

Peter P. Pranis, Jr. • Lower Rio Grande Valley Power Squadron • Texas

Banana Waffles

1½	cups all-purpose flour
2	teaspoons baking powder
½	teaspoon salt
2	tablespoons sugar
3	egg yolks
1	teaspoon lemon juice
4	tablespoons butter, melted
1½	cups milk
1	medium banana, thinly sliced
3	egg whites, stiffly beaten
	Honey for topping

Sift together flour, baking powder, salt and sugar. Make a well in dry ingredients. Add egg yolks, juice, butter and milk to well. Stir until just moistened. Add banana. Fold in egg whites. Cook batter on a hot waffle griddle. Serve with honey.

Yield: 4 to 6 servings

Tish Cullen • Las Vegas Sail & Power Squadron • Nevada

Bluefield Tomato/Eggplant Casserole

1	medium eggplant, 1½ pounds, peeled and cut into ½-inch slices	1	tablespoon chopped onion
½	cup boiling water	½	teaspoon ground oregano
1½	teaspoons salt	½	cup crushed saltine crackers, about 8
2	tablespoons butter, melted	6	medium slices tomatoes
2	eggs, beaten	½	cup grated Parmesan or shredded American cheese
¼	teaspoon pepper		

Cook eggplant in boiling water and salt 20 minutes or until tender. Drain and mash eggplant. Add butter, eggs, pepper, onion, oregano and cracker crumbs. Spoon mixture into a 1-quart casserole dish. Top with tomato slices. Sprinkle with cheese. Bake at 375 degrees 25 minutes or until browned.

Yield: 6 servings

Marjorie L. Mullin • Long Bay Power Squadron • South Carolina

Crab Supreme

8	slices white sandwich bread, crust removed and cubed	½	bell pepper, chopped
		½	cup mayonnaise
1	pound crabmeat	4	eggs
1	onion, chopped	3	cups milk
1	cup chopped celery, sautéed	1	(10¾-ounce) can cream of mushroom soup
			Shredded Cheddar cheese

Place one-half bread cubes in the bottom of a 13 x 9 x 2-inch baking dish. Combine crabmeat, onion, celery, bell pepper and mayonnaise. Spoon mixture over bread. Top with remaining bread cubes. Whisk together eggs and milk. Pour over bread. Cover and refrigerate overnight.

Bake at 325 degrees 15 minutes. Remove from oven and spread soup on top. Sprinkle with cheese. Bake at 350 degrees an additional 1 hour.

Yield: 8 to 10 servings

Joan V. Cooke • Ocean City Power Squadron • Maryland

Cheese & Artichoke Oven Omelet

¾ cup picante salsa	1 cup shredded Cheddar cheese
1 cup coarsely chopped artichoke hearts	5 large eggs
¼ cup grated Parmesan cheese	1 (8-ounce) container sour cream
1 cup shredded Monterey Jack cheese	Tomato wedges and parsley sprigs

Preheat oven to 350 degrees. Butter a 9 or 10-inch pie pan or quiche dish. Spread picante salsa over bottom of pan. Arrange artichokes over salsa. Sprinkle with Parmesan cheese, Monterey Jack cheese and Cheddar cheese. Whisk eggs until smooth. Add sour cream and mix well. Pour over cheeses. Bake, uncovered, 30 to 40 minutes or until set in the middle. Cut into wedges and garnish with tomato and parsley.

Yield: 6 to 8 servings

Phyllis Davis • Winooski Valley Power Squadron • Vermont

DID YOU KNOW?

The longer the VHF antenna the great its range. Also, the higher it is mounted on the vessel the greater the range. VHF signals are line-of-sight. The Power Squadron boating course provides information on VHF radio installation, operation and uses.

Eggs à la Suisse

1 tablespoon butter	2 tablespoons shredded Cheddar cheese
½ cup dry white wine	Toasted bread or English muffins
4 eggs Salt, pepper and cayenne pepper to taste	

Melt butter in a skillet. Stir in wine. Carefully place each egg in the skillet. Season with salt, pepper and cayenne. Cook eggs until the whites are nearly firm. Sprinkle cheese over each egg. Spoon wine sauce over each egg. Put one egg over toast or muffin. Pour a small amount of wine sauce over each serving.

Yield: 2 servings

Duane O. Leathers • San Diego Power Squadron • California

 Curried Eggs

8	hard-cooked eggs, peeled	½	teaspoon dry mustard
1	(8-ounce) package sliced mushrooms, rinsed	⅛	teaspoon ground ginger
		¼	cup milk
2	tablespoons butter		Salt and pepper to taste
2	(10¾-ounce) cans cream of mushroom soup	2	tablespoons sour cream
		4	English muffins, halved
¾	teaspoon curry powder		

Cut each egg into one-eighths. Set aside. Sauté mushrooms in butter. Add mushroom soup and heat thoroughly. Stir eggs, curry powder, mustard and ginger. Pour in milk and heat thoroughly. Season with salt and pepper. Stir in sour cream prior to serving. Serve over muffins.

Yield: 4 servings

Nancy Miner • Birmingham Power Squadron • Michigan

Portuguese Poached Eggs

2	tablespoons butter	1	teaspoon salt
2	onions, minced	½	teaspoon pepper
2	garlic cloves, minced	1	(16-ounce) can sweet peas, drained
1	cup water		
2	tomatoes, chopped	4	eggs
1	pound Italian sausage, cut into ½-inch slices	4	slices French bread, 1-inch thick
1	teaspoon beef bouillon crystals		

Melt butter in a large skillet over medium heat. Sauté onion and garlic 5 minutes. Add water, tomato, sausage, beef bouillon, salt and pepper. Bring to boil. Reduce heat, cover and simmer 15 minutes. Add peas and heat thoroughly. Break one egg at a time into a cup. Carefully slide egg into the skillet. Cover and simmer 5 minutes or until eggs are set. Serve each egg with meat sauce over each bread slice.

Yield: 4 servings

Carolyn & Joel Wilbe • Tip of the Mitt Power Squadron • Michigan

Denver Sandwich

4 eggs
¼ cup diced ham
¼ cup diced onion
¼ cup diced bell pepper

Salt and pepper to taste
1 tablespoon butter
4 slices white sandwich bread

Beat eggs in a bowl. Add ham, onion, bell pepper, salt and pepper. Melt butter in a skillet. Pour mixture into hot skillet. Scramble mixture until cooked. Divide cooked egg mixture to make two sandwiches.

Yield: 2 servings

Jan Johnson • Lansing Power Squadron • Michigan

Christmas Morning Wife Saver

16 slices white sandwich bread, crust removed
8 slices Canadian bacon or thin sliced ham
8 slices sharp Cheddar cheese
6 eggs
½ teaspoon salt
½ teaspoon pepper
½ teaspoon dry mustard

¼ cup minced onion
¼ cup finely chopped bell pepper
2 teaspoons Worcestershire sauce
3 cups whole milk
Dash of Tabasco sauce
1 stick butter, melted
Crushed cornflakes

Place 8 bread slices in the bottom of a buttered 13 x 9 x 2-inch baking dish, covering bottom of dish entirely. Layer bacon, then cheese slices and top with remaining bread slices. Beat together eggs, salt and pepper. Add mustard, onion, bell pepper, Worcestershire sauce, milk and Tabasco. Pour over bread. Cover and refrigerate overnight.

Before baking, pour butter over bread and top with corn flake crumbs. Bake, uncovered, at 350 degrees 1 hour. Cool 10 minutes before serving.

Yield: 8 servings

Dorothea Clarke • Sebastian Inlet Sail & Power Squadron • Florida

Delicious Mexican Chili Cheese Breakfast

2 (7-ounce) cans whole
   chilies, halved and seeds
   removed
4 eggs
¼ cup all-purpose flour
1 (12-ounce) can
   evaporated milk

2 (8-ounce) packages
   shredded Colby cheese
2 (8-ounce) packages
   shredded Monterey Jack
   cheese
2 (7-ounce) cans salsa

Arrange chili halves close together in a 13 x 9 x 2-inch baking dish. Beat eggs, flour and milk. Stir in Colby and Monterey Jack cheeses. Pour mixture over chilies. Bake at 350 degrees 45 minutes. Spread salsa on top and cut into squares.

Yield: 8 to 10 servings

Bobby Shaw • Beaverton Power Squadron • Oregon

Vidalia Onion Torte

¼ cup white wine
5 medium Vidalia onions,
   thinly sliced
6 tablespoons butter
1 tablespoon all-purpose
   flour
1 cup half & half
1 teaspoon salt

¼ teaspoon pepper
½ teaspoon ground nutmeg
4 eggs, slightly beaten
10 slices bacon, cut into
   1-inch pieces, cooked
   and drained
1 (9-inch) pie crust, unbaked

Boil wine until reduced by half. Set aside. Sauté onion in butter until translucent. Whisk in flour until blended. Slowly add half & half, whisking constantly, until mixture thickens. Add reduced wine, salt, pepper and nutmeg. Cook 2 minutes. Remove from heat and cool. Stir in eggs and bacon. Pour mixture into pie crust. Bake at 400 degrees 20 minutes or until tester comes out clean. Cool 10 minutes before serving.

Yield: 6 to 8 servings

Leslie H. McCarthy • Brooklyn Power Squadron • New York

Breakfast Casserole

1   pound seasoned sausage
1   small onion, chopped
½   package croutons
18   eggs

1¼   cups milk
1   teaspoon salt
1   cup shredded Cheddar
       cheese

Crumble sausage and cook in skillet until browned. Add onion and cook 5 minutes. Drain well. Spread sausage mixture into the bottom of a greased 13 x 9 x 2-inch baking dish. Scatter croutons over sausage. Whisk together eggs, milk and salt. Pour mixture over sausage. Sprinkle with cheese. Bake at 350 degrees 45 minutes or until tester comes out clean.

Yield: 8 to 10 servings

BJ Baden • Boca Ciega Sail & Power Squadron • Florida

DID YOU KNOW?

When reading a chart with a symbol showing a symbol RW "NC" Mo (A) GONG the RW stands for red and white vertical stripes, the "NC" is the buoy name or markings, the Mo (A) means the light flashes the morse signal "A" (a short then long flash) and the GONG means the sea action causes the gong to sound. A safe boating course may help you identify chart symbols.

Sunday Morning Machacca

1   pound stir-fry beef, chopped
1   tablespoon olive oil
½   jalapeño pepper, finely chopped
     Dash of cayenne pepper
     Dash of Tabasco sauce
1   sweet red pepper, diced
1   yellow pepper, diced
1   bell pepper, diced
½   white onion, diced

3   green onions, chopped
1   stalk celery, diced
5   garlic cloves, crushed, divided
⅓   cup chopped cilantro
4   eggs, slightly beaten
¼   cup white wine
     Salt and pepper to taste
     Avocado for garnish
     Warm tortillas and salsa

Brown beef in a hot skillet with oil and jalapeño. Stir in cayenne and Tabasco. Add all peppers, onion, green onion, celery and 4 garlic cloves. Sauté until tender. Remove from heat and strain beef mixture. Set aside. Wipe skillet with a paper towel. Heat oil and cook cilantro and 1 garlic clove. Whisk together eggs, wine, salt and pepper. Add to skillet. Stir until eggs are cooked. Return beef mixture to skillet and heat thoroughly. Serve with warm tortillas, avocados and top with salsa.

Yield: 4 to 6 servings

Dan Moore • Tacoma Power Squadron • Washington State

Corned Beef Hash

8-10	ounces corned beef, chopped	1	tablespoon chopped parsley
½	cup diced salt pork or bacon	1	tablespoon Worcestershire sauce
1½	cups diced beets	¼	cup half & half
2½	cups diced cooked potatoes		Salt and pepper to taste
1	medium/large onion, diced	¼	cup vegetable oil or bacon drippings

Combine corned beef, salt pork, beets, potato, onion, parsley, Worcestershire sauce, half & half, salt and pepper. Heat oil in a large skillet over medium heat. Pour in mixture and cook into a cake. Serve with poached eggs.

Yield: 4 servings

This is an easy recipe to cook on the boat since all the ingredients can be prepared ahead and then combined before cooking. May substitute bacon bits for salt pork.

Thomas Dougherty • Absecon Island Sail & Power Squadron New Jersey

Blintz Soufflé

	Butter	5	eggs
2	(10-ounce) packages frozen cheese or blueberry blintzes, thawed	⅔	cup sugar
		1	teaspoon vanilla
		1	(3-ounce) package cream cheese, softened
1½ cups sour cream			

Spread butter on top and bottom of blintzes. Lay flat in a buttered 13 x 9 x 2-inch baking dish. Combine sour cream, eggs, sugar, vanilla and cream cheese. Spoon mixture over blintzes. Bake at 350 degrees 1 hour.

Yield: 8 to 10 servings

Leslie McCarthy • Brooklyn Power Squadron • New York

Apple Lilies

6	baking apples	½	cup maple syrup
2	tablespoons butter		Whipped cream for garnish
1	cup raisins		
½	cup chopped nuts		

Use an apple cutter and push almost through each apple to give a lily shape with 8 apple slices. Place each apple in a buttered dish. Fill apple center with raisins and nuts. Pour in syrup to reach halfway up sides of dish. Place cups on a foil-lined baking sheet. Bake at 350 degrees 40 minutes or until tender. Serve with whipped cream.

Yield: 6 servings

Jim Elwood • Kentucky Lake Power Squadron • Kentucky

Cranberry Apple Casserole

3	cups peeled and chopped apples	1	cup sugar
2	cups fresh cranberries	3	packages instant cinnamon spice oatmeal
½	cup plus 2 tablespoons all-purpose flour, divided	¾	cup chopped pecans
		½	cup packed brown sugar
		1	stick butter, melted

Combine apples, cranberries and 2 tablespoons flour. Toss to coat. Stir in sugar. Pour mixture into a 2-quart casserole dish. Combine oatmeal, pecans, ½ cup flour, brown sugar and butter. Mix well. Spoon over fruit mixture. Bake, uncovered, at 350 degrees 45 minutes.

Yield: 6 servings

Beth Cummins • Winston-Salem Power Squadron • North Carolina

DID YOU KNOW?

If a vessel becomes beneaped or goes aground on a "spring" high tide, she may have to wait 14 days for the next high tide sufficient to float her off. Spring refers to a specific kind of tide not the time of year. USPS advanced courses teach students about tides and currents.

Chocolate Gravy

1	cup sugar		Dash of salt
2	tablespoons all-purpose flour	1	tablespoon cocoa
		1½	cups whole milk

Combine sugar, flour, salt and cocoa in a large saucepan. Cook and stir over low heat. Slowly pour in milk and cook until thickened. Serve over hot biscuits.

Yield: 3 servings

Ronald K. Roeseler • Oklahoma City Sail & Power Squadron
Oklahoma

Cheese Grits

4	cups water	4	tablespoons butter
½	teaspoon salt	1	tablespoon dried onion flakes
1	cup quick-cooking grits	½	cup milk
1	(8-ounce) package shredded Cheddar cheese	2	eggs, beaten

Bring water and salt to boil. Stir in grits and cook according to package directions. Remove from heat. Stir in cheese, butter and onion. Pour in milk. Stir in eggs in batches to not cook the eggs. Mix well. Pour mixture into a greased 2½-quart casserole dish. Bake at 350 degrees 40 minutes or until set.

Yield: 6 to 8 servings

Carolyn Knaggs • Port Huron Sail & Power Squadron • Michigan

Honey Chicken Salad

4   cups chopped cooked
      chicken
3   stalks celery, diced
1   cup sweetened dried
      cranberries
½   cup chopped pecans

1½ cups mayonnaise
⅓   cup orange-blossom honey
¼   teaspoon salt
¼   teaspoon pepper
      Chopped toasted pecans
        for garnish

Combine chicken, celery, cranberries and pecan. Whisk together mayonnaise, honey, salt and pepper. Pour dressing over chicken mixture and toss to coat. Garnish with pecans.

Yields: 4 servings

The mayonnaise and honey mixture is reminiscent of a poppy seed dressing. Reduce the amount of honey for a less sweet taste.

Mary Beth Poole   •   Richmond Sail & Power Squadron
                            Virginia

Greek Chicken Salad

3   cups cubed cooked
      chicken
2   medium cucumbers,
      peeled, seeded and
      chopped
1¼ cups feta cheese, crumbled
⅔   cup sliced pitted olives

¼   cup chopped parsley
1   cup mayonnaise
½   cup plain yogurt
1   tablespoon dried oregano
3   garlic cloves, minced
      Lettuce leaves
      Pita bread halves

Combine chicken, cucumber, feta cheese, olives and parsley. In a separate bowl, whisk together mayonnaise, yogurt and oregano. Add mayonnaise mixture to chicken and toss to coat. Cover and refrigerate. To serve, line pita halves with lettuce leaves. Spoon chicken mixture into pita halves.

Yields: 4 to 6 servings

Carol Sanfilippo   •   Peconic Bay Power Squadron
                            New York

Maple Ham Peaches

1	egg, beaten	1	pound ground ham
½	cup soft bread crumbs	12	peach halves, drained
¾	cup maple syrup, divided		Chopped parsley for
	Dash of ground cloves		garnish
1	teaspoon prepared mustard		

Combine egg, bread crumbs, ½ cup syrup, cloves, mustard and ham. Shape mixture into 12 balls. Place a ham ball in the center of each peach half. Place in a 13 x 9 x 2-inch baking dish. Sprinkle with parsley. Bake at 350 degrees 25 minutes. Drizzle with ¼ cup syrup while baking to prevent drying.

Yields: 6 servings

Jim Elwood • Kentucky Lake Power Squadron
Kentucky

Swedish Doughnuts with Mashed Potatoes

4½	cups all-purpose flour	1	cup mashed potatoes
4	teaspoons baking powder	2	tablespoons vegetable shortening, melted
½	teaspoon nutmeg		
½	teaspoon baking soda	¾	cup buttermilk
1	teaspoon salt	½	teaspoon vanilla
3	medium eggs		Powdered sugar
2	cups sugar		

Sift flour, measure and sift again with baking powder, nutmeg, baking soda and salt. Set aside. Beat eggs until light and fluffy. Add sugar, mashed potato, shortening, buttermilk and vanilla. Add dry ingredients to potato mixture. Mix well. Roll dough on a lightly floured surface to ½-inch thickness. Cut dough with a round cutter. Cook in hot oil until browned. Dip in powdered sugar.

Yields: 2 dozen, depending on cutter size

Ruth Elizabeth Zeiss • St. Louis Sail & Power Squadron
Missouri

soups & salads

education
lessons we've learned

Some wise person once said the key to success is knowledge. Certainly the key to boating fun and safety is knowledge. Statistics have proven the reverse. A focus on safety resulting from knowledge persists today in USPS, an organization which has three primary interests.......Education, Civic Service and Family Fun.

USPS members enjoy learning the finer points of boating, albeit for sailing, canoeing, kayaking or power boating. Family fun is the cornerstone of the educational program at USPS. Some ascribe to knowledge of the maintenance, knots, weather and smooth handling of a boat. Others are fascinated by charts, tides, currents, electronics and the piloting from place to place. Even other boaters are eager to know about navigation using only celestial bodies.

Where ever your interests lie in fun on the water, simple river and lake boating, coastal navigation or off shore distance sailing with all the necessary information for fun and safety, USPS educational courses are the best available presented in the newest and most user friendly methodologies and may be studied at a rate defined by the boater.

Why not join us and see for yourself?

For more information call 1-888-367-8777. Thanks for listening!

Creamy Pumpkin Soup

¼ cup minced onion

2 tablespoons minced leek, white and some green

2 tablespoons butter

2 cups chicken broth

2 cups canned pumpkin

½ teaspoon ground mace

½ teaspoon sugar

Salt and pepper to taste

Half & half

Ground nutmeg for garnish

Sauté onion and leek in butter until tender in a saucepan. Add broth and pumpkin. Mix well and heat thoroughly. Purée in batches in the blender. Return to pan. Add mace, sugar, salt and pepper. Stir in half & half if necessary to thin soup. Serve hot and sprinkle with nutmeg.

Yield: 6 servings

Anne Magyar • Vero Beach Power Squadron • Florida

DID YOU KNOW?

When a vessel flips over, end for end, bow under first, it is referred to as "pitchpoling". If the vessel is hit from the side by a wave and rolled over it is said to have been broached. These and other terms are part of the USPS Boat Smart course.

Winter Soup

2 slices bacon, diced

2 cups diced onion

½ cup diced celery

2 pounds smoked beef sausage, cut into ¾-inch slices

3 cups water or 1½ cups water and 1½ cups white wine

¼ cup chopped parsley

½ teaspoon cracked peppercorns

¼ teaspoon salt

4-5 carrots, coarsely sliced

2 parsnips, peeled and coarsely sliced

1 rutabaga, peeled and cubed

3-4 turnips

4-5 potatoes, peeled and cubed

1 head cabbage, cut into wedges

Salt and pepper to taste

Brown bacon in a 4-quart saucepan or Dutch oven. Sauté onion and celery 2 minutes, stirring constantly. Add sausage and cook 5 minutes. Stir in water, parsley, peppercorns and salt. Reduce heat, cover and simmer 20 minutes. Add carrot, parsnip, rutabaga, turnip and potato. Cover and simmer 12 to 15 minutes. Arrange cabbage on top and cook 15 minutes or until cabbage is tender. Season with salt and pepper.

Yield: 6 to 8 servings

Edie Oathout • Music City Power Squadron • Tennessee

DID YOU KNOW?

*An EPIRB
(Emergency Positioning
Identifying Radio Beacon)
can send a signal as far as
200 miles, alerting land
stations, rescue vessels and
passing aircraft that an
emergency exists and
will lead searchers to the
distress scene.*

Mary's Portuguese Kale Soup

1	large shank bone	½	teaspoon ground allspice
1	pound linguiça (garlic sausage)	½	teaspoon dried basil
1	pound chorizo	½	teaspoon dried oregano
3	quarts water	1	large bunch kale, chopped
	Salt and pepper to taste	1	medium head cabbage, chopped
3	large potatoes, diced	¼	cup vinegar (optional)
1	(15-ounce) can kidney beans	½	cup ketchup (optional)

Combine shank bone, linguiça and chorizo and water in a stockpot. Simmer until meats are cooked. Add salt, pepper, potatoes, kidney beans, allspice, basil, oregano, kale and cabbage. Cook until kale and cabbage are tender. Add vinegar and or ketchup after cooking if desired.

Yield: 8 servings

George Cambra • Taunton River Power Squadron • Massachusetts

Joan's Maryland Crab Soup

3	(28-ounce) cans crushed tomatoes	1	bunch celery, chopped
4	(12½-ounce) cans diced tomatoes	6	(32-ounce) packages frozen mixed vegetables, thawed
4	gallons water	1	thyme leaf
1	cup chicken broth	3-4	tablespoons pepper
1	medium head cabbage, chopped	¼	cup Old Bay seasoning
6	medium onions, chopped	5	pounds crabmeat

Combine tomato, water, broth, cabbage, onion and celery in a large stockpot. Simmer until onion and celery are tender. Add mixed vegetables, thyme leaf, pepper and seasoning, Simmer until vegetables are cooked. Add crabmeat and heat thoroughly.

Yield: 12 to 15 servings

Joan Yeigh • Kent Narrows Sail & Power Squadron • Maryland

Sweet Potato Minestrone
with Turkey Sausage

½	pound smoked turkey sausage, cut into ¼-inch slices		½	teaspoon coarsely ground pepper
1	cup diced onion		¼	teaspoon salt
1	cup diced carrot		2	(14½-ounce) cans no sodium diced tomatoes, undrained
¾	cup thinly sliced celery		1	(15-ounce) can cannellini beans
3	cups water			
2	cups peeled and sliced sweet potatoes		8	cups coarsely chopped spinach
1	teaspoon dried oregano			

Sauté sausage, onion, carrot and celery in a Dutch oven over medium heat 7 minutes or until sausage is browned. Add water, sweet potato, oregano, pepper, salt, tomato and beans. Bring to boil. Reduce heat, cover and simmer 30 minutes or until vegetables are tender. Add spinach and cook an additional 2 minutes.

Yield: 8 servings

The Griffin Family • Marblehead Sail & Power Squadron
Massachusetts

Scallop and Carrot Soup

1	large shallot or ½ white onion, chopped		1¼	pounds fresh scallops, well rinsed and chopped
1	tablespoon butter, divided		3	tablespoons heavy cream
2	carrots, grated			Pepper and Old Bay seasoning to taste
1	cup dry white wine			
1	cup fish or vegetable broth			Chopped parsley for garnish

Gently sauté shallot in 1 teaspoon butter. Add carrot and cook 5 minutes. Stir in wine and broth. Bring to boil. Reduce heat and simmer 5 minutes. Add scallops and return to boil. Cook 30 seconds. Stir in remaining 2 teaspoons butter, cream, pepper and seasoning. Ladle into bowls and garnish with parsley.

Yield: 6 servings

Patricia Tuller • Cape Coral Power Squadron • Florida

Minestrone Soup

2	tablespoons olive oil		1	(14½-ounce) can diced tomatoes
1	onion, chopped		1	(15-ounce) can cannellini beans, rinsed and drained
¾	teaspoon crushed red pepper		1	(14-ounce) can low-sodium beef broth
2	carrots, peeled and chopped		1	ounce piece Parmesan cheese rind
2	stalks celery, chopped		2	tablespoons chopped flat-leaf parsley
3	ounces thinly sliced pancetta, coarsely chopped			Salt and pepper to taste
3	garlic cloves, minced			Grated Parmesan cheese for garnish
½	pound baby spinach leaves and Swiss chard			
1	russet potato, peeled and cubed			

Heat oil over medium heat in a large stockpot. Add onion, red pepper, carrot, celery, pancetta and garlic. Sauté 10 minutes until onion is translucent. Add spinach, Swiss chard and potatoes and cook 2 minutes. Stir in tomato and simmer 10 minutes until spinach is wilted and tomato broken down. Add beans, broth and Parmesan rind. Simmer 15 minutes, stirring occasionally. Stir in parsley and cook 2 minutes. Season with salt and pepper. Discard rind. Serve with grated Parmesan cheese.

Yield: 4 to 6 servings

Richard Gallop • Mount Clemens Power Squadron • Michigan

Cream of Zucchini Soup

1	stick butter	2	tablespoons all-purpose flour	
2	leeks, cut into ½-inch pieces	1	cup dry white wine	
3	teaspoons chicken bouillon crystals	1	zucchini, unpeeled and chopped	
½	tablespoon white pepper	1	quart half & half	
1	tablespoon ground nutmeg	1	egg white	
1	cup peeled and chopped potato	2	cups zucchini, unpeeled and grated	

Melt butter in a 6-quart stockpot. Add leeks and cook until tender. Add bouillon, white pepper, nutmeg, potato, flour, wine, chopped zucchini and half & half. Simmer, uncovered, 30 minutes. Place mixture in blender. Add egg white and blend until smooth. Return to pot and add grated zucchini. Simmer 15 minutes. Serve hot or cold.

Yield: 6 to 8 servings

Dorothy J. Lewis   •   Mattapoisett Power Squadron   •   Massachusetts

Slow Cooker Beef Stew

5	carrots, chopped	1	bay leaf	
5	medium potatoes, cubed	1	tablespoon salt	
2	pounds stew meat, cut into 1-inch cubes	½	teaspoon pepper	
1	teaspoon Worcestershire sauce	1	teaspoon paprika	
1	garlic clove, minced	1	large onion, diced	
		1	(16-ounce) can green peas, undrained	

Place carrot, potato, meat, Worcestershire sauce, garlic, bay leaf, salt, pepper, paprika, onion and peas in a crockpot. Cover and cook on low 12 hours. Remove bay leaf. Pour into a large casserole dish for serving. Individual servings can be frozen and reheated in the microwave.

Yield: 6 servings

Carrol Walker   •   Everett Sail & Power Squadron   •   Washington State

DID YOU KNOW?

The following channels should be used for VHF communications, channel 13 for bridges, 16 for hailing and emergencies, 71 and 72 for information exchange between vessels and channels 24 and 27 to contact the marine operator. These and other bits of information about VHF radio are taught as part of the Power Squadron Boating Course.

Mushroom Soup

½	cup chopped onion	1	pound mushrooms, sliced
4	tablespoons butter	1	cup chopped celery
2	tablespoons all-purpose flour	1	cup diced potato
1	teaspoon salt	1	cup diced carrots
½	teaspoon pepper	½	cup half & half
3	cups water	¼	cup grated Parmesan cheese
2	chicken bouillon cubes		

Sauté onion in butter until tender. Add flour, salt and pepper. Stir to make a smooth paste. Gradually add water and bouillon, stirring constantly. Bring to boil. Cook and stir 1 minute. Add mushrooms, celery, potato and carrot. Reduce heat, cover and simmer 30 minutes or until vegetables are tender. Stir in half & half and cheese. Heat thoroughly.

Yield: 4 to 6 servings

Mt Clemens Power Squadron members recommend this be eaten with a fork. It is a must for the Frost Bite Cruises.

Mary LaPlante • Mt. Clemens Power Squadron • Michigan

Frogmere Stew

12-15	new potatoes, skin on	1	(12-ounce) can beer
12	(3-inch) slices sausage	1	package crab boil mix
6	ears corn, broken in half	1-2	pounds medium shrimp in shells

Fill a large stockpot about two-thirds full with water. Bring to boil. Cook potatoes 10 minutes. Add sausage and cook 5 minutes. Add corn, beer and crab boil mix. Cook 2 to 3 minutes longer. Turn off heat, add shrimp and cook 2 to 3 minutes until shrimp turn pink.

Yield: 12 servings

Martie Barnard • Atlanta Sail & Power Squadron • Georgia

Creamy Carrot Soup with Chives

3 tablespoons olive oil	4 cups chicken broth
1 tablespoon butter	1 vegetable bouillon cube
1 cup diced onion	½ teaspoon sugar
3 medium garlic cloves, diced	¼ teaspoon salt
3 cups peeled and sliced carrots, ½-inch pieces	¼ teaspoon white pepper
	2 tablespoons dry sherry
1 cup peeled and diced potatoes	½ cup sour cream
	¼ cup chopped fresh chives

Heat oil and butter in a large stockpot. Sauté onion and garlic 2 to 3 minutes until tender. Do not brown. Add carrot and potato and sauté 2 to 3 minutes. Stir in broth, vegetable bouillon, sugar and salt and bring to a simmer. Reduce heat to low and gently simmer 20 to 25 minutes. Remove from heat and cool slightly. Working in batches, purée in a blender until smooth. Add pepper. Stir in sherry just prior to serving. Ladle into soup bowls. Garnish each with 1 to 2 spoonfuls sour cream and chives.

Yield: 4 servings

Ellen Pate • Venice Sail & Power Squadron • Florida

Oyster Stew with Sherry

2 tablespoons butter	¼ teaspoon Tabasco sauce
1 pint shucked oysters, well-drained	1¾ cups half & half
	¼ cup sherry
½ teaspoon salt	Dash of paprika
½ teaspoon Worcestershire sauce	

Melt butter in a saucepan. Cook oysters 5 minutes or until edges begin to curl. Add salt, Worcestershire sauce, Tabasco, half & half and sherry. Cook, stirring occasionally, 15 minutes until hot. Sprinkle with paprika and serve.

Yield: 4 appetizer or 2 entrée servings

Evan Croft • Cape Cod Sail & Power Squadron • Massachusetts

DID YOU KNOW?

*Heaving a line from one
vessel to another or to a
dock can be a difficult task.
Adding a Monkey's Fist to
the end of the line gives
weight and aids in the task.
The USPS Boat Smart
course aids the boater with
docking and undocking ideas
and tips on safety.*

Fish Stew

6	cups hot water			Pepper to taste
6	chicken bouillon cubes		1	cup sliced mushrooms
1	cup thin sliced carrots		1	tomato, wedged
2	medium onion, cut into eighths		2	tablespoons stuffed olives, sliced
2	tablespoons cornstarch		1	pound cod or haddock, cut into 2 x 2-inch squares
¼	cup cold water			
2	cups broccoli florets			Plain yogurt and French bread slices
½	teaspoon dried basil			

Combine water, bouillon, carrot and onion. Bring to boil. Reduce
heat, cover and simmer until tender. Stir together cornstarch and cold
water. Whisk into soup. Add broccoli, basil, pepper, mushrooms, tomato
and olives. Cook 5 minutes. Add fish. Cover and cook 5 to 8 minutes
until fish flakes. Serve with a dollop of yogurt and French bread.

Yield: 6 servings

Phyllis Davis • Winooski Valley Power Squadron • Vermont

Northwest Salmon Chowder

½	cup chopped celery		1½	teaspoons salt
½	cup chopped onion		½	teaspoon pepper
½	cup chopped bell pepper		½	teaspoon dried dill
1	garlic clove, minced		1	(14-ounce) can cream style corn
3	tablespoons butter		2	cups half & half
1	(14-ounce) can chicken broth		1¾-2	cups cooked salmon chunks or 1 (14-ounce) can salmon, drained, bones and skin removed
1	cup peeled and diced potatoes			
1	cup shredded carrots			

Sauté celery, onion, bell pepper and garlic in butter until tender. Add
broth, potato, carrot, salt, pepper and dill. Bring to boil. Reduce heat,
cover and simmer 40 minutes. Stir in corn, half & half and salmon.
Simmer 15 minutes or until heated thoroughly.

Yield: 8 servings

Sandy Haskins • Susquehannock Power Squadron • Pennsylvania

Beef and Onion Stew

1 cup chopped onion, large chop

2 garlic cloves, finely chopped

3 tablespoons olive oil

2 pounds stew beef, cut into 1-inch cubes

½ cup dry red wine

2 tablespoons red wine vinegar

½ teaspoon salt

½ teaspoon pepper

1 bay leaf

1 stick cinnamon

1 (8-ounce) tomato sauce

1 (15-ounce) jar small pearl white onion or fresh, cooked until tender.

Crumbled feta or gorgonzola cheese

Sauté onion and garlic in oil in a large stockpot until tender. Using a slotted spoon, transfer vegetables to a bowl. Brown meat in oil about 20 minutes. Drain drippings. Return onion and garlic to pot. Add wine, vinegar, salt, pepper, bay leaf, cinnamon stick and tomato sauce. Bring to boil. Reduce heat, cover and simmer 1 hour, 15 minutes. Add pearl onion and simmer 30 minutes. Remove bay leaf and cinnamon stick before serving.

Yield: 4 servings

Peggy Farber • Atlanta Sail & Power Squadron • Georgia

Corn-Potato-Crab Chowder

½ pound finely chopped onions

3 tablespoons butter

¼ cup all-purpose flour

4 medium potatoes, finely diced

1½ quarts half & half

1 bay leaf

1 tablespoon Old Bay seasoning

Dash of salt and pepper

1 (16-ounce) can whole kernel corn

1 pound crabmeat

⅓ cup sherry

Sauté onion in butter until tender. Add flour to a make a roux. Cook 5 minutes, stirring constantly. Stir in potatoes. Add half & half, bay leaf, seasoning, salt and pepper. Simmer 20 minutes. Stir in corn, crabmeat and sherry. Remove bay leaf before serving.

Yield: 4 servings

Margi Zimmerman • Lancaster Power Squadron • Pennsylvania

Hatteras Clam Chowder

1	teaspoon onion powder	1	medium onion, diced
½	teaspoon garlic powder	6	stalks celery, diced
½	teaspoon white pepper	2	(6½-ounce) cans clams
½	teaspoon dried oregano	2	large potatoes, sliced
¾	cup water	3	cups water
6-8	large chowder clams	½	teaspoon pepper
8-10	slices bacon, diced	2	tablespoons dried parsley
¼	teaspoon dried oregano		

Combine onion powder, garlic powder, pepper and oregano in water. Bring to boil. Add clams and steam until well opened. Remove shells and boil liquid until reduced by half. Remove from pan and purée in blender. Set aside clam base.

Brown bacon in a large stockpot. Sauté onion and celery in drippings. Add canned clams. Whisk in clam base and add potatoes. Pour in water. Bring to rolling boil 5 minutes. Add pepper, parsley and oregano. Cool slightly and serve.

Yield: 6 to 8 servings

Tom Moore • Virginia Beach Power Squadron • Virginia

French Egg Chowder

2	medium potatoes, diced	1	tablespoon butter
2	large stalks celery, diced	½	teaspoon parsley
2	medium onions, chopped		Dash of pepper
6-8	hard-cooked eggs, peeled and sliced		Assorted crackers or sliced French bread
1	quart milk		

Combine potato, celery and onion in a stockpot. Cover with just enough water to cook until tender. Do not drain. Add eggs, milk, butter, parsley and pepper. Heat thoroughly, do not boil. Serve with crackers or bread.

Yield: 4 servings

Marge Broyer • Anclote Key Power Squadron • Florida

Red Saunders' Famous Clam Chowder

3   pounds onions, diced

3   pounds potatoes, peeled and diced

2   bushels chowder clams

20   gallons hot water

3   pounds diced salt pork

3   (28-ounce) cans tomatoes

3   (15-ounce) cans cream style corn

Rinse onion and potato three times. Set aside. Scrub each clam. Add water to a G. I. can to 2-inches. Steam one bushel clams in water. Save broth. Steam second bushel of clams. Shuck clams. Place all but 8 quarts clams in a meat grinder. Coarsely chop clams. Add 20 gallons water to a G. I. can. Add all clams, reserved broth, onion, potatoes, salt pork and tomato. Stir and cook 2 hours.

Raise can on brick and cool chowder overnight. Skim off salt pork. Bring to boil, adding water if needed. Stir in corn. Boil 20 minutes. Serve 2 bowls of chowder to a person.

Yield: 250 servings

Robert Ware   •   Penfield Power Squadron   •   Connecticut

New England Fish Chowder

1   stick butter, divided

3   medium onion, sliced

5   medium potatoes, peeled and diced

4   teaspoons salt

½   teaspoon pepper

3   cups boiling water

2   pounds fresh or frozen haddock filets, cut into large chunks

1   quart milk, scalded

1   (12-ounce) can evaporated milk

Melt 4 tablespoons butter in a 6 to 8-quart stockpot. Sauté onion until translucent but not browned. Add potatoes, salt, pepper and water. Top with fish. Simmer, covered, 25 minutes or until potatoes are fork tender. Stir in milk, evaporated milk and remaining butter. Heat thoroughly. Season with additional salt and pepper.

Yield: 4½ quarts

Bruce Sjoquist   •   Bellingham Sail & Power Squadron   •   Michigan

★ Barnes' Down East Clam Chowder

3	gallons water or more as needed	6	pounds white or red potatoes, peeled and cubed
5	pounds clams, cleaned, chopped with juice	8-10	slices turkey bacon, cooked and crumbled
4	large white onions, diced		Garlic salt, pepper, salt and seafood seasoning to taste
1	pound sliced carrots		Plain white cornmeal
1	bunch celery, chopped		

Combine water and clams with juice. Simmer 1 hour, 30 minutes. Add onion, carrot, celery, potato and bacon. Season with garlic salt, pepper, salt and seafood seasoning. Simmer an additional 2 hours, 30 minutes. Add water as needed. When chowder is ready, prepare cornbread dumplings using cornmeal and water. Drop batter into simmering chowder.

Yield: 4 gallons

L. M. Barnes • Rocky Mount Sail & Power Squadron • North Carolina

Awesome White Chili

4	(15-ounce) cans great Northern beans, drained		Salt and pepper to taste
4	(14½-ounce) cans chicken broth	4	boneless, skinless chicken breast halves
½	cup diced onions	6	tablespoons olive oil
3	tablespoons ground cumin	1	(6-ounce) box wild rice mix
7	garlic cloves, minced		Shredded Monterey Jack cheese for garnish

Combine beans, broth, onion, cumin, garlic, salt and pepper in a stockpot. Simmer 30 minutes over medium heat. Cook chicken in oil until done. Cool and chop chicken. Add to soup and simmer an additional 30 minutes. Prepare rice according to package directions. Stir rice into soup. Ladle into soup bowls and top with cheese.

Yield: 6 to 8 servings

Carolyn Ross • Ft. Meyers Power Squadron • Florida

Turkey and Black Bean Chili

1 tablespoon olive oil
1 cup chopped onion
2 cups diced sweet red and bell pepper
1 cup diced carrots
1 garlic clove, chopped
3 tablespoons chili powder
1 tablespoon ground cumin
1 pound ground turkey breast
1 (12-ounce) jar mild fresh salsa
3 cups low-sodium chicken broth
1 (16-ounce) can black beans, drained and rinsed
1 tablespoon low-sodium tomato paste

Heat oil in a stockpot. Sauté onion, red and bell pepper, carrot and garlic 8 minutes, stirring often, until tender. Stir in chili powder and cumin. Add turkey and stir to break up meat. Cook 5 to 7 minutes until meat is cooked. Add salsa, broth, beans and tomato paste. Bring to boil. Reduce heat and simmer 45 minutes until liquid is reduced and chili is thickened.

Yield: 8 servings

Richard Salter • Beverly Sail & Power Squadron • Massachusetts

Lobster Bisque

1 (10¾-ounce) can cream of asparagus soup
1 (10¾-ounce) can cream of mushroom soup
1 cup half & half
Dash of cayenne pepper
½ pound lobster meat
2 tablespoons chopped chives
2 tablespoons sherry, Calvados or brandy
2 tablespoons butter

Combine asparagus and mushroom soup, half & half and cayenne. Bring to simmer over medium heat. Add lobster and chives. Heat, stirring occasionally, to simmer. Stir in sherry. Swirl in butter and serve immediately.

Yield: 2 to 4 servings

Joan Cooke • Ocean City Power Squadron • Maryland

DID YOU KNOW?

There are 6,067 feet in a nautical mile or about 13% longer than the statute mile. Thus if one is going 30 knots you are traveling about 34 miles per hour. Sometimes speed on the water is dangerous. Boat safely, take a boating course.

Serendipity's Real Russian Cabbage Borscht

2	pounds cabbage, shredded	1	(28-ounce) can tomato purée
1	tablespoon kosher salt		
½	teaspoon pepper	1	large potato, cubed
1	onion, chopped	2	teaspoons sour salt
1½	quarts water	1	cup sugar
1½	pounds beef chuck, cubed	2	garlic cloves, minced
1	large soup bone		

Combine cabbage, salt, pepper, onion and water. Cover and bring to boil. Add beef, bone and tomato purée. Reduce heat, cover and simmer 1 hour. Add potato, cover and simmer 40 minutes. Stir in salt and sugar. Simmer 15 minutes. Stir in garlic and simmer 5 minutes.

Yield: 8 servings

May substitute vinegar and lemon juice for sour salt.

Howard Bernbaum • Coco Beach Power Squadron • Florida

Gazpacho Grande

1	large cucumber, peeled, halved lengthwise and seeded	3	cups tomato juice, divided
		⅓	cup red wine vinegar
2	large tomatoes, peeled, cored and seeded	1	tablespoon olive or vegetable oil
1	bell pepper, halved and seeded	¼	teaspoon Tabasco sauce
		¼	teaspoon salt
1	medium onion, peeled and halved	⅛	teaspoon pepper
		3-4	garlic cloves, crushed
1	(2-ounce) jar diced pimentos		Croutons for garnish

Combine half cucumber, 1 tomato, half bell pepper, half onion, pimento and 1 cup tomato juice in a blender. Purée at high speed. Chop the remaining vegetables and place in a bowl. Cover and refrigerate. Pour purée in a separate large bowl. Stir in remaining tomato juice, vinegar, oil, Tabasco, salt, pepper and garlic. Cover and refrigerate at least 2 hours. Before serving, add chopped vegetables to soup. Garnish with croutons.

Yield: 6 servings

Claire Finkel • Fort Vancouver Power Squadron • Washington State

Greek Chicken Salad

3 cups cooked cubed chicken breast
2 medium cucumbers, peeled, seeded and chopped
1¼ cups feta cheese, crumbled
⅔ cup pitted ripe olives, sliced
¼ cup snipped parsley
1 cup mayonnaise
½ cup plain yogurt
1 teaspoon dried oregano
3 garlic cloves, minced
   Pita bread halves and lettuce leaves

Combine chicken, cucumber, feta cheese, olives and parsley in a large bowl. In a separate bowl, whisk together mayonnaise, yogurt, oregano and garlic. Add to chicken mixture and toss to coat. Cover and refrigerate. Serve with pita halves lined with lettuce.

Yield: 4 to 6 servings

Carol Sanfilippo • Peconic Bay Power Squadron • New York

Rendezvous Seafood Salad

1 pound crabmeat
1 cup diced celery
3 hard-cooked eggs, peeled and chopped
½ teaspoon Worcestershire sauce
¼ teaspoon prepared mustard
1 pound chopped shrimp
1 bell pepper, chopped
¾ cup mayonnaise
½ cup chopped onion
   Salt and pepper to taste
   Shredded lettuce

Combine crabmeat, celery, eggs, Worcestershire sauce, mustard, shrimp, bell pepper, mayonnaise, onion, salt and pepper. Mix well. Serve on a bed of shredded lettuce.

Yield: 8 servings

June Reasons • Cape Lookout Sail & Power Squadron • North Carolina

HOT BACON DRESSING

6 slices bacon
1 egg
¼ cup all-purpose flour
¼ cup vinegar
¼ cup sugar
½ teaspoon salt
½ teaspoon dry mustard

Cook bacon until crisp. Cool and crumble. Reserve bacon drippings in skillet. Beat egg in a 2-cup measuring cup. Add flour, vinegar, sugar, salt and mustard and mix well. Add enough water to equal 2-cups. Add to heated drippings. Cook and stir constantly until thickened. Add bacon. Store in the refrigerator. Serve over shredded lettuce, Swiss chard, spinach, endive and dandelion greens.

Yield: 2 cups

Dorothy M. Bonstedt
Fort Meyers Power Squadron
Florida

Hot Crab Salad

White Sauce

1	tablespoon butter	1½	cups milk
2	tablespoons all-purpose flour	1	teaspoon salt
		½	cup mayonnaise

Melt butter in a saucepan. Whisk in flour to make a roux. Stir in milk and salt. Cook, stirring constantly, over low heat until smooth. Remove from heat and stir in mayonnaise. Set aside.

Crab Salad

2	cups cooked noodles	2	tablespoons minced onion
3	eggs, beaten	2	tablespoons diced bell pepper
1½	cups milk	5⅓	tablespoons butter
1	cup breads crumbs	⅓	cup mayonnaise
1	teaspoon salt	1	cup shredded Cheddar cheese
1½	cups crabmeat		

Combine noodles, eggs, milk, bread crumbs, salt and crabmeat. Sauté onion and pepper in butter. Add to crabmeat mixture. Stir in mayonnaise and cheese. Mix well. Pour mixture into a greased 13 x 9 x 2-inch baking dish. Pour white sauce over mixture and gently toss to coat. Bake at 350 degrees 45 to 60 minutes.

Yield: 10 servings

Lynn Stewart • Skagit Bay Sail & Power Squadron • Washington State

Peas and Cauliflower Salad

1 (10-ounce) package frozen baby peas, thawed
1 cup cauliflower florets
½ cup minced onion
¼-½ cup chopped cashews
½ cup chopped celery
  Sliced mushrooms
1 cup fat free mayonnaise
½ cup sugar
2 tablespoons white vinegar

Combine peas, cauliflower, onion, cashews, celery and mushrooms. Whisk together mayonnaise, sugar and vinegar. Pour dressing over salad and toss to coat.

Yield: 4 servings

M. Wright • Delaware River Power Squadron • Pennsylvania

Greek Spinach Pasta Salad

Dressing

½ cup extra virgin olive oil
¼ teaspoon dried oregano
2 garlic cloves, crushed
1 teaspoon Dijon mustard
½ cup white vinegar
  Salt and pepper to taste

Whisk together oil, oregano, garlic, mustard, vinegar, salt and pepper. Refrigerate dressing.

Pasta Salad

1 (12-ounce) package bow tie pasta, cooked al dente
½ cup grated Parmesan cheese
1 (6-ounce) package feta cheese, crumbled
1 bunch green onions, chopped
1 (12-ounce) bag spinach leaves
1 pint cherry tomatoes, halved
1 medium cucumber, chopped
½ cup Greek olives
2-3 cups cooked cubed chicken

Combine pasta, Parmesan cheese, feta cheese, onion, spinach, tomato, cucumber, olives and chicken. Mix well. Cover and refrigerate. Just before serving, pour in dressing and toss to coat.

Yield: 8 servings

Ellie Lemoine • Lake Charles Power Squadron • Louisiana

HARD-COOKED EGGS

12 eggs

Cover eggs with cold water in a saucepan. Bring to a quick boil. Remove from heat and cover. Let stand 3 minutes. Run under cold water.

Yield: 12 eggs

Carole Biddick

Door County Sail & Power Squadron

Wisconsin

Pasta e Fagioli

3 cups dry cannellini beans	1 large stalk celery with leaves, diced
3 tablespoons extra virgin olive oil and more for serving	1 medium onion, diced
½ teaspoon crushed red pepper	6 garlic cloves, minced
½ cup minced pancetta or bacon	3 quarts water
1 medium carrot, diced	¾ teaspoon sea salt
	Pepper to taste
	⅓ cup small dry pasta

Rinse beans, remove pebbles and place in a bowl. Cover with boiling water and set aside 1 hour. Drain and rinse beans. Discard water. In a large stockpot, combine oil, red pepper, pancetta, carrot, celery, onion and garlic. Cook 5 minutes until tender. Add beans and water. Bring to simmer, cover and cook 30 minutes. Add salt and pepper. Simmer until beans are soft. Cook 45 minutes, stirring occasionally. Remove from heat.

Working in batches, purée soup in an immersion mixer until creamy, leaving some beans whole. Return to pot. Add pasta and cook 8 minutes until pasta is tender. Add water if too thick. Serve very hot and drizzle each serving with oil.

Yield: 6 to 8 servings

Richard P. Gallop • Mount Clemens Power Squadron • Michigan

78 ● SALADS

Celery Salad

1   bunch celery with leaves, sliced on a diagonal
½   cup sliced mushrooms
2   tablespoons Italian dressing
½   cup cherry tomatoes, halved
1   medium onion, thinly sliced and halved
2   tablespoons ranch or blue cheese dressing

Place celery in a bowl and refrigerate. Toss mushrooms with Italian dressing and refrigerate. Place halved tomatoes in the refrigerator. One hour before serving, add tomato and onion to mushrooms and toss to coat. Return to refrigerator. Just before serving, drain off dressing and add to celery. Toss well. If serving in individual salad bowls, drizzle with 2 tablespoons ranch dressing. If serving in a large salad bowl, serve dressing separately.

Yield: 4 to 6 servings

Variation: Add bacon bits or chopped nuts just prior to serving.

Joyce Bradshaw • Nansemond River Power Squadron • Virginia

Japanese Coleslaw

Dressing

¼   cup sugar
1   teaspoon salt
1   teaspoon pepper
6   tablespoons rice vinegar
¾   cup vegetable oil

Combine sugar, salt, pepper, vinegar and oil and mix well.

Coleslaw

1   small head cabbage, shredded
½   cup toasted almonds
½   cup toasted sunflower seeds
8   green onions, chopped
1   (3-ounce) package Ramen noodles, broken up, discard flavor packet

Just before serving, combine cabbage, almonds, sunflower seeds, onion and noodles. Toss with dressing. Serve immediately.

Yield: 4 servings

Joan Druker • Lake Candlewood Power Squadron • New York

 Maurice Salad

Maurice Dressing

1 egg	1 cup olive or vegetable oil, divided
2 tablespoons lemon juice	1 hard-cooked egg, peeled
½ teaspoon dry mustard	1 small gherkins pickle, sliced
1 teaspoon salt	Parsley without stems
1 green onion	

Process egg, juice, mustard and salt in blender. Add onion and ¼ cup oil. Blend 5 minutes. Add remaining oil, hard-boiled egg, pickle and parsley and blend until smooth. Set aside.

Salad

Shredded or torn lettuce	Cooked shredded chicken
Shredded ham	Tomato wedges and hard-cooked eggs, sliced
Shredded gherkins pickles	
Shredded Swiss cheese	

Mix together lettuce, ham, gherkins, Swiss cheese and chicken. Pour on dressing and toss to coat. Top with tomato wedges and hard-cooked eggs.

Yield: 6 servings

Nancy Miner • Birmingham Power Squadron • Michigan

Ramen Noodle Salad

1 (1-pound) package broccoli coleslaw	½ cup toasted almonds
2 (3-ounce) packages Ramen noodles, broken up	4 green onions, chopped
	⅓ cup cider vinegar
	½ cup vegetable oil
½ cup toasted sunflower seeds	½ cup sugar
	2 flavor packets from noodles

Combine coleslaw, noodles, sunflower seeds, almonds and onion. In a separate bowl, whisk together vinegar, oil, sugar and flavor packets. Pour dressing over coleslaw. Toss well. Cover and refrigerate.

Yield: 12 servings

Barbara McGhee • Ocala Sail & Power Squadron • Florida

Kim's Strawberry-Spinach Salad

Dressing

½ cup sugar
1 tablespoon poppy seeds
1 teaspoon salt
⅓ cup red wine vinegar
1 cup vegetable oil

Whisk together sugar, poppy seeds, salt, vinegar and oil. Mix well and refrigerate.

Pecans

1 egg white
½ cup packed brown sugar
Dash of vanilla
4 cups pecans
Salt to taste

Preheat oven to 275 degrees. Beat together egg white, brown sugar and vanilla until smooth. Add pecans and toss to coat. Spread mixture onto a parchment paper-lined baking sheet. Bake at 350 degrees 10 to 15 minutes until browned. Remove from oven and sprinkle with salt.

Salad

1 bunch spinach, rinsed
10 large strawberries, sliced

Toss together spinach, strawberries and pecans. Pour on dressing just before serving.

Yield: 6 servings

Carol Allen • Sanibel/Captiva Power Squadron • Florida

Sunset Salad

1 bunch broccoli, cut into florets
1 red onion, chopped
¼ cup sugar
1 cup mayonnaise
1 pound bacon, cooked and crumbled
½ cup golden raisins

Combine broccoli, onion, sugar, mayonnaise, bacon and raisins. Refrigerate until ready to serve.

Yield: 4 servings

A simple and tasty treat while anchored in a secluded cove, watching a sunset.

Dianne Marshburn • Tar River Power Squadron • North Carolina

★ **HOMEMADE MUSTARD**

1 cup dry mustard
1 cup cider vinegar
¼ cup sugar
¾ cup packed brown sugar
3 eggs, well beaten

Combine mustard, vinegar, sugar, brown sugar and eggs in the top of a double boiler. Whisk mixture constantly until it reaches 165 degrees for 1 minute. Do not boil. Spoon mustard into a jar and seal tightly. Refrigerate before serving. Store in refrigerator.

Yield: 1½ cups

Mary Lou and Les Johnson
Diablo Power Squadron
California

MOM PEOPLES
MAYONNAISE

½ cup water
1 cup vinegar
1 cup sugar
1 tablespoon
all-purpose flour
2 teaspoons dry mustard
4-5 eggs

Combine water, vinegar,
sugar, flour, mustard and
eggs in a saucepan. Cook
and stir until thickened.
Cool and refrigerate. For
a thicker consistency, use
egg yolks for eggs.

Yield: 2 cups

Linda Peoples

Banana River Power
Squadron

Florida

Fresh Vegetable Pasta Salad

Marinade

1½ cups vegetable oil	1 teaspoon garlic powder
1½ cups sugar	1 teaspoon seasoned salt
1½ cups vinegar	1 (16-ounce) package
1 teaspoon salt	rotini, cooked al dente
1 teaspoon pepper	

Whisk together oil, sugar, vinegar, salt, pepper, garlic powder and seasoned salt. Pour over cooked pasta. Cover and refrigerate until ready to serve or overnight.

Vegetables

2 cucumbers, sliced	1 cup broccoli florets
1 cup sliced mushrooms	2 stalks celery, chopped
2 carrots, sliced	3-4 green onions, chopped
1 cup cauliflower florets	Cherry tomatoes

Just before serving, add vegetables to pasta and toss to coat. Serve immediately.

Yield: 8 to 10 servings

Mary L. McAllister   •   Beaver Lake Power Squadron   •   Arkansas

Layered Lettuce Salad

1 head lettuce, torn into small pieces	8 slices bacon, cooked and crumbled
1 cup diced celery	2 cups mayonnaise
4 hard-cooked eggs, sliced	1-2 tablespoons sugar
1 (10-ounce) package frozen green peas, thawed and drained	1 cup shredded Cheddar cheese
½ cup diced bell pepper	Chopped parsley for garnish
1 medium red onion, diced	

Layer ingredients in order in a 13 x 9 x 2-inch glass dish, starting with lettuce, celery, eggs, peas, bell pepper, onion and bacon. Mix together mayonnaise and sugar. Spread evenly over salad. Sprinkle with cheese. Cover and refrigerate 8 to 12 hours. Top with parsley before serving.

Yield: 12 servings

Alice J. Pardoe   •   Singing River Sail & Power Squadron   •   Mississippi

Barnacle Bill's Offshore Salad

¾ cup red wine vinegar
½ cup olive oil
1 cup sugar
1 (8½-ounce) can very young peas
1 (11-ounce) can shoe peg corn
1 (14½-ounce) can French style green beans
1 cup chopped celery
1 cup bell pepper
1 cup chopped green onion
1 (4-ounce) jar sliced pimentos
¾ cup chopped parsley
3 bay leaves
1 teaspoon dried basil
Pepper to taste

Combine vinegar, oil and sugar in a saucepan. Bring to boil. Remove from heat and cool. Combine peas, corn, beans, celery, bell pepper, green onion, pimentos, parsley, bay leaves and basil in a large bowl. Pour cooled marinade over salad. Toss to coat. Cover and refrigerate at least 8 hours or overnight. Remove bay leaves before serving. Season with pepper when serving.

Yield: 6 to 8 servings

"D" and Don Wogaman • Columbus Power Squadron • Ohio

Chick or Not Pasta Salad

Dressing
1 teaspoon Dijon mustard
¼ cup red wine vinegar
1 cup olive oil
2 teaspoons honey
1 garlic clove, crushed
Pepper to taste

Whisk together mustard, vinegar, oil, honey, garlic and pepper. Let stand 15 minutes.

Salad
1 pound bow tie pasta, cooked al dente
2 cups cooked chopped chicken
10-12 slices bacon, cooked and crumbled
2 cups coarsely shredded spinach
1 cup pitted black olives, sliced or whole
1 (4-ounce) package crumbled blue cheese

Combine pasta, chicken, bacon, spinach, olives and blue cheese. Mix well. Pour on dressing and gently toss to coat.

Yield: 12 servings

Marjorie Brandt • Clearwater Power Squadron • Florida

MOTHER'S FRENCH DRESSING

½ cup vegetable oil
6 tablespoons sugar
¼ cup ketchup
2 tablespoons vinegar
1 teaspoon salt
¼ teaspoon dry mustard
¼ teaspoon cayenne pepper
Juice of one lemon
1 small onion, quartered

Combine oil, sugar, ketchup, vinegar, salt, mustard, cayenne, juice and onion in a large jar. Seal lid and shake until well blended. Pour over sliced tomato or green salad with orange slices and red onion.

Yield: 1½ cups

Carolyn Knaggs
Port Huron Power Squadron
Michigan

$150.00 Cabbage Slaw

Dressing

2	teaspoons sugar	1	tablespoon salt
1	teaspoon dry mustard	1	cup vinegar
1	teaspoon celery seed	¾	cup vegetable oil

Combine sugar, mustard, celery seed, salt, vinegar and oil in a saucepan. Bring to boil. Reduce heat and keep warm.

Slaw

1	head cabbage, shredded	½	cup shredded carrots
1	onion, thinly sliced or 1 tablespoon instant onion flakes	½	cup chopped bell pepper
		1	cup sugar

Place cabbage, onion, carrot and bell pepper in a bowl. Top with sugar. Pour hot dressing over salad. Cover tightly and refrigerate 4 to 5 hours.

Yield: 4 servings

Slaw is better after the third day when flavors have blended. May store slaw in the refrigerator for 2 to 3 weeks.

Martha & Lee Dreier • Cincinnati Power Squadron • Ohio

Sweet and Sour Dressing

¼	cup extra virgin olive oil	1	tablespoon dried parsley
¼	cup vegetable oil	1	teaspoon salt
¼	cup sugar		Pepper to taste
2	tablespoons balsamic vinegar	12	dashes of Tabasco sauce
2	tablespoons Heinz salad vinegar	1	garlic clove, minced

Combine olive oil, vegetable oil, sugar, vinegars, parsley, salt, pepper, Tabasco and garlic in a jar. Seal lid tightly and shake well. Refrigerate until ready to use.

Yield: 1 cup

Susan Skeoch • St. Lucie River Power Squadron • Florida

JANUARY 1996

THE ENSIGN®

OFFICIAL MAGAZINE OF UNITED STATES POWER SQUADRONS

Sail and Power Boating

vegetables
& sides

the ensign®

read all about it!!!

Charles and Shirley just took a terrific trip from Pittsburgh to Louisville and back on the Ohio. Did you read about it in The Ensign®*? Articles like these and others of general interest to the recreational boater are printed monthly in the USPS magazine* The Ensign. *Each month the magazine devotes itself to topics about which the recreational boater is interested.*

Some months the topic is engine maintenance, others the maintenance of sails or the servicing of electronic equipment. As fall approaches there are articles on preparing the boat for winter storage and in the spring, writers give tips on getting ready for the season. These and other articles are all prepared by knowledgeable experienced boaters who maintain their own vessels.

This is a magazine about boating, written by members of USPS who are boaters. The Ensign *is not a professional publication designed to sell members products, but a newsletter with items of interest for its members.*

Do you have an interesting story to tell about a great cruise, a tip on how to easily change the impeller in a water pump or how to make repairs in fiberglass?

Then why not join us and be part of the writing staff of The Ensign*?*

For more information call 1-888-367-8777. Thanks for listening!

Broccoli-Pepper Jack Cheese Casserole

1½ cups ricotta cheese
3 eggs
4 tablespoons butter
⅓ cup all-purpose flour
5 cups broccoli, steamed until tender
1 (11-ounce) can shoe peg corn or whole kernel corn

2½ cups shredded pepper jack cheese
½ cup chopped onion
½ cup chopped sweet red pepper
½ teaspoon salt

Combine ricotta cheese, eggs, butter and flour in a blender. Process until smooth. Mix broccoli, corn, pepper cheese, onion, red pepper and salt in a bowl. Stir in ricotta cheese mixture and toss to coat. Spoon mixture into a lightly greased 13 x 9 x 2-inch baking dish. Bake at 350 degrees 45 minutes.

Yield: 8 to 10 servings

Anne Wolski • Northern Neck Provisional Power Squadron • Virginia

DID YOU KNOW?

At crowded marinas an open cleat for securing your line is rare. So as not to disturb your neighbor's boat, just run a line under the neighbor's dock line and secure it with a bowline. These and other knots and docking techniques are taught in the Squadron Boating Course.

Carrot Casserole

8 carrots, steamed until tender and sliced
½ cup mayonnaise
1 tablespoon horseradish
2 tablespoons minced onion

½ teaspoon salt
½ teaspoon pepper
Buttered bread crumbs, slivered almonds and paprika

Combine carrots, mayonnaise, horseradish, onion, salt and pepper and mix well. Spoon mixture into an 11 x 7 x 2-inch baking dish. Top with bread crumbs, almonds and sprinkle with paprika. Bake at 350 degrees 25 minutes or until bubbly.

Yield: 8 servings

Doris Smith Hallister • Des Moines Power Squadron • Iowa

Baked Corn

3	(14¾-ounce) cans cream style corn	1½	cups milk
4	eggs	2	cups sugar

Combine corn, eggs, milk and sugar and mix well. Pour mixture into a 3-quart casserole dish. Bake at 350 degrees 2 hours or until center is firm.

Yield: 6 to 8 servings

Anne McQuade • Palisades Power Squadron • New Jersey

Country Corn Pudding

3	eggs	1	teaspoon salt
2	cups heavy cream	2	(15-ounce) cans whole kernel corn, drained
1	tablespoon all-purpose flour	2	tablespoons butter, melted
¼	cup sugar		

Beat eggs until pale yellow. Add cream, flour, sugar and salt. Mix well. Stir in corn and butter. Pour mixture into a buttered 1½-quart casserole dish. Cover and bake at 325 degrees 1 hour.

Yield: 4 to 6 servings

Janell F. Boyd • Cape Fear Power Squadron • North Carolina

Al's Summer Garden Vegetables

1	tablespoon vegetable shortening	5-6	hot yellow peppers, sliced
1	small head cabbage, sliced	3	large tomatoes, sliced
3	large yellow onions, sliced	½	teaspoon salt
		¼	teaspoon paprika

Melt shortening in a stockpot. Layer in order the cabbage, onion, pepper and tomato. Add salt and paprika. Stir and cook until tender. Serve over mashed potatoes or with sausage.

Yield: 6 servings

Donna Selden • Richmond Sail & Power Squadron • Virginia

Cabbage Au Gratin

4	cups shredded cabbage	½	teaspoon salt
6	tablespoons butter, divided and melted	1	cup milk
1½	tablespoons all-purpose flour	1	cup shredded Cheddar cheese
		2	cups bread crumbs

Boil cabbage 5 minutes. Drain well. Combine 2 tablespoons butter, flour, salt and milk in a saucepan. Cook and stir until smooth and thickened. Arrange alternating layers of cabbage, cheese and sauce in a 1½-quart casserole. Mix together bread crumbs and remaining 4 tablespoons butter. Sprinkle over casserole. Bake at 350 degrees 25 minutes.

Yield: 6 servings

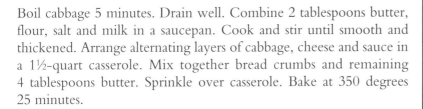

Louise Sewell • Atlanta Sail & Power Squadron • Georgia

German Style Red Cabbage

2	pounds red cabbage	2	tablespoons all-purpose flour
4-6 slices bacon		⅔	cup vinegar
½	cup diced red onion	⅔	cup packed brown sugar

Slice cabbage into quarters. Remove white core and julienne the cabbage. Cook cabbage in water 10 minutes. Drain well and place in a serving bowl. Cook bacon in a skillet. Remove bacon and crumble. Add onion to bacon drippings and sauté 15 minutes. Whisk in flour and cook 5 minutes. Add vinegar and bring to boil. Cook 2 minutes. Stir in brown sugar. Add bacon and onion mixture to cabbage. Toss to coat.

Yield: 4 servings

Mary Evans • Austin Power Squadron • Texas

Popeye's Spinach Soufflé

1	(16-ounce) container cottage cheese	Dash of ground nutmeg
3	eggs, beaten	Salt to taste
3	(10-ounce) packages frozen chopped spinach, thawed and squeezed dry	1½ cups shredded Cheddar cheese, divided

Combine cottage cheese and eggs. Stir in spinach, nutmeg, salt and 1 cup cheese. Mix well. Pour mixture into a greased 11 x 7 x 2-inch baking dish. Sprinkle ½ cup remaining cheese. Bake at 350 degrees 30 to 40 minutes or until set.

Yield: 4 to 6 servings

Patricia Blanchard • Peconic Bay Power Squadron • New York

 Spinach Squares

2	(10-ounce) packages frozen chopped spinach, thawed and squeezed dry	1	tablespoon chopped onion
3	eggs, slightly beaten	2	(8-ounce) packages shredded sharp Cheddar cheese
1	cup all-purpose flour		Dash of seasoned salt
1	cup milk	2	tablespoons butter, melted
1	teaspoon salt		
1	teaspoon baking powder	2	tablespoons olive oil

Combine spinach, eggs, flour, milk, salt, baking powder, onion, cheese and salt. Mix well. Blend butter and oil and spread on the bottom of a 13 x 9 x 2-inch baking dish. Pour spinach mixture into dish. Bake at 350 degrees 30 minutes or until bubbly and slightly browned.

Yield: 8 servings

Nancy Miner • Lakes Region Power Squadron • New Hampshire

Spinach Pie (Spanakopita)

1 pound feta cheese, cubed
1 (16-ounce) container ricotta cheese
2 (10-ounce) packages fresh spinach or frozen, thawed and squeezed dry

8 eggs, beaten
¼ cup milk
½ cup Romano cheese
½ cup olive oil
4 sticks butter
1 (16-ounce) package frozen phyllo dough, thawed

Combine feta cheese and ricotta cheese. Rinse, remove stems and finely chop fresh spinach. Add spinach, eggs, milk, Romano cheese and oil to cheese mixture. Mix well. Melt butter in a saucepan. Set aside. Butter a 15 x 10 x 1-inch baking sheet. Lay one sheet of phyllo dough into pan and smooth with fingers. Brush butter over sheet. Repeat dough and butter layers for a stack of 6 to 8 phyllo sheets. Spread spinach mixture evenly over dough. Top with 6 to 8 phyllo sheets, brushing each with butter. Bake at 350 degrees 1 hour, 15 minutes. Cool and cut into squares.

Yield: 20 to 24 servings

Mary and Theophilos Kuliopulos • Beverly Power Squadron
Massachusetts

Asparagus-Tomato Stir-Fry

2 tablespoons plus 1 teaspoon vegetable oil
½ teaspoon grated ginger
¾ pound asparagus, cut into 1-inch slices
4 green onion, thinly sliced into 1-inch pieces

1½ cups sliced mushrooms
¼ cup chicken broth
2 teaspoons soy sauce
1 teaspoon cornstarch
2 small tomatoes, cut into wedges

Heat 2 tablespoons oil in a skillet. Cook ginger 30 seconds. Add asparagus and green onion and cook 3 minutes. Stir in mushroom and cook 1 minute. Pour in broth. Blend soy sauce, 1 teaspoon oil and cornstarch until smooth. Pour sauce into the center of the skillet. Stir until thickened. Add tomato and stir until coated and heated thoroughly.

Yield: 4 servings

Carol Thranhardt • Southport Power Squadron • North Carolina

BUTTER SAUCE

1 stick butter

3 tablespoons fish broth

2 hard-cooked eggs, chopped or ¼ cup chopped green onion

2 tablespoons capers, drained or 2 tablespoons lemon juice

Combine butter, broth, eggs and capers in a saucepan. Cook and stir until butter melts. Heat thoroughly.

Yield: 1 cup sauce

Tish Cullen

Las Vegas Power Squadron

Nevada

Asparagus Casserole Supreme

3	pounds asparagus, trimmed	1	teaspoon Worcestershire sauce
1	(10¾-ounce) can cream of mushroom soup	¼	teaspoon pepper
¾	cup mayonnaise	1½	cups shredded Cheddar cheese
2	tablespoons lemon juice		

Steam asparagus about 3 minutes. Drain well. Arrange in a lightly greased 13 x 9 x 2-inch baking dish. Blend soup, mayonnaise, juice, Worcestershire sauce and pepper. Pour over asparagus. Cover and refrigerate 8 hours.

Bake at 350 degrees 15 to 20 minutes. Sprinkle with cheese and bake an additional 5 minutes or until cheese melts.

Yield: 12 servings

Sue Acheson • Port Huron Power Squadron • Michigan

Green Bean Bundles

1	pound green beans, trimmed	3	tablespoons butter or bacon drippings
8	slices bacon, partially cooked	1	tablespoon white wine vinegar
1	tablespoon finely chopped onion	1	tablespoon sugar
		¼	teaspoon salt

Cook beans until crisp-tender. Wrap a bacon slice around 15 beans and secure with a toothpick. Place on a foil-lined baking sheet. Sauté onion in butter until tender. Stir in vinegar, sugar and salt and heat thoroughly. Bake bundles at 400 degrees 10 to 15 minutes or until bacon is cooked. Remove to a platter and pour sauce over beans. Serve immediately.

Yield: 8 servings

Pat Halligan Kroeger • Quad City Power Squadron • Iowa

Green Beans and Swiss Cheese

3 tablespoons butter,
   divided
1 tablespoon all-purpose
   flour
½ teaspoon pepper
¼ cup milk
½ teaspoon grated onion

½ cup sour cream
2 (16-ounce) cans whole
   green beans, drained
1 (8-ounce) package
   shredded Swiss cheese
⅓ cup french-fried onion
   rings, crumbled

Melt 1 tablespoon butter in a saucepan. Whisk in flour and pepper.
Cook and stir until smooth and bubbly. Blend in milk. Remove from
heat and add onion and sour cream. Stir in beans and cheese. Pour
mixture into a buttered 1½-quart casserole dish. Top with onion rings
and drizzle with 2 tablespoons melted butter. Bake at 400 degrees
20 minutes.

Yield: 6 to 8 servings

Paula and Jeff Crosby • Port Clinton Power Squadron • Ohio

★ New-Wave Green Beans

2 tablespoons butter
1½ pounds green beans,
   trimmed
1 (¾-ounce) package
   cremini mushroom,
   rinsed and sliced
1 cup heavy cream

½ teaspoon salt
¼ teaspoon pepper
1 (8-ounce) package Brie
   cheese, rind removed
   and cubed
3 tablespoons walnuts,
   toasted and chopped

Melt butter in a large skillet. Sauté beans, stirring occasionally, 7 minutes
or until crisp-tender. Add mushroom and cook 5 minutes. Stir in
cream, salt and pepper. Remove from heat. Add Brie cheese and stir
until cheese melts. Top with walnuts. Serve immediately.

Yield: 4 servings

To toast walnuts, spread nuts on a baking sheet. Bake at 350
degrees 7 to 10 minutes. Cool slightly before chopping.

Sandy Kennedy • St. Petersburg Sail & Power Squadron • Florida

Sweet Peas

1	tablespoon olive oil	1	tablespoon cornstarch
½	cup diced celery	½	cup chicken broth
½	cup diced onion	2	teaspoons honey
⅓	cup orange juice	½	teaspoon salt
1	(16-ounce) package frozen baby sweet peas, thawed	⅛	teaspoon pepper
		⅓	cup craisins

Heat oil in a saucepan. Sauté celery and onion 5 minutes or until tender. Add juice and peas. Cook 5 minutes, stirring frequently. Whisk together cornstarch and broth. Stir into pea mixture. Remove from heat. Add honey, salt, pepper and craisins. Serve immediately.

Yield: 4 to 6 servings

Eva "Frankie" Foster • Santana Sail & Power Squadron • California

Grilled Marinated Portobello Mushrooms

2	tablespoons balsamic vinegar	2	teaspoons chopped basil or 1 teaspoon dried
⅓	cup olive oil		Salt and pepper to taste
½	teaspoon minced garlic	4	whole portobello mushrooms

Combine vinegar, oil, garlic, basil, salt and pepper. Arrange mushrooms smooth side down in a baking dish. Pour marinade over mushrooms. Let stand 10 minutes, turning once. Grill mushroom 5 to 7 minutes, turning once.

Yield: 4 servings

Serve sliced in a sandwich, on pizza or salads or as a dinner side dish.

Clorinda McVinna • Ft. Worth Power Squadron • Texas

Eggplant Casserole

1	medium or large eggplant, peeled and sliced
	Salt and pepper to taste
1	small onion, diced
2	tablespoons butter
¾	cup milk
3	tablespoons shredded sharp Cheddar cheese
1	cup crushed buttery round crackers
4	slices American cheese or shredded mozzarella cheese

Cook eggplant in salted water until tender. Drain and mash. Add salt, pepper, onion, butter, milk, Cheddar cheese and cracker crumbs. Mix well. Spoon mixture into a greased 1-quart casserole dish. Bake at 350 degrees 50 minutes. Arrange cheese slices on top and bake an additional 10 minutes.

Yield: 4 servings

Marianne Bartley • Crystal River Power Squadron • Florida

Eggplant and Tomato Casserole

2	medium eggplant, peeled and cut into 2-inch cubes
2	garlic cloves, finely chopped
¼	cup vegetable oil
2	(32-ounce) cans stewed tomatoes, undrained
3	tablespoons all-purpose flour
	Salt and pepper to taste
2	teaspoons sugar
1	teaspoon paprika
½	teaspoon dried basil
½	cup grated Parmesan cheese

Steam eggplant in salted water 10 minutes. Drain well and set aside. Sauté garlic in oil 3 minutes until golden browned. Remove from heat. Stir in tomato, flour, salt, pepper, sugar, paprika and basil. Bring to boil. Reduce heat and simmer until sauce thickens. Add eggplant and mix well. Pour into a greased 2-quart casserole. Top with cheese. Bake at 375 degrees 20 minutes or until lightly browned.

Yield: 6 to 8 servings

Rosemary Stevenson • Lake Hartwell Sail & Power Squadron
South Carolina

HOT BACON DRESSING

6 slices bacon
1 egg, beaten
¼ cup all-purpose flour
¼ cup vinegar
¼ cup sugar
½ teaspoon salt
¼ teaspoon mustard

Cook bacon and remove to a plate. Crumble bacon. Reserve drippings. Blend egg, flour, vinegar, sugar, salt and mustard in a 2 cup measuring cup. Add enough water to equal 2 cups. Stir mixture into hot bacon drippings. Cook and stir until thickened. Return bacon and mix well. Serve over shredded lettuce, Swiss chard, spinach, endive or dandelion greens. Store in the refrigerator.

Yield: 1 cup dressing

Dorothy M. Bonstedt
Ft. Meyers Power Squadron
Florida

Vidalia Onion Pie

6 tablespoons butter, divided	2 eggs, slightly beaten
1 cup finely crushed saltine crackers	1 teaspoon salt
	Dash of pepper
3 cups thinly sliced Vidalia onion	Dash of ground nutmeg
¾ cup milk	1 cup shredded sharp Cheddar cheese

Melt 4 tablespoons butter and mix with cracker crumbs. Press crumbs into the bottom and up sides of a 9-inch pie plate. Melt 2 tablespoons of butter in a skillet. Sauté onion about 15 minutes. Do not brown. Spoon onion into pie shell. Heat milk, eggs, salt, pepper and nutmeg. Pour over onion. Sprinkle with cheese. Bake at 350 degrees 30 minutes. Cut into wedges and serve immediately.

Yield: 6 to 8 servings

Dorothy B. Willis • Vero Beach Power Squadron • Florida

 Tomato Pie

4-6 tomatoes, sliced	1 cup mayonnaise
1 Vidalia onion, sliced	1 cup shredded Cheddar cheese
Fresh basil leaves	
1 (9-inch) deep dish pie crust, baked	1 cup shredded mozzarella cheese
Salt and pepper to taste	

Layer tomato slices, onion and basil in pie crust. Season with salt and pepper. Blend together mayonnaise, Cheddar cheese and mozzarella cheese. Spread over filling. Bake at 350 degrees 30 minutes. Serve hot or cold.

Yield: 8 servings

Ann Bailey • Raleigh Sail & Power Squadron • North Carolina

Tomato and Potato Tart

6 small ripe tomatoes, halved and seeded
   Extra virgin olive oil
1 teaspoon finely ground toasted coriander seeds
   Sea salt and pepper to taste

1 pound Yukon gold or new red potatoes, very thinly sliced
1 teaspoon fresh thyme leaves

DID YOU KNOW?

If you experience fire, flooding, collision or crew-overboard will you know what to do? It usually happens to the other guy, but occasionally it happens to us. A boating course can help.

Place tomato, cut side up, close together in the center of a baking sheet. Sprinkle with 2 tablespoons oil, coriander, salt and pepper. Roast at 400 degrees 1 hour, 30 minutes until wilted and browned. Cool completely.

Layer one half of potato in a 10-inch cast-iron skillet. Begin layering in the center and working in circles, layer potato like fish scales. Season with salt and pepper. Layer remaining potato in the same fashion. Roast at 400 degrees 30 minutes or until browned. Remove from oven. Arrange tomato over potato in a single layer near center. Pour any tomato juice on top. Return to oven and roast an additional 20 minutes. Remove from oven and top with thyme. Cut into wedges and serve.

Yield: 6 servings

Rose Closter • Manhasset Bay Power Squadron • New York

Cream Cheese Potatoes

8 medium potatoes
1 (8-ounce) package low-fat cream cheese, softened
1 (8-ounce) container low-fat sour cream

1 stick butter, softened
¼ teaspoon garlic salt
1 cup shredded sharp Cheddar cheese

Boil potato in unsalted water until tender. Mash potato in a bowl. Add cream cheese, sour cream, butter and garlic salt. Mix well. Spread mixture in a buttered 9 x 9 x 2-inch baking dish. Top with Cheddar cheese. Bake at 325 degrees 1 hour. Cover with foil during last 15 minutes to prevent over browning.

Yield: 8 to 9 servings

Juanita Henning • Marco Island Power Squadron • Florida

Potatoes Au Gratin

8	potatoes, peeled and sliced	1	pint half & half
2	yellow onions, chopped Salt, black pepper and white pepper to taste	1	stick butter, sliced
		1	(12-ounce) package shredded mozzarella cheese

Place a single layer of potato and onion in a buttered 13 x 9 x 2-inch baking dish. Sprinkle with salt, black pepper and white pepper. Continue with layers of potato and onion, leaving the nicest potato slices for the top. Pour half & half over all. Dot with butter slices and top with mozzarella cheese. Cover with foil and bake at 350 degrees 1 hour, 15 minutes or until tender. Remove foil and bake until lightly browned.

Yield: 6 servings

Eva Hult • Everglades Power Squadron • Florida

Blue Cheese Baked Potatoes

4	medium-large potatoes	3	tablespoons minced green onion
⅔	cup non-fat plain yogurt		Paprika for garnish
3	tablespoons crumbled blue cheese		

Pierce potatoes with a knife. Bake at 425 degrees 50 minutes or until tender. Cool slightly. Slice off top of each potato and remove pulp. Do not break the skin. Mash potato pulp. Add yogurt, blue cheese and green onion. Mix well. Return potato mixture to skin, mounding up the top. Sprinkle with paprika. Broil 5 minutes or until lightly browned.

Yield: 4 servings

Norm Menchel • Kingsway Power Squadron • New Jersey

Hacienda Executive Potato Casserole

6 medium potatoes
6 tablespoons butter, divided
1 (8-ounce) package
   shredded Cheddar
   cheese
1 (16-ounce) container sour
   cream
⅓ cup chopped chives
½ teaspoon salt
¼ teaspoon white pepper

Boil potatoes in salted water until tender. Refrigerate. When cool, peel and grate potatoes. Combine 4 tablespoons melted butter, cheese, sour cream, chives, salt and pepper. Pour over potatoes and mix gently. Pour mixture into a 13 x 9 x 2-inch baking dish. Dot with 2 tablespoons butter. Bake at 350 degrees 30 to 35 minutes.

Yield: 8 to 10 servings

Baked potatoes may be prepared in advance and frozen.

Judy Griffing • Santana Power Squadron • California

DID YOU KNOW?

Working together to keep our water clean…in the US territorial waters you must be at least 3 miles off shore before dumping raw sewage overboard. Rules on spills and dumping waste are covered in boating courses.

Sweet Potato Casserole

3 cups cooked mashed
   sweet potatoes
1 cup sugar
1 stick plus 2 tablespoons
   butter, melted
2 eggs, well beaten
1 teaspoon vanilla
⅓ cup milk
½ cup packed brown sugar
¼ cup all-purpose flour
½ cup chopped pecans

Combine sweet potatoes, sugar, 1 stick melted butter, eggs, vanilla and milk. Mix well. Pour mixture into a greased 2-quart casserole dish. Mix together brown sugar, flour and 2 tablespoons melted butter until crumbly. Sprinkle over potato. Top with pecans. Bake at 350 degrees 25 minutes.

Yield: 8 servings

Ruth C. Wentworth • Green Bay Sail & Power Squadron • Wisconsin

Stovies
(a Scottish one-pot stove-top dish)

Bacon slices, chopped
Potatoes, thinly sliced
Carrots, thinly sliced
Onion, thinly sliced

Smoked sausage, sliced
  lengthwise
Salt, pepper and seasoned
  salt to taste

Layer bacon on the bottom of a saucepan. Alternate layers of potato, carrot, onion and sausage. Season each layer with salt, pepper and seasoned salt. Cover with a tight fitting lid. Cook over low heat 1 hour or until vegetables are tender.

Yield: 6 to 8 servings

William Berry • Santa Barbara Power Squadron • California

Avocado Goat Cheese Baguette

1   large ripe avocado,
    peeled and pitted
¼   teaspoon minced garlic
    Salt and pepper to taste
1   tablespoon lemon juice

1   (16-ounce) loaf crusty
    sourdough baguette
    Olive oil
1   (3½-ounce) log soft goat
    cheese
1   tomato, sliced

Lightly mash avocado. Stir in garlic, salt, pepper and juice. Slice baguette on the diagonal into 4 lengthwise pieces. Slice each piece in half. Drizzle both sides with olive oil. Spread goat cheese on one side and sprinkle with pepper. Spread avocado mixture on other side and top with tomato slices. Place halves together to make a sandwich. Wrap in foil or plastic wrap.

Yield: 4 servings

Kathy Hall • Susquehannock Power Squadron • Pennsylvania

Vegetable Spaghetti Pie

1 medium pepper, chopped (choice of bell, sweet red or yellow)
1 cup sliced mushrooms
½ cup chopped onion
½ cup thinly sliced carrots
1 tablespoon olive oil
1 (15-ounce) can tomato sauce
2 cups cooked spaghetti
1 cup shredded mozzarella cheese

Sauté pepper, mushroom, onion and carrot in oil 5 minutes or until tender. Stir in tomato sauce. Bring to boil. Reduce heat and simmer, uncovered, 10 minutes. Arrange spaghetti in the bottom and up the sides of a greased 9-inch deep dish pie plate. Pour vegetable mixture over spaghetti. Top with cheese. Bake at 375 degrees 20 minutes. Cool 5 minutes before cutting into 6 wedges.

Yield: 6 servings

Marti Katterhenry • Anna Maria Island Power Squadron • Florida

Herb Butter

4 tablespoons butter, softened
4 tablespoons cream cheese, softened
¼ cup feta cheese
1 teaspoon garlic powder
1 teaspoon chopped chives

Combine butter, cream cheese, feta cheese, garlic powder and chives in a blender. Process until smooth.

Yield: 1 cup butter

Richard Salter
Beverly Power Squadron
Massachusetts

Rendezvous Beans

4-5 (15-ounce) cans lima beans, drained
2 (15-ounce) cans tomato sauce
1 cup packed dark brown sugar
1 medium onion, chopped
3-4 squirts prepared mustard
4-5 slices bacon
1 (16-ounce) package hot dogs

Combine lima beans, tomato sauce, brown sugar, onion and mustard. Mix well. Pour mixture into a 13 x 9 x 2-inch baking dish. Lay bacon over mixture. Bake at 350 degrees 1 hour, 15 minutes. Place hot dogs on top and spoon some sauce over hot dogs. Bake an additional 45 minutes to 1 hour.

Yield: 8 to 10 servings

Sharon Smola • Mountaineer Power Squadron • West Virginia

Santa Fe Spicy Baked Black Beans

1	large white onion, diced	2	dried ancho chilies, softened in hot water, drained and stemmed
1	tablespoon vegetable oil		
1-2	tablespoons puréed chipotle chiles in adobo sauce		Salt to taste
½	cup ketchup	½	cup water
½	cup tomato juice	3	(15-ounce) cans low-sodium black beans, rinsed and drained
2	tablespoons packed dark brown sugar		
1	tomato, seeded and diced		Corn tortillas, diced tomatoes, cilantro, green onion and sour cream for garnish
¼	cup cider vinegar		
¼	cup molasses		

Sauté onion in oil in a saucepan 4 minutes until tender. Add 1 tablespoon chipotle purée, ketchup, tomato juice, brown sugar, tomato, vinegar, molasses, ancho chilies, salt and water. Mix well. Add more chipotle purée if desired. Simmer 10 minutes. Cool slightly. Purée mixture in a food processor. Pour into a 2-quart casserole. Stir in beans. Cover and bake at 350 degrees 1 hour. Add up to ½ cup more water if mixture is too thick. Serve as a side dish or in a warm corn tortilla. Garnish with diced tomato, cilantro, green onion and sour cream.

Yield: 8 to 10 servings

Joyce Koehler • Redondo Beach Power Squadron • California

Kathy Semple's White Bean Dish

½	cup diced onion	1	(15½-ounce) can small white beans, undrained
2	tablespoons olive oil		
2	garlic cloves, chopped	1	tablespoon chopped flat-leaf parsley
1	(14½-ounce) can Italian style diced tomatoes		

Sauté onion in oil until tender. Add garlic and sauté 1 minute. Stir in tomato and beans. Simmer, uncovered, 20 to 30 minutes, stirring occasionally. Cook until sauce thickens. Add parsley 5 minutes before serving.

Yield: 4 to 6 servings

Maria Semple • Somerset Sail & Power Squadron • New Jersey

Barbecued Beans

½ pound ground beef
½ cup chopped onion
⅓ cup packed brown sugar
½ cup barbecue sauce
2 tablespoons molasses
1 (15-ounce) can kidney beans, drained
1 (15-ounce) can lima beans, drained
1 (15-ounce) can baked pork and beans, undrained
10 slices bacon, cooked and crumbled
¼ cup ketchup
½ teaspoon salt
½ teaspoon pepper
½ teaspoon chili powder
1 teaspoon Dijon mustard

Brown beef and onion, stirring to crumble meat. Drain and place in a large bowl. Add brown sugar, barbecue sauce, molasses, kidney beans, lima beans, pork and beans, bacon, ketchup, salt, pepper, chili powder and mustard. Mix well. Pour mixture into a lightly greased 2½-quart casserole dish. Bake at 350 degrees 1 hour, stirring once.

Yield: 8 to 10 servings

Julie Tompkins • Kent Narrows Power Squadron • Maryland

★ Polly's New England Baked Beans

1 pound dried beans (navy, great Northern or chick pea)
1 teaspoon baking soda
1 stick butter
1 teaspoon packed light brown sugar
1 teaspoon salt
1 teaspoon dry mustard
1 small onion

Prepare beans according to package directions by soaking overnight or parboiling. Rinse beans. Cover beans with water in a stockpot. Add baking soda and cook 15 minutes or until skin lifts up. Do not overcook. Rinse again. Place beans in an ovenproof pot. Add butter, brown sugar, salt, mustard and onion. Cover with warm water and stir. Cook at 300-325 degrees for several hours. Add more water if needed to stay moist. Check frequently.

Yield: 8 servings

Robert L. Woods • Saybrook Power Squadron • Connecticut

HOT CHILI SAUCE

4 large bell peppers, chopped
1 large sweet red pepper, chopped
2 large onions, chopped
⅓ cup vegetable oil
2 tablespoons hot chili powder
3 cups tomato sauce
1 cup chicken broth
4 jalapeño peppers, chopped

Sauté bell pepper, red pepper and onion in oil until tender. Add chili powder, tomato sauce and broth. Simmer 10 minutes. Stir in jalapeño pepper.

Yield: 4 cups sauce

For a great cheese dip, mix half of chili sauce with 1-1½ pounds of processed cheese loaf. Melt in the microwave.

Cindy Tauscher
Johnson City Power Squadron
Tennessee

Southern Style Black-Eyed Peas

1	pound dried black-eyed peas	1	large onion, chopped
4	cups water	2	stalks celery, chopped
2	teaspoons salt	½	pound salt pork, sliced
¼	teaspoon pepper		Hot cooked rice and cornbread

Soak beans in water overnight. Drain and place in a crockpot. Add 4 cups water, salt, pepper, onion, celery and salt pork. Cover and cook on high 1 to 2 hours. Reduce to low heat and cook 8 to 10 hours. Serve over rice and with cornbread.

Yield: 6 to 8 servings

May substitute 3 (10-ounce) packages frozen black-eyed peas for dried peas and use only 2 cups water.

Mary King • Iroquois Power Squadron • New York

Pineapple Casserole

6	tablespoons all-purpose flour	1	(8-ounce) package shredded Cheddar cheese
½	cup sugar	1	stick butter, softened
2	(20-ounce) cans pineapple chunks, drained, saving 6 tablespoons juice	1½	sleeves buttery round crackers, crushed

Combine flour, sugar and pineapple juice. Stir in pineapple and cheese. Pour mixture into a 1½-quart casserole dish. Mix together butter and cracker crumbs until crumbly. Sprinkle over pineapple. Bake at 350 degrees 30 minutes.

Yield: 6 to 8 servings

Billie J. Kearney • Galveston Bay Power Squadron • Texas

Cranberry Casserole

6 apples, sliced not peeled
1 (12-ounce) package fresh cranberries
2 cups sugar
1 stick butter, softened
1 cup pecans or walnuts, chopped
1 cup old-fashioned rolled oats

Arrange apple slices in the bottom of a 13 x 9 x 2-inch baking dish. Scatter cranberries over apples. Sprinkle with sugar. Mix together butter, nuts and oats. Sprinkle over cranberries. Cover and bake at 350 degrees 2 hours or until all juice is absorbed.

Yield: 10 to 12 servings

Virginia Moore • Cross Country Power Squadron • New York

Cranberry Sauce à la Grand Marnier

4 cups cranberries
2 cups sugar
1 cup chopped dried apricots
1 cup water
1 cup orange juice
1 tablespoon orange zest
1 tablespoon Grand Marnier

Combine cranberries, sugar, apricots, water, juice and zest in a saucepan. Cook and stir over medium heat until sugar dissolves. Cover and bring to boil. Boil, stirring occasionally, 8 minutes until cranberries pop open. Stir in Grand Marnier. Transfer to a bowl. Cover and refrigerate until cold. Sauce will thicken as it cools.

Yield: 12 to 15 servings

Charlotte Ward • Hilton Head Power Squadron • South Carolina

DID YOU KNOW?

Be especially careful when shrink-wrapping a vessel not to get too close to the fuel vents. The heat from the torch may ignite the fumes in the vent. Boat Smart, take a boating course.

 Turkey Dressing

1	medium onion, diced	2	cups milk
4	stalks celery, diced	2	tablespoons poultry
1	stick butter		seasoning
1	(24-ounce) loaf white sandwich bread		

Sauté onion and celery in butter until tender. Toast the bread. Break bread into small pieces. Add onion mixture to bread. Pour in milk. Mix thoroughly with hands. Add poultry seasoning and mix well. Spoon mixture into a 9 x 9 x 2-inch baking dish. Bake at 350 degrees 1 hour, 15 minutes or until browned. Serve with homemade turkey gravy.

Yield: 6 to 8 servings

Audrey and Bill Selden • Richmond Power Squadron • Virginia

Lively Lemony Linguine

½	cup extra virgin olive oil	1	pound linguine (farfalle or other shaped pasta), cooked al dente and keep warm
	Zest from one lemon		
	Juice of two lemons		
¼	cup chopped parsley		Salt and pepper to taste
½	cup chopped green onion	¾	cup grated Parmesan cheese

Combine oil, zest, juice, parsley and green onion in a bowl. Add hot pasta and toss well. Season with salt and pepper. Top with cheese.

Yield: 6 servings

May add barbecued chunks of chicken, diced tomato, chopped red onion, shrimp, or asparagus tips.

Bob Owens • Lake Pontchartrain Sail & Power Squadron • Louisiana

Sandy's Dumplings

2   cups all-purpose flour
¼   cup vegetable shortening
1   tablespoon baking
      powder
1   teaspoon salt
1   cup milk
2   (14½-ounce) cans
      chicken broth, hot

Blend flour and shortening until crumbly. Add baking powder and salt. Stir in milk and mix well. Heat broth in a saucepan until hot. Drop batter by tablespoonfuls into hot broth. Cook, uncovered, 15 minutes. Cook, covered, an additional 10 minutes.

Yield: 4 servings

Joseph Beran   •   Tri-Lakes Power Squadron   •   West Virginia

Pasta Puttanesca

1   tablespoon olive oil
3   garlic cloves, minced
¼-½ teaspoon crushed red
        pepper
6   anchovies, rinsed
        (optional)
1   (28-ounce) can whole
        tomatoes, undrained
1   tablespoon capers
½   cup chopped pitted
        kalamata olives
1   pound spaghetti,
        cooked al dente
      Salt and pepper to taste

Heat oil in a large skillet. Add garlic, red pepper and anchovies. Mash anchovies. Cook and stir 2 minutes. Add tomato with juice. Break tomato with spoon. Add capers and olives. Bring to boil. Reduce heat and simmer 5 to 10 minutes until thickened. Toss with pasta and season with salt and pepper.

Yield: 6 servings

Michael Olexsy   •   Birmingham Power Squadron   •   Michigan

Noodle Pudding Supreme

1	pint sour cream	1	cup sugar
1	(8-ounce) package cream cheese, softened	8	eggs
1	tablespoon vanilla	8	ounces egg noodles, cooked al dente
2	sticks butter, melted		

Process sour cream, cream cheese, vanilla, butter, sugar and eggs at high speed in the blender until smooth. Arrange cooked noodles in a 13 x 9 x 2-inch baking dish. Pour mixture over noodles. Cover and bake at 350 degrees 1 hour.

Yield: 12 servings

M. C. Bardsley • Homestead Power Squadron • Florida

Risotto Verde

1	cup chopped spinach	1	cup dry long-grain rice
¼	cup minced celery	1	tablespoon chopped parsley
¼	cup minced onion	½	teaspoon ground nutmeg
¼	cup minced carrot		Dash of pepper
2	garlic cloves, crushed	1	teaspoon herbal salt
1	tablespoon olive oil		Grated Parmesan cheese
1	cup chicken broth		

Sauté spinach, celery, onion, carrot and garlic in oil until tender. Add broth, rice, parsley, nutmeg, pepper and salt. Simmer over low heat 35 minutes until rice is tender. Top with Parmesan cheese.

Yield: 6 to 8 servings

Anne Magyar • Vero Beach Power Squadron • Florida

Ham Fried Rice

2   eggs, slightly beaten
¼   cup vegetable oil, divided
¼   cup chopped green onion
1   cup dry rice, cooked
      until tender
2   tablespoons soy sauce
½   teaspoon sugar
¼   teaspoon seasoned salt
      flavor enhancer
1   cup diced cooked ham

Scramble eggs in 1 tablespoon oil in a skillet. Add green onion and cook 1 minute. Add cooked rice and remaining oil. Stir quickly to coat rice in oil. Add soy sauce, sugar, seasoned salt and ham. Heat thoroughly.

Yield: 4 servings

Albert Basier   •   Muscogee Power Squadron   •   Georgia

Fresh Vegetable Risotto

2   cups sliced mushrooms
½   cup chopped onion
2   garlic cloves, minced
1   tablespoon olive oil
1   cup dry Arborio rice
3   cups water or vegetable
      broth, divided
2   cups bite-size asparagus
      pieces or broccoli
      florets
¾   cup chopped tomato
¼   cup shredded carrots
¾   cup shredded low-fat
      mozzarella cheese
3   tablespoons grated
      Parmesan cheese
3   tablespoons snipped basil
      or parsley
    Parmesan cheese shavings

Sauté mushroom, onion and garlic in oil until onion is tender. Stir in rice. Cook and stir 5 minutes. Heat water or broth in a separate saucepan. Slowly add 1 cup hot broth to rice mixture, stirring constantly. Cook and stir until liquid is absorbed. Add ½ cup more broth and asparagus. Cook until liquid is absorbed. Repeat with remaining broth, adding one half cup at a time and allowing broth to be absorbed before adding more. This will take about 15 minutes.

Stir in tomato and carrot. Cook until creamy and vegetables are tender. Add mozzarella cheese, grated Parmesan cheese and basil. Mix well. Top with Parmesan cheese shavings and serve immediately.

Yield: 4 servings

Sally Ratty   •   St. Petersburg Power Squadron   •   Florida

DID YOU KNOW?

Sometimes, when a pleasure boat has been on a long cruise, a green or brown stain forms and is referred to as a moustache. This should be cleaned quickly or a permanent stain may develop. Boat maintenance is one of the chapters in the Squadron Boating Course.

Couscous with Plums, Goat Cheese and Fresh Mint

1½ cups water
1 cup whole wheat couscous
3 ripe plums, chopped
2 green onions, thinly sliced

½ cup goat cheese, crumbled
¼ cup chopped mint
3 tablespoons honey
3½ tablespoons balsamic vinegar
Salt and pepper to taste

Bring water to boil. Stir in couscous. Cover and remove from heat. Let stand 10 minutes. Fluff couscous with a fork and transfer to a bowl. When cool, add plums, green onion, goat cheese and mint. Whisk together honey and vinegar until honey dissolves. Pour over couscous and toss gently. Season with salt and pepper.

Yield: 6 servings

Pat Blake • Barnegat Bay Power Squadron • New Jersey

United States Power Squadrons

90th Anniversary

1914-2004

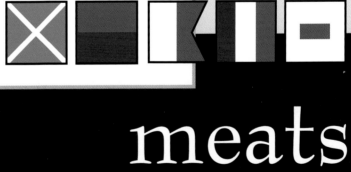

meats

membership

meet the USPS family

Our family is about as diverse as one could imagine. We are secretaries, shop foremen, doctors, accountants, lawyers, business people, and teachers. We live in suburban communities, condominiums in uptown USA, and rural areas of this great land. Our common interest is a love of the water and boating.

So what attracts folks to join USPS and become members? Membership in USPS brings with it opportunities to learn about the fine points of the sport, it gives one the opportunity to share knowledge and experiences, and maybe even a new recipe that can be prepared on a boat. Membership in USPS puts one in a family of boaters who enjoy sailing, racing, fishing, canoeing and handling boats in a skillful and safe manner, but most of all, generally the fun of knocking about in boats.

There are other benefits which await the member, let's just mention a few. Members enjoy discounts on marine supplies, fuel, travel, and electronic items. Towing services and insurance companies provide discounts and services at reduced rates to members of USPS.

Membership in USPS is family fun with picnics, outings, socials and a comradery only possible as part of the society of boaters keen on learning and serving others.

Won't you join us?

For more information call 1-888-367-8777. Thanks for listening!

Toni Dean-Shaw's Taco Lasagna

1 pound ground beef, pork
   or turkey
1 (1-ounce) package taco
   seasoning mix
1 (15-ounce) can non-fat
   refried beans
2 (8-ounce) packages
   shredded Mexican
   cheese

1 (16-ounce) container
   cottage cheese, drained
1 (12-ounce) jar salsa
9 corn or flour tortillas
   Sour cream, guacamole
   and chopped jalapeño
   peppers for garnish

Brown meat and add seasoning mix. Pour beans into a bowl and add enough water to thin mixture to spreading consistency. Combine Mexican cheese and cottage cheese. Spoon enough salsa to cover the bottom of a 13 x 9 x 2-inch baking dish. Stir remaining salsa into meat. Cut three tortillas in half, place cut sides along edges of the pan and place whole tortilla in the center. Spread a layer of beans over tortillas. Spoon meat over beans. Spread a layer of cheese mixture. Repeat two more times, ending with cheese. Top with small amount of salsa. Bake at 250 degrees 30 minutes. Cool 10 to 15 minutes. Serve with sour cream, guacamole and peppers.

Yield: 8 to 10 servings

Bobby Shaw • Beaverton Power Squadron • Oregon

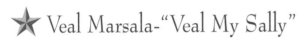 Veal Marsala-"Veal My Sally"

1 pound thin sliced veal
   cutlets, pounded
1 cup bread crumbs
½ cup grated Romano cheese
3 tablespoons butter
6 tablespoons water

1 cup Vendace or Marsala
   wine
   Lemon juice, parsley and
   butter to taste
   Hot cooked rice or
   vermicelli

Coat cutlets with crumbs and cheese. Brown in butter in a skillet. Add water. Cover and simmer until fully cooked. Blend wine, juice, parsley and butter in a saucepan. Cook and stir until butter melts. Pour sauce over cutlets. Serve over rice or vermicelli.

Yield: 4 servings

Emery E. Ellis • Ashtabula Power Squadron • Ohio

Shipwreck Kelly

4-6 medium to large potatoes, peeled and sliced less then ¼-inch thick	2 (14-ounce) cans dark kidney beans Diced onion (optional)
1-2 pounds ground beef	1-3 (8-ounce) cans tomato sauce

Arrange a thin layer of potato in a 13 x 9 x 2-inch baking dish. Spread a thin layer of meat. Spoon a thin layer of beans. Top with onion and a thin layer of tomato sauce. Repeat layers to about 1-inch from top of casserole dish. Cover with foil and bake at 400 degrees about 3 hours.

Yield: 6 servings

Gary Brown • Auburn Power Squadron • New York

Rose Bay Shish Kebabs

2	pounds beef	¼	teaspoon dried oregano
½	medium onion, thinly sliced	¼	cup olive oil
½	cup chopped parsley	1	pint cherry tomatoes
¼	cup sherry	¼	pound small white onions, parboiled
2	garlic cloves, minced	¼	pound mushrooms
1	teaspoon salt	1	bell pepper, cut into 1½-inch squares
½	teaspoon pepper		Butter, melted
¼	teaspoon ground thyme		

Combine beef, onion, parsley, sherry, garlic, salt, pepper, thyme and oregano in a bowl. Let stand 10 minutes. Add oil and toss lightly. Cover and refrigerate 24 to 36 hours. Skewer beef alternately with tomato, onion, mushroom and bell pepper. Brush lightly with butter. Broil or grill kebabs until desired degree of doneness, turning frequently.

Yield: 6 to 8 servings

Ernie Marshburn • Tar River Power Squadron • North Carolina

★ Spaghetti Pie

6   ounces spaghetti, broken
    in half and cooked al
    dente
2   eggs, beaten
¼   cup grated Parmesan
    cheese
2   tablespoons butter
⅓   cup chopped onion

1   cup sour cream
1   pound bulk Italian
    sausage
1   (6-ounce) can tomato
    paste
1   cup water
1   cup shredded mozzarella
    cheese

Combine warm spaghetti with eggs and cheese. Pour mixture into a greased 10-inch pie plate. Press mixture up sides of plate. Melt butter in a skillet. Sauté onion until tender. Stir in sour cream and spoon over spaghetti. Cook sausage, breaking up meat. Drain well. Add tomato paste and water to meat. Simmer 10 minutes. Spread over sour cream. Bake at 350 degrees 25 minutes. Top with cheese and return to oven until cheese melts.

Yield: 6 servings

Pam Miner • Birmingham Power Squadron • Michigan

Ervin's Spaghetti

4   sweet Italian sausages,
    casing removed
½   cup green onion,
    chopped
2   garlic cloves
1   cup chopped cilantro
1   cup chopped parsley

1   cup coarsely chopped
    tomatoes
½   cup spaghetti or other
    fine pasta
    Olive oil
    Grated Parmesan cheese
    or Romano cheese

Break up and brown sausage in a skillet. Add green onion, garlic, cilantro and parsley. Cook and stir until onion is tender. Add tomato and heat thoroughly. Cook pasta al dente, drain and toss with olive oil. Mix pasta with meat mixture. Serve with additional sauce on the side. Top with cheese.

Yield: 4 servings

Jerry Ervin • Arrowhead Power Squadron • California

MGR Spaghetti

4	medium onions, chopped	1	teaspoon salt
	Butter, melted	1	teaspoon pepper
2	pounds ground beef	2	tablespoons packed
1	bell pepper, chopped		brown sugar
3	(4-ounce) jars sliced mushrooms or fresh	¼	cup Worcestershire sauce
3	(16-ounce) cans diced tomatoes	1	pound block Parmesan cheese, grated
4	(15-ounce) cans tomato sauce		Dash of chili powder (optional)
		½	cup sherry or port

Sauté onion in butter until tender. Add beef and cook until meat is browned. Stir in bell pepper and mushroom and cook until tender. Add tomato, tomato sauce, salt, pepper, brown sugar and Worcestershire sauce. Heat thoroughly until hot. Slowly stir in cheese to avoid clumping. Simmer over low heat 1 hour. Stir in chili powder and sherry. Simmer an additional 1 hour. Dish freezes well.

Yield: 8 servings

Maury Rice • Central Wisconsin Sail & Power Squadron • Wisconsin

Taco Casserole

1½	pounds lean ground beef	1	cup low fat shredded Cheddar cheese
1	(1¼-ounce) package taco seasoning mix	1	(16-ounce) can fat free refried beans
1	cup water	1	cup salsa
10	flour or corn tortillas, fajita size		

Brown beef and drain drippings. Stir in seasoning and water. Simmer 10 minutes. Spread half of beef in a greased 2-quart casserole dish. Layer with 2 tortillas, overlapping to fill the dish. Layer with the following: half of cheese, 2 tortillas, half of beans, 2 tortillas, remaining beef, 2 tortillas, remaining beans and 2 tortillas. Top with remaining cheese and salsa. Bake, uncovered, at 350 degrees 40 minutes. Cool 5 minutes before serving.

Yield: 6 servings

Janet Dougherty • Absecon Island Power Squadron • New Jersey

"In Case She Stays" Spaghetti Sauce

1 pound lean ground beef
1 large onion, chopped
1 garlic clove, minced
2 (1-pound) cans tomatoes, cut up
1 (8-ounce) can tomato sauce
1 (12-ounce) can tomato paste
1 cup beef bouillon
2 tablespoons minced parsley
1 tablespoon packed brown sugar
1 teaspoon dried oregano
1 teaspoon dried basil
1 teaspoon salt
¼ teaspoon pepper
1 bay leaf
   Hot cooked spaghetti

Crumble meat in a large skillet. Add onion and garlic and cook until meat is cooked thoroughly. Drain off drippings. Transfer to crockpot. Add tomato, tomato sauce, tomato paste, bouillon, parsley, brown sugar, oregano, basil, salt, pepper and bay leaf. Cover and cook on low 6 to 8 hours. Remove bay leaf. Serve over hot spaghetti. May be made in advance and frozen.

Yield: 6 to 8 servings

Bill Neef • Anclote Key Sail & Power Squadron • Florida

Tangy Glazed Meatloaf

¼ cup bread crumbs
⅓ cup milk
1 pound lean ground turkey
1 egg, beaten
1 small onion, chopped
   Salt and pepper to taste
½ teaspoon poultry seasoning
¼ cup plus 2 tablespoons ketchup
3 tablespoons packed brown sugar
¼ teaspoon ground nutmeg
1 teaspoon dry mustard

Combine bread crumbs and milk. Add turkey, egg, onion, salt, pepper, poultry seasoning and 2 tablespoons ketchup. Mix well. Shape mixture into a loaf and place in a 9 x 5-inch loaf pan. Bake at 350 degrees 40 minutes. Blend ¼ cup ketchup, brown sugar, nutmeg and mustard. Spoon glaze over meatloaf. Bake an additional 20 minutes.

Yield: 6 servings

Regina Wiegert • Saybrook Power Squadron • Connecticut

Chili Over Crispy Potatoes and Crumbled Blue Cheese

2	tablespoons vegetable oil	1	tablespoon chili powder
2	cups chopped yellow onions	2	teaspoons ground cumin
2	teaspoons salt, divided	2	teaspoons dried oregano
⅓	teaspoon cayenne pepper	⅓	teaspoon crushed red pepper
1	pound beef bottom round, cut into ½-inch cubes	1	(15½-ounce) can kidney beans
½	cup tomato paste	2½	pounds potatoes, rinsed and thinly sliced
1	(28-ounce) can whole tomatoes with juice	5	ounces crumbled blue cheese
2	cups beef broth	1	tablespoon chopped parsley
2	tablespoons chopped garlic		

Heat oil in a large heavy stockpot. Sauté onion with 1 teaspoon salt and cayenne 4 minutes until tender and golden browned. Season meat with remaining salt. Add beef and cook 4 minutes until browned on all sides. Add tomato paste and cook 2 minutes. Stir in tomato, broth, garlic, chili powder, cumin, oregano, red pepper and beans. Bring to boil. Reduce heat and simmer, uncovered, 2 hours, stirring occasionally. Skim off fat from surface. Keep chili warm.

Cook potato in a large skillet in batches until golden browned. Remove and seasoning with salt and pepper. To serve, mound the potato in the bottom of individual dishes. Top with chili and sprinkle with blue cheese and parsley.

Yield: 8 to 10 servings

Lynn Keltner • Balboa Power Squadron • California

Lallaralle

1 large onion, finely chopped
2 tablespoons vegetable oil
  Dash of garlic salt
1 pound ground beef
1 teaspoon chili powder
1 (8-ounce) can tomato sauce
1 cup water
1 cup noodles, uncooked
1 teaspoon salt
1 (15¾-ounce) can cream style corn, undrained
1 (2¼-ounce) can sliced black olives, undrained
½ cup shredded Cheddar cheese
  Paprika for topping

Sauté onion in oil until tender. Season with garlic while cooking. Add beef and cook until browned. Stir in chili powder, tomato sauce, water, noodles and salt. Cover and cook 8 minutes until noodles are tender. Add corn and olives. Pour mixture into a buttered 2-quart casserole dish. Top with cheese and sprinkle with paprika. Bake at 300 degrees 30 minutes or until cheese melts.

Yield: 6 to 8 servings

Judy Griffing • Santana Power Squadron • California

Admiral's Favorite-Steak Au Poivre

4 (8 to 10-ounce) filet mignon steaks
4 tablespoons butter
½ cup brandy or cognac
¼ cup green peppercorns, ground
1 shallot, diced
2-3 cups heavy cream
2 tablespoons spicy mustard
  Salt and pepper to taste

Sear steaks over high heat in butter 2 to 3 minutes for medium rare. Transfer to a warm oven. Deglaze the pan with brandy, being careful of spills which can ignite. Add shallot and peppercorns. Reduce alcohol from mixture. Add cream and reduce until thick and bubbly. Stir in mustard, salt and pepper. Pour sauce over steak and serve immediately.

Yield: 4 servings

Norm Menchel • Kingsway Power Squadron • New Jersey

Bakalla Hash

3	pounds frozen hash-brown potatoes or fresh shoestring	¼	teaspoon dried tarragon
1	large onion, diced	½	teaspoon dried basil
½	medium bell pepper, diced	½	teaspoon crushed red pepper
3-4	garlic cloves, minced	1	(14-ounce) can stewed tomatoes, diced
1	pound ground beef, pork or sausage	½	cup rum
¼	teaspoon ground cumin	3	eggs
		½	cup shredded Cheddar cheese

Cook potatoes in a skillet until lightly browned. Transfer to a 13 x 9 x 2-inch baking dish. Sauté onion, pepper and garlic until tender. Add meat, cumin, tarragon, basil, red pepper, tomato and rum. Simmer 15 minutes. Combine eggs and cheese. Pour into meat mixture. Spread over potatoes and mix well. Bake at 350 degrees 30 minutes. Cool 15 minutes before serving.

Yield: 10 to 15 servings

Variation: May add carrots or parsnips to vegetable mixture.

Elmer Bakalla • Titusville Sail & Power Squadron • Florida

Sauerbraten

1	boneless beef rump roast	14-16	black peppercorns
	Apple cider vinegar	10-14	whole cloves
	Water		Crushed gingersnaps
5	bay leaves		Potato dumplings

Place meat in a large non-metallic bowl. Cover with equal parts vinegar and water. Add bay leaves, peppercorns and cloves. Cover and refrigerate at least 4 days or up to 1 week, turning meat daily.

Simmer in a Dutch oven in the marinade until done. Add more water if necessary. Remove meat and keep warm. Strain marinade to remove spices. Return to pan and heat. Stir in gingersnap crumbs to thicken gravy. Serve sliced meat with gravy and potato dumplings.

Yield: 4 to 6 servings

Jean Roeber • Spokane Power Squadron • Washington State

Grandma's Goulash

3	pounds beef round or chuck, cubed
¼	cup all-purpose flour
¼	cup vegetable oil
4	cups chopped onions
4	cups water
4	beef bouillon cubes
2	teaspoons browning sauce
2	tablespoons paprika
1	tablespoon salt
2	bay leaves
2	garlic cloves, minced
	Hot cooked egg noodles

Dredge meat in flour. Heat oil in a heavy stockpot and brown meat in batches. Add onion and cook until tender. Blend water, bouillon cubes and browning sauce. Pour into meat mixture. Add paprika, salt, bay leaves and garlic. Cover and simmer 2 hours, 30 minutes to 3 hours, stirring occasionally, until meat is tender. Remove bay leaves. Serve over noodles.

Yield: 4 to 6 servings

Lynne Lapierre   •   Jones Beach Power Squadron   •   New York

Pepper Steak Caballero

1½	pounds sirloin steak, cut into ⅛-inch thick strips
1	tablespoon paprika
2	garlic cloves, crushed
2	tablespoons butter
1	cup sliced green onion with tops
2	bell peppers, julienned
2	large tomatoes, diced
1	cup beef broth
¼	cup water
2	tablespoons cornstarch
2	tablespoons soy sauce
3	cups hot cooked rice

Season steaks with paprika. Brown steak and garlic in butter. Add green onion and bell pepper. Cook until vegetables are tender. Stir in tomato and broth. Cover and simmer 15 minutes. Blend water with cornstarch and soy sauce. Slowly pour into steak mixture and stir until thickened. Serve over a bed of rice.

Yield: 6 servings

Marilyn Kerr   •   Fostoria Power Squadron   •   Ohio

Green Enchilada Casserole

1½ pounds lean ground beef
¼ teaspoon garlic powder
1 (10¾-ounce) can cream of chicken soup
1 (5-ounce) can evaporated milk
1 (8-ounce) package processed cheese loaf
1 (1-ounce) package ranch salad dressing mix
1 (4-ounce) can chopped mild green chilies
1 (4-ounce) jar diced pimentos
1 (8-ounce) package shredded Cheddar cheese
1 large onion, chopped
1 (10-ounce) package tortilla chips

Brown beef with garlic powder. Drain and set aside. Combine soup, milk and cheese loaf in a saucepan. Cook and stir over low heat until cheese melts. In a bowl, combine dressing mix, chilies and pimentos. Stir into cheese sauce. Add Cheddar cheese and onion to meat mixture.

Place a layer of chips in a 13 x 9 x 2-inch baking dish. Spread a layer of meat mixture over chips. Pour cheese sauce over meat, smoothing over edges. Repeat layers, ending with cheese sauce. Cover with foil and bake at 350 degrees 30 minutes.

Yield: 8 to 12 servings

Mary K. Russ • Houston Power Squadron • Texas

 # Hamburger Tater Tot Casserole

1 pound ground beef
¼ cup chopped onion
1 (12-ounce) package frozen tater tot potatoes, thawed
1 (10¾-ounce) can cream of mushroom soup
¾ cup milk

Crumble beef in a skillet. Add onion and cook until beef is browned. Drain well. Spread beef mixture into the bottom of a 13 x 9 x 2-inch baking dish. Scatter tater tots over meat. Blend together soup and milk. Pour over beef mixture and mix well. Bake at 350 degrees 30 minutes.

Yield: 6 servings

Peggy Davenport • Mansfield Power Squadron • Ohio

Mini Beef Wellingtons

Madeira Sauce

4	tablespoons butter	¼	teaspoon browning sauce (optional)
5	tablespoons all-purpose flour		Dash of ground cloves
2	cups beef consommé	½	cup Madeira wine or beef broth
1	tablespoon tomato paste	2	cups sliced mushrooms
¼	teaspoon dried thyme	2	tablespoons olive or vegetable oil
¼	teaspoon dried rosemary, crushed		

Melt butter in a saucepan. Whisk in flour until smooth. Stir in consommé, tomato paste, thyme, rosemary, browning sauce and cloves. Bring to boil. Cook and stir 2 minutes or until thickened. Stir in wine. Sauté mushroom in the oil in a skillet until tender. Add to sauce. Keep warm.

Beef

3	eggs, divided	¾	pound ground veal
½	cup ketchup	¾	pound ground pork
2½	teaspoons seasoned salt	⅓	cup chopped onion
2	teaspoons Worcestershire sauce	¾	cup dry bread crumbs
¼	teaspoon dry mustard	1	(17¼-ounce) package frozen puff pastry, thawed
⅛	teaspoon pepper		
¾	pound lean ground beef		

Beat together 2 eggs, ketchup, seasoned salt, Worcestershire sauce, mustard and pepper. Crumble beef, veal and pork into mixture and mix well. Stir in onion and bread crumbs. Shape mixture into 8 loaves about 4 x 2 x 1-inch.

Roll out each pastry sheet to an 18 x 16-inch rectangle on a lightly floured surface. Cut one pastry sheet into 4 pieces. Invert a meatloaf in the center of each pastry piece. Fold short sides over loaf. Fold long sides over loaf and cut away excess pastry. Seal the seams. Place seam-side down on a rack in a 15 x 10 x 1-inch roasting pan. Repeat with second pastry sheet and remaining 4 meatloaves. Pierce the top and sides of pastry. Beat remaining egg and brush over pastry. Bake at 350 degrees 1 hour to 1 hour, 10 minutes or until meat thermometer reaches 160-170 degrees. Pour Madeira sauce over meatloaves when ready to serve.

Yield: 8 meatloaves and 2½ cups sauce

Charlotte Ward • Hilton Head Sail & Power Squadron • South Carolina

DID YOU KNOW?

In the strictest sense of the word, pleasure vessels that are "documented" are required to fly the yacht ensign when in US territorial waters. This and other flag etiquette topics are covered in the USPS learning guide on "Flags". These inexpensive learning guides are available at many discount marine stores.

Crockpot Brisket of Beef in Tomato Onion Gravy

1 (4 to 5-pound) beef brisket, trimmed	1 (10¾-ounce) can cream of tomato soup
¼ cup all-purpose flour	¼ cup beef broth or water
1 (1½-ounce) package dry onion soup mix	2 tablespoons packed brown sugar
½ teaspoon black peppercorns, crushed	2 tablespoons balsamic or red wine vinegar

Dredge brisket in flour coating on all sides. Place in a crockpot. Combine soup mix, pepper, tomato soup, and broth in a bowl. Pour over brisket. Cover and cook on low 12 hours or on high 6 hours, until beef is tender.

Thinly slice brisket and keep warm. Stir brown sugar and vinegar into sauce in crockpot. Pour sauce over meat or serve in a gravy boat.

Yield: 8 to 10 servings

For a thicker sauce, pour mixture into a saucepan. Blend 2 tablespoons cornstarch with ¼ cup hot cooking liquid, 2 tablespoons at a time. Whisk cornstarch mixture into sauce. Cook and stir until thickened.

Sally A. Williams • Palm Beach Power Squadron • Florida

⚓ Skillet Lasagna

1 pound ground beef	1 teaspoon dried oregano
1 (16-ounce) container cottage cheese	1 teaspoon salt
3 cups medium noodles, uncooked	3 (8-ounce) cans tomato sauce
1 tablespoon dried basil	1 cup water
1 tablespoon dried parsley	1 cup shredded mozzarella cheese

Brown beef in a salted skillet. Spread cottage cheese over meat. Layer noodles on top. Sprinkle with basil, parsley, oregano and salt. Pour in tomato sauce and water. Cover and simmer 30 to 35 minutes. Remove from heat. Top with cheese, cover and let stand 10 to 15 minutes.

Yield: 8 servings

Betty Y. Bush • Hilton Head Power Squadron • South Carolina

Spanish Noodles

1 medium onion, chopped
½ cup chopped bell pepper
½ cup chopped celery
2 tablespoons vegetable oil
1 pound ground beef
1 (4-ounce) jar mushrooms, drained
1 teaspoon chili powder
1 tablespoon packed brown sugar

1 tablespoon vinegar
1 teaspoon salt
1 (15¼-ounce) can whole kernel corn, drained
2 (8-ounce) cans tomato sauce
2 cans water (from tomato cans)
6 ounces noodles, uncooked

Sauté onion, bell pepper and celery in oil until tender. Remove vegetables. Brown beef in skillet. Drain well. Return vegetables to meat. Add mushroom, chili powder, brown sugar, vinegar, salt, corn, tomato sauce and water. Mix well. Stir in noodles. Cover and simmer 25 to 30 minutes until noodles are tender.

Yield: 10 servings

Johanna B. Chapin • Anclote Key Sail & Power Squadron • Florida

Chili Spaghetti

1 pound ground beef
½ cup chopped onion
2 garlic cloves, mined
3 cups tomato juice
1 (16-ounce) can kidney beans, rinsed and drained

6 ounces spaghetti, broken into 3-inch pieces
1 tablespoon Worcestershire sauce
2-3 teaspoons chili powder
1 teaspoon salt
½ teaspoon pepper

Cook beef, onion and garlic until meat is fully cooked. Drain well. Transfer to a greased 1½-quart baking dish. Stir in tomato juice, beans, spaghetti, Worcestershire sauce, chili powder, salt and pepper. Cover and bake at 350 degrees 1 hour, 5 minutes to 1 hour, 10 minutes or until spaghetti is tender. Cool, covered, 10 minutes.

Yield: 6 servings

A great potluck dish for a boat outing.

Ron Werner • Phoenix Sail & Power Squadron • Arizona

Beef Stroganoff

4	tablespoons butter, divided	1	tablespoon ketchup
2	pounds filet of beef, cut into strips	½	teaspoon salt
		⅛	teaspoon pepper
1	cup chopped onion	1	(10½-ounce) can beef broth
1	garlic clove, finely chopped		
		½	cup dry white wine
1	(8-ounce) package sliced mushrooms	¾	teaspoon dried dill
		1½	cups sour cream
2	tablespoons all-purpose flour		Cognac to taste (optional)
2	tablespoons meat extracts paste or bouillon crystals		

Melt 1 tablespoon butter in a large skillet. Brown beef strips in batches until browned. Transfer to a plate. Melt remaining 3 tablespoons butter. Sauté onion, garlic and mushroom 3 to 5 minutes until onion is tender. Remove from heat. Stir in flour, meat extract, ketchup, salt and pepper. Slowly add broth and bring to boil, stirring constantly. Reduce heat and simmer 5 minutes. Stir in wine, dill and sour cream. Return beef strips and heat thoroughly. Add cognac if desired.

Yield: 6 to 8 servings

Marianne Killen • Naples Sail & Power Squadron • Florida

Bob's Smothered Pork Chops

4	boneless pork chops, trimmed	1	(10½-ounce) can beef broth
1	medium onion, chopped		Cornstarch for thickening
1	teaspoon French herbs (thyme, rosemary, basil, fennel, tarragon, savory)	½	cup sour cream or to taste

Brown pork in a greased skillet. Top with onion and herbs. Slowly pour in broth. Cover and simmer 1 hour, 30 minutes to 3 hours. Thicken sauce with cornstarch. Add sour cream.

Yield: 4 servings

Jane Schnoor • Cocoa Beach Power Squadron • Florida

 Pork Tenderloin

2	pork tenderloins	¼	cup olive oil
	Italian sausage (enough to stuff tenderloin)	¼	teaspoon salt
3	tablespoons prepared mustard	¼	teaspoon pepper

Butterfly tenderloins from end-to-end. Boil sausage until cooked. Place sausage inside tenderloin and tie to close opening. Combine mustard, oil, salt and pepper in a plastic bag. Place pork in bag and marinate 3 hours in the refrigerator.

Sear pork on the grill over high heat. Reduce heat to medium and cooked to desired degree of doneness. Transfer to a serving platter. Cool 3 minutes before slicing.

Yield: 6 to 8 servings

Mary Lou and Les Johnson • Diablo Sail & Power Squadron • California

Kapusta and Kielbasa (Sauerkraut and Sausage)

1	(2-pound) bag sauerkraut	2	tablespoons bacon drippings or butter
1	(16-ounce) package fresh or smoked polish sausage		Salt and pepper to taste
1	large yellow onion, chopped	1	tablespoon caraway seeds (optional)

Place sauerkraut in a large saucepan and cover with water. Simmer over low-medium heat 30 minutes. If using fresh sausage, simmer 30 minutes. Roast sausage in small amount of water at 350 degrees 45 minutes. Drain kraut and squeeze dry. Sauté onion in drippings until tender. Add kraut and mix well. Season with salt, pepper and caraway seeds. Slice sausage into 1-inch chunks and toss with kraut or arrange on a platter with whole sausage.

Yield: 6 to 8 servings

Walter Cosdon • San Fernando Valley Power Squadron • California

BULGOGI (KOREAN MEAT MARINADE)

3 tablespoons sesame seed oil

4-5 tablespoons soy sauce

2-3 teaspoons sesame seeds

3 garlic cloves, minced

3 tablespoons sugar

½ teaspoon pepper

2 green onion, chopped

Blend together oil, soy sauce, sesame seeds, garlic, sugar, pepper and green onion. Pour over tri-tip, sirloin steaks or short ribs. Marinate overnight in the refrigerator. Grill to desired degree of doneness.

Yield: 4 to 6 servings

Jeanette L. Myers

Agate Pass Sail & Power Squadron

Washington State

SPAMWICHES

1 (12-ounce) can
spam, ground or
finely chopped
1 (8-ounce) package
shredded Cheddar
cheese
2 teaspoons sweet
or dill relish
2 teaspoons finely
chopped onion
Mayonnaise
to moisten
6 hamburger buns
Finely chopped
bell pepper, sliced green
or black olives

Combine spam,
cheese, relish, onion and
mayonnaise. Spread on
hamburger buns. Top with
bell pepper and olives. To
serve hot, bake or broil
until cheese melts and spam
is heated thoroughly.
May serve cold also.

Yield: 4 to 6 servings

Nancy Thompson
Ventura Power Squadron
California

---

3 tablespoons chili powder	1¼ cups white vinegar
1 tablespoon dried oregano	3 tablespoons Worcestershire sauce
1 teaspoon pepper	⅔ cup packed brown sugar
2 tablespoons paprika	3 tablespoons Tabasco sauce
1 tablespoon sugar	1 (12-ounce) bottle chili sauce
1 tablespoon ground cumin	
1 tablespoon salt	1 teaspoon salt
1 (5 to 6 pounds) lean pork shoulder arm or picnic roast	20 thick slices soft white bread or soft rolls
1 tablespoon vegetable oil	
½ cup finely chopped onion	

Combine chili powder, oregano, pepper, paprika, sugar, cumin and salt in a plastic bag. Trim skin and excess fat from pork leaving ⅛-inch thick layer of fat. Place meat in bag with seasonings. Seal and toss to coat meat. Refrigerate overnight.

Heat oil in a 3-quart saucepan. Sauté onion 4 to 5 minutes until tender. Add vinegar, Worcestershire sauce, brown sugar, Tabasco, chili sauce and salt. Bring to boil. Reduce heat and simmer 30 minutes until slightly thickened. Place roast in a 13 x 9 x 2-inch baking dish. Pour sauce over top. Cover tightly with foil. Bake at 325 degrees 3 hours, 30 minutes to 4 hours until meat is tender enough to pull away from the bone.

Transfer roast to a cutting board. Using two forks, pull meat off bone breaking into large shreds. Discard bone and return meat to pan. Stir into sauce. Bake, uncovered, 25 minutes longer. Serve pork over bread slices or soft rolls.

Yield: 10 servings

Spencer P. Anderson • Banana River Power Squadron • Florida

Pork Tenderloin in Spiced Bourbon Sauce

2 pounds pork tenderloin	1 teaspoon minced ginger or ½ teaspoon ground
¼ cup bourbon	
¼ cup soy sauce	1 teaspoon Worcestershire sauce
¼ cup packed brown sugar	
3 garlic cloves, minced	¼ cup olive oil
¼ cup Dijon mustard	

Pierce tenderloin all over with a fork. Combine bourbon, soy sauce, brown sugar, garlic, mustard, ginger, Worcestershire sauce and oil in a zip-top plastic bag. Place tenderloin in bag and refrigerate overnight. Grill 15 to 20 minutes or until desired degree of doneness. Do not overcook. While meat is cooking, boil marinade and pour over cooked slices of pork.

Yield: 6 servings

Shelia and Ken Link   •   Fort Macon Sail & Power Squadron
North Carolina

Pork 'n' Corn Roasts

1 tablespoon prepared mustard	2 tablespoons finely chopped onion
4-6 pork chops, ½-inch thick	1 tablespoon finely chopped bell pepper
1 cup water	
1 (14¾-ounce) can cream style corn	1 teaspoon salt
	Dash of pepper
⅔ cup soft bread crumbs	

Lightly spread mustard over pork. Brown in a skillet. Arrange chops in a 13 x 9 x 2-inch baking dish. Drain dripping from skillet. Add water and heat to boil, scraping any browned bits. Pour around chops. Combine corn, bread crumbs, onion, pepper, salt and pepper. Top each chop with corn mixture. Cover and bake at 350 degrees 15 minutes. Uncover and bake an additional 45 minutes.

Yield: 4 to 6 servings

Jan Keller   •   Boca Ciega Sail & Power Squadron   •   Florida

Did you know?

Paint and varnish cans which develop a skin on the top cause waste and make use difficult. It is possible to reduce this by storing the can upside down or by floating a small amount of linseed oil or paint thinner on the top to keep the skin from forming. Helpful suggestions appear monthly in the Power Squadron newsletter the Ensign®.

Stuffed Pork Loin

4-6 pound boneless pork loin roast	1 tablespoon salt
1 yellow onion, finely chopped	1 teaspoon coarse ground pepper
3 stalks celery, finely chopped	2 (8-ounce) packages baby portobello mushrooms
5 garlic cloves, sliced	1 (18-ounce) jar apricot preserves
½ cup wine vinegar	

Butterfly roast and place in a roasting pan. Combine onion, celery, garlic, vinegar, salt and pepper. Pour mixture over roast, some will drip into pan. Close and secure roast with toothpicks. Bake at 375 degrees 45 minutes. Scatter mushroom around roast and bake an additional 45 minutes or until fully cooked. Transfer roast to a platter and immediately brush with preserves. Arrange mushroom around roast.

Yield: 6 servings

Maureen Miller • Austin Power Squadron • Texas

Spiedes

1 pound cubed pork or chicken	¼ cup ketchup
¼ cup vinegar	1 teaspoon dried basil
¼ cup vegetable oil	1 teaspoon dried oregano
¼ cup wine	½ teaspoon dried marjoram
¼ cup lemon juice	½ teaspoon garlic powder
	1 teaspoon onion powder

Combine pork, vinegar, oil, wine, juice, ketchup, basil, oregano, marjoram, garlic powder and onion powder in a zip-top plastic bag or covered dish. Refrigerate overnight. Thread meat onto skewers and grill to desired degree of doneness. Wrap in Italian bread.

Yield: 4 servings

Nancy Harvey • Cambridge Sail & Power Squadron • Delaware

Southwestern Stuffed Peppers

8   Cabanelle bell peppers
1   pound bulk sausage
¼   cup chopped onion
¾   teaspoon chili powder
1   (8-ounce) package
    shredded Cheddar
    cheese, divided

3   eggs, beaten
1   cup all-purpose flour
1   (32-ounce) jar salsa
    Hot cooked mashed
    potatoes

Cut tops off peppers and remove seeds. Set aside. Combine sausage, onion, chili powder and 1 cup cheese. Stuff mixture into peppers. Dip peppers into egg, roll in flour and re-dip in egg. Place in a greased shallow baking dish. Bake at 400 degrees 35 to 40 minutes or until sausage is cooked. Remove peppers and drain drippings. Place in a 13 x 9 x 2-inch baking dish. Pour salsa over peppers. Sprinkle with remaining cheese. Bake an additional 5 to 10 minutes or until cheese melts and salsa is hot. Serve with mashed potato and additional salsa.

Yield: 8 servings

Sharon Bates • Youngstown Power Squadron • Ohio

Sausage Supreme

1   pound Italian sweet
    sausage
1   small onion, thinly sliced
3   garlic cloves, minced
3   tablespoons olive oil
1   (28-ounce) can tomato
    sauce
1   (28-ounce) can crushed
    tomatoes
2   large bell peppers, cut
    into strips

1   sweet red pepper, cut
    into strips
1   yellow pepper, cut into
    strips
    Salt and pepper to taste
3   small zucchini, chopped
1   pound linguine, cooked
    al dente
    Grated Parmesan cheese

Cook sausage, onion and garlic in oil, breaking up sausage as it cooks. Add tomato sauce and crushed tomato. Stir in all peppers, salt and pepper. Cook, uncovered, 10 minutes. Add zucchini and cook, covered, 20 to 30 minutes longer. Serve over linguine and top with cheese.

Yield: 6 to 8 servings

Pat O'Neil • Mosquito Lake Power Squadron • Ohio

All-Purpose Rub

6 tablespoons paprika

4 teaspoons
garlic powder

4 teaspoons
seasoned salt

4 teaspoons pepper

2 teaspoons
cayenne pepper

2 teaspoons dried
oregano

2 teaspoons
dry mustard

1 teaspoon
chili powder

Combine paprika,
garlic powder, seasoned
salt, pepper, cayenne,
oregano, mustard and
chili powder.

*Yield: Enough rub for
2 slabs of pork back ribs.*

Cindy Tauscher

Johnson City Power Squadron

Tennessee

Sweet and Sour Pork Roast

¾	cup corn syrup	5	garlic cloves, minced
1	cup packed brown sugar	½	teaspoon cornstarch
1	cup applesauce	2-2½	pounds boneless pork roast
1	cup orange juice		
7	tablespoons soy sauce		Hot cooked mashed potatoes
3	tablespoons white vinegar		

Combine corn syrup, brown sugar, applesauce, juice, soy sauce, vinegar, garlic and cornstarch in a zip-top plastic bag. Place roast in the bag, turning to coat. Refrigerate at least 3 hours. Place roast and marinade in a shallow roasting pan so marinade covers bottom half of roast. Roast at 350 degrees about 25 minutes per pound or desired degree of doneness. Boil marinade in a saucepan and serve over mashed potato.

Yield: 8 servings

The Griffin Family • Marblehead Sail & Power Squadron
Massachusetts

Hurry-Up Ham 'n' Noodles

4	tablespoons butter	¼	cup thinly sliced green onion
1	cup heavy cream		
1½	cups julienned fully cooked ham	¼	teaspoon salt
½	cup grated Parmesan cheese	⅛	teaspoon pepper
		5-6	cups wide egg noodles, cooked al dente

Melt butter in a skillet. Stir in cream and bring to boil. Cook and stir 2 minutes. Add ham, cheese, green onion, salt and pepper. Stir in noodles. Heat thoroughly.

Yield: 4 servings

Ron Werner • Phoenix Sail & Power Squadron • Arizona

Pork Tenderloin
with Mustard Cream Sauce

1	pork tenderloin		1	shallot, minced
2-3	tablespoons Dijon mustard		¼	cup dry white wine
¼	cup all-purpose flour		½-¾	cup chicken broth
2	tablespoons olive oil		2-3	tablespoons half & half
2	teaspoons butter, divided		2	tablespoons chopped parsley

Cut tenderloin into 1 to 2-inch thick medallions. Spread mustard over pork and dust with flour. Heat oil and 1 teaspoon butter in a skillet. Brown pork on all sides until golden browned. Remove to a plate and keep warm. Pour off drippings. Heat remaining teaspoon butter. Sauté shallot. Add wine and deglaze pan. Stir in broth and cook until sauce is reduced. Stir in half & half and parsley. Return pork to pan and heat 3 to 5 minutes, stirring occasionally.

Yield: 2 servings

Serve with red bliss potatoes, a green vegetables and sautéed apples. Recipe may be doubled.

Julie McGarr • Venice Power Squadron • Florida

Bacon Spaghetti Sauce

4-6 slices bacon		1	(28-ounce) can whole tomatoes, chopped with juice
1	stick butter			
¼	cup olive oil		½	teaspoon salt
1	large onion, diced		½	teaspoon pepper
4	garlic cloves, minced			Hot cooked noodles or penne pasta

Cook bacon in a large skillet. Remove bacon and crumble. Add butter and oil to bacon drippings. Sauté onion and garlic until tender. Add tomato and juice, salt and pepper. Return bacon to sauce. Simmer 15 to 20 minutes. Serve over noodles or penne.

Yield: 4 servings

Henry Stuart • Raritan Bay Power Squadron • New Jersey

Cranberry Pork

1	(16-ounce) can whole cranberry sauce	¼	cup French dressing
1	(1¼-ounce) package dry onion soup mix	2	(1½-pound) pork tenderloins

Combine cranberry sauce, soup mix and dressing. Pour over tenderloins. Cover and bake at 350 degrees 1 hour. Uncover and bake an additional 30 minutes. Check for doneness with a meat thermometer.

Yield: 6 servings

Kay Henry • Kentucky Lake Power Squadron • Kentucky

BBQ SAUCE

1 (32-ounce) bottle
ketchup
5 tablespoons
Worcestershire sauce
2 tablespoons dry
mustard
5 tablespoons vinegar
⅔ cup oil
⅓ bottle Tabasco sauce
7 tablespoons sugar
1½ teaspoons onion salt
1½ teaspoons garlic salt
1½ teaspoons seasoned
salt flavor enhancer
¼ cup molasses

Combine ketchup,
Worcestershire sauce,
mustard, vinegar, oil,
Tabasco, sugar, onion salt,
garlic salt, seasoned salt and
molasses. Mix well.

Yield: 6 cups

Cindy Tauscher

Johnson City Power Squadron

Tennessee

Barbecued Ribs à la Crockpot

2	cups ketchup	6	tablespoons Worcestershire sauce
¾	cup packed brown sugar		
½	cup red wine vinegar	2	tablespoons chili powder
3	tablespoons olive oil		
1	medium onion, chopped	2	teaspoons liquid smoke
2	garlic cloves, minced	3½-4	pounds pork baby back ribs, cut into 3 to 4 rib pieces
1	tablespoon Tabasco sauce		

Combine ketchup, brown sugar, vinegar, oil, onion, garlic, Tabasco, Worcestershire sauce, chili powder and liquid smoke in a saucepan. Bring to boil. Reduce heat and simmer 20 minutes. Remove from heat. Grill or broil ribs 5 minutes per side until browned. Coat ribs in sauce and place in a crockpot. Reserve some sauce for dipping. Cook on low 8 to 10 hours or until meat falls from the bone.

Yield: 4 to 6 servings

Thomas R. Dougherty • Absecon Island Power Squadron • New Jersey

Quick & Easy Pork Tenderloin with Apples & Grapes

1	pork tenderloin	1	Fuji apple, sliced
	All-purpose flour	20	red grapes, halved
	Chicken bouillon crystals to taste		Cooked rigatoni or sweet potato
	Dried oregano to taste		

Slice tenderloin into 2-inch slices. Dredge in flour. Brown in hot oil 10 to 15 minutes in a skillet. While cooking, sprinkle with bouillon and oregano. Add apple slices and grapes. Remove from heat and let stand 5 to 8 minutes for favors to blend. Serve with rigatoni or sweet potato.

Yield: 2 servings

Zdenka L. Sellenraad • Saginaw Bay Power Squadron • Michigan

Pork Chop Skillet Dinner

1	tablespoon vegetable oil	1	(15-ounce) can sliced carrot, drained
8	pork chops	1	(15½-ounce) can green beans, drained
1	small diced onion (optional)		Liquid butter spray
2	(15-ounce) cans sliced or whole potatoes, drained		Dried parsley

Using an electric skillet, heat oil and brown chops on both sides. Add onion. Cover and cook 5 to 8 minutes until chops are fully cooked. Stir in potato, carrot and green beans. Cover and simmer until heated thoroughly. Just before serving, spray with liquid butter and sprinkle with parsley. Serve from skillet.

Yield: 4 servings

Dolores Cope • Fort Meyer Power Squadron • Florida

★ Stuffed Bell Peppers with Spiced Lamb, Currants and Feta Cheese

4	quarts water
1	tablespoon salt
4	medium sweet red, yellow or orange peppers
1	cup long-grain white rice
1½	tablespoons olive oil
1	medium onion, finely chopped
12	ounces ground lamb
1	tablespoon ground cumin
1	teaspoon ground cardamom
½	teaspoon ground cinnamon
½	teaspoon crushed red pepper
3	medium garlic cloves, minced
1	(1-inch) piece fresh ginger, minced
¼	cup currants
1	(14½-ounce) can diced tomatoes, drained
1	(6-ounce) package feta cheese, crumbled
2	tablespoons chopped cilantro
	Salt and pepper to taste
⅓	cup chopped salted cashews

Bring water and salt to boil in a large stockpot. Trim ½-inch off tops of peppers. Core, seed and slightly trim the bottom to make a good standing base. Cook peppers in water 3 to 5 minutes until softened. Remove with a slotted spoon and place cut-side up to drain on paper towels. Return water to boil and add rice. Cook 13 minutes until tender. Drain rice and transfer to a large bowl. Set aside.

In same stockpot, add oil and swirl to coat. Sauté onion until beginning to brown. Add lamb, cumin, cardamom, cinnamon and crushed red pepper. Cook and stir, breaking up meat until no longer pink. Stir in garlic, ginger and currants. Cook 30 seconds. Transfer to bowl with rice. Stir in tomato, feta cheese, cilantro, salt and pepper. Mix well.

Arrange peppers cut-side up in a 9 x 9 x 2-inch square baking dish. Divide filling evenly among peppers. Top each with cashews. Bake at 350 degrees 25 to 30 minutes or until filling is heated thoroughly. Serve immediately.

Yield: 4 servings

Lance J. Jensen • Bellevue Sail & Power Squadron • Washington State

⭐ Lamb Shanks à la Arturo

4	lamb shanks	1	bay leaf
1	garlic clove		Salt and pepper to taste
	Olive oil	12	small red potatoes
½	cup diced onion	6	carrots, diced
2	cups beef broth		All-purpose flour

Rub lamb with garlic and dredge in flour. Sear lamb in oil with onion. Place lamb in a roasting pan. Pour in broth. Add bay leaf, salt and pepper. Cover and bake at 325 degrees 1 hour, 45 minutes. During last 45 minutes, add potato and carrot. Combine flour with water and slowly add to thicken sauce.

Yield: 4 servings

Art Farr • Rocky River Power Squadron • Florida

⭐ Lamb Chops en Farce

2	hard-cooked eggs, finely chopped	1	garlic clove, minced
½	cup dry bread crumbs	¼	teaspoon salt
2	tablespoons butter, melted	4	lamb loin chops, 1½-inches thick, trimmed
1	tablespoon chopped parsley		Paprika to taste

Combine eggs, bread crumbs, butter, parsley, garlic and salt. Press mixture on the top and bottom of each chop. Individually wrap each chop in foil. Bake at 400 degrees 20 to 25 minutes for medium rare. Open foil packet, sprinkle with paprika and broil 2 to 3 minutes until browned.

Yield: 4 servings

Joseph Kennedy • St. Petersburg Sail & Power Squadron • Florida

Did you know?

Knots are used for various purposes. Do you know the best for your application? Slippery hitches and knots are useful in temporary situations and can be untied quickly, even under load. The USPS Learning Guide on Bends, Hitches and Knots is useful for learning about marlinspike.

Aft Deck Lamb Chops

¼	cup olive oil	2	garlic cloves, minced
¼	cup Worcestershire sauce	1	teaspoon lemon juice
1	tablespoon ground thyme		Dash of salt and pepper
1	tablespoon dried basil	4	lamb loin chops

Blend together oil, Worcestershire sauce, thyme, basil, garlic, juice, salt and pepper. Pour over chops and refrigerate at least 1 hour. Grill, basting with marinade, until desired degree of doneness.

Yield: 4 servings

Ernie Marshburn • Tar River Power Squadron • North Carolina

Butterflied Leg of Lamb

1	cup Dijon mustard	2	garlic cloves, chopped
2	tablespoons dried rosemary, crumbled	3	tablespoons soy sauce
		3	tablespoons peanut oil
2	tablespoons finely chopped ginger	1	whole leg of lamb, boned, about 5 pounds

Blend together mustard, rosemary, ginger, garlic, soy sauce and oil. Spread mixture all over lamb. Place in a plastic bag or bowl and refrigerate overnight. Grill or broil 15 minutes on each side. Use a thermometer for desired degree of doneness. Lamb will be dark brown or black around the edges and rare inside.

Yield: 10 to 12 servings
Marinade is good with lamb chops also.

Linda Wehrum • Memphis Power Squadron • Tennessee

poultry

squadrons
we gather together

Fun and fellowship are why most folks get together. As with any organization, there must be some structure to hold the group together. The Power Squadron is no different. By the way, why is it a squadron? Well that is a part of our heritage. Our roots go back to the days of the Boston Yacht Club and the founders of our organization. Their first power boating unit was called the Power Squadron of the Boston Yacht Club. This name has lasted for nine decades.

The Squadron is a group of local members who boat in generally the same area, live in close proximity and have common interests in education, civic service and family boating. USPS currently has 455 such units spread across the United States, the Caribbean and Japan. The local squadrons have a group of officers much like any organization, an executive committee comprised of the officers and elected members at large, and committees that see to the workings of the desires of the members and in concert with the bylaws and constitution of USPS.

The local squadrons organize and plan boating educational classes, boating activities, picnics, rendezvous, parties, provide civic service in many ways described in another section of the book and generally see to the workings of the organization.

The squadron meetings are social gatherings where ideas are exchanged, information on activities is shared, updates on the workings of the committees are presented and possible services are aired and discussed for future implementation. Speakers are invited to present information of general interest to the membership or to provoke action by the unit.

All in all, the squadron is the grass roots organization where the work of USPS is presented, discussed, planned, organized and executed. It is a social group whose purpose is to promote safe boating for its members and the boating public. Why not see for yourself.

For more information call 1-888-367-8777. Thanks for listening!

Marinated Raspberry Chicken

¼ cup Dijon mustard
2 tablespoons packed
   brown sugar
3 tablespoons water
1 tablespoon raspberry
   wine vinegar
1 teaspoon olive oil
2 garlic cloves, minced
¼ teaspoon pepper
4 boneless, skinless chicken
   breast halves

Combine mustard, brown sugar, water, vinegar, oil, garlic and pepper. Mix well. Pour marinade over chicken, coating all sides. Cover and refrigerate least 2 hours or overnight.

Remove chicken from marinade. Heat marinade to boil. Remove from heat and cool. Grill chicken over medium-high heat, basting occasionally with marinade.

Yield: 4 servings

Shelia & Ken Link • Fort Macon Sail & Power Squadron
North Carolina

Raspberry Chicken

6 boneless skinless chicken
   breast halves or thighs
   (1½ pounds)
½ cup raspberry preserves
½ cup frozen pineapple
   juice concentrate,
   thawed
½ cup low-sodium soy sauce
1 tablespoon rice wine
   vinegar
½ teaspoon chili powder
½ teaspoon curry powder
½ teaspoon garlic powder
¼ cup fresh raspberries,
   mashed

Place chicken in a 13 x 9 x 2-inch baking dish. In a bowl, combine preserves, pineapple juice, soy sauce, vinegar, chili powder, curry, garlic powder and raspberries. Mix well. Pour over chicken. Cover tightly with foil. Marinate in the refrigerator at least 2 hours or overnight.

Bake, covered, at 350 degrees 30 to 40 minutes. Transfer chicken to a serving platter and top with pan juices.

Yield: 6 servings

Kay Simkins • Patuxent River Power Squadron • Maryland

TOMATILLO RELISH FOR GRILLED FISH OR CHICKEN

1½ pounds tomatillos,
   husked, rinsed and
   chopped
1½ pounds roma
   tomatoes, chopped
1 large onion, chopped
½ cup olive oil
¼ cup white vinegar
1 bunch cilantro, leaves
   only, chopped
¼ cup sugar
6 garlic cloves, minced
2 jalapeño peppers,
   stemmed, seeded and
   diced
1 sweet red pepper,
   chopped
2 teaspoons salt
1 teaspoon pepper

Combine tomatillos, tomato, onion, oil, vinegar, cilantro, sugar, garlic, jalapeño pepper, red pepper, salt and pepper in a large saucepan. Cover and simmer 1 hour. Cool to room temperature. Serve as a condiment to fish or chicken. May be stored in the refrigerator for up to one week.

Yield: 8 servings or 4½ cups

Julie Cheehan

Lower Rio Grand Valley
Power Squadron

Texas

Santa Fe Chicken

1	large onion, chopped	1	cup uncooked rice
1	tablespoon butter or vegetable oil	⅛	teaspoon garlic powder
1¼	cups chicken broth	4	boneless skinless chicken breast halves
1	cup salsa	¾	cup shredded Cheddar cheese

Sauté onion in butter in a skillet until tender. Add broth and salsa. Bring to boil. Stir in rice and garlic powder. Place chicken over rice, cover and simmer 10 minutes. Add water if rice begins to stick. Turn chicken and simmer an additional 15 minutes or until meat juices run clear. Remove from heat. Cover and let stand 5 minutes. Sprinkle with cheese.

Yield: 4 servings

David H. Bergen • Alamitos Sail & Power Squadron • California

Chicken Carlotta

1	tablespoon olive oil	½	cup fresh diced tomatoes
2	whole chicken breasts, halved		Juice of one lemon
½	pound mushrooms, sliced	¼	cup chopped green onion
3	garlic cloves, minced	1	teaspoon dried dill
2	tablespoons capers	¼	teaspoon cinnamon
1	(14-ounce) jar artichoke hearts, halved	⅛	teaspoon ground nutmeg
			Hot cooked brown rice
1	cup dry white wine	⅓	cup feta cheese

Coat a large skillet with cooking spray and add oil. Brown chicken, remove and keep warm. Add mushroom, garlic, capers and artichokes. Mix well. Pour in wine. Add tomato, juice, green onion, dill, cinnamon and nutmeg. Cook and stir until sauce thickens. Return chicken to pan and heat thoroughly. Serve over brown rice and top with feta cheese.

Yield: 4 servings

Charlotte Ward • Hilton Head Sail & Power Squadron
South Carolina

Baked Chicken Poupon

¼ cup grey poupon mustard
2 tablespoons vegetable oil
    or water
1 teaspoon garlic powder

½ teaspoon Italian seasoning
1 pound boneless skinless
    chicken breast halves

Combine mustard, oil, garlic powder and seasoning in a bowl or plastic bag. Add chicken and turn to coat all sides. Bake at 375 degrees 20 minutes or until done.

Yield: 4 servings

Nila Jane Shaw • Gainesville Sail & Power Squadron • Florida

Chicken Chasseus

¼ cup all-purpose flour
1 teaspoon salt
⅛ teaspoon pepper
¼ teaspoon dried oregano
2 boneless skinless chicken
    breast halves

3 tablespoons butter
1 small onion, chopped
6-8 mushrooms, sliced
⅔ cup white wine or
    chicken broth
1 tablespoon lemon juice

Blend flour, salt, pepper and oregano. Reserve 1 tablespoon flour mixture. Coat chicken in remaining flour mixture. Melt butter in a skillet and brown chicken. Transfer chicken to a plate. Sauté onion and mushroom. Sprinkle with 1 tablespoon flour mixture. Cook and stir a few seconds. Pour in wine and juice. Bring to boil. Return chicken to skillet. Cover and simmer 30 to 40 minutes until chicken is tender.

Yield: 2 servings

Grace Smithgall • Banana River Power Squadron • Florida

DID YOU KNOW?

Recreational boats have horns or other sound devices for numerous reasons. There are signals to indicate passing, crossing and overtaking situations to alert the other boat which course you will take. You should sound one short blast if you are changing to starboard. The Power Squadron Boat Smart course helps the student learn about signals.

Old-Fashioned Chicken Fricassee

4	tablespoons butter, divided	1	(8-ounce) package mushrooms, trimmed
2	tablespoons vegetable oil	1	teaspoon lemon juice
2½-3	pounds chicken, cut into pieces	16-24	small white onion
		½	cup water
3	tablespoons all-purpose flour	1	teaspoon sugar
1	cup dry white wine	6	tablespoons heavy cream
3	cups chicken broth		Salt to taste
1	bouquet garni	2	tablespoons chopped parsley
	Salt to taste		
¼	teaspoon white pepper		

Melt 2 tablespoons butter and oil in a large skillet. Brown half the chicken 10 minutes until golden. Remove to a plate and brown the remaining chicken. Return all chicken to skillet and sprinkle with flour, turning to coat. Cook, stirring occasionally, 4 minutes. Pour in wine and bring to boil. Pour in broth and push chicken to side of pan. Scrape browned bits from bottom. Bring to boil again. Add bouquet garni, salt and white pepper. Cover and simmer 25 to 30 minutes until chicken is tender.

Meanwhile, melt remaining butter in another skillet. Sauté mushroom with juice 3 to 4 minutes until golden. Transfer mushroom to a bowl. Add onion, water and sugar and mix well. Simmer 10 minutes until onion is tender. Pour onion and pan juice into bowl containing mushroom. Set aside.

Transfer cooked chicken to a deep serving dish and cover with foil. Discard bouquet garni. Pour vegetable cooking juice into chicken skillet. Bring to boil, stirring frequently, until sauce is reduced by half. Whisk in cream and cook 2 minutes. Add mushroom and onion and cook 2 minutes longer. Season with salt. Pour sauce over chicken and sprinkle with parsley.

Yield: 4 to 6 servings

Patricia Tuller • Cape Coral Power Squadron • Florida

Chicken à la Marie

Chicken

1 cup chicken broth	3 tablespoons olive oil
1 cup tomato sauce	Salt, pepper and garlic
1 cup Marsala wine	powder to taste
1½ pounds chicken cutlets	Mozzarella cheese slices
Italian seasoned bread	Grated Parmesan cheese
crumbs	Hot cooked rice or pasta
2 tablespoons butter	

Combine broth, tomato sauce and wine. Pour half into the bottom of a 13 x 9 x 2-inch baking dish. Pound cutlets to ¼-inch thickness. Coat in bread crumbs. Melt butter and oil in a skillet. Lightly brown the chicken. Transfer to baking dish. Season with salt, pepper and garlic powder. Cover each chicken piece with a mozzarella cheese slice. Pour remaining half broth mixture in skillet, scraping bits from the bottom. Pour broth and bits over chicken. Sprinkle with Parmesan cheese. Bake at 325 degrees 20 minutes. Serve over pasta or rice and sauce on the side.

Sauce

1 (8-ounce) can tomato	1 tablespoon butter
sauce	1-2 tablespoons tomato paste
1 cup chicken broth	½ teaspoon dried tarragon

Combine sauce, broth, butter, paste and tarragon in a small saucepan. Simmer over low heat 15 minutes. Pour over pasta or rice.

Yield: 4 to 6 servings

Marie Ragone • San Carlos Bay Sail & Power Squadron • Florida

South of the Border Turkey Casserole

10-12	ounces ground turkey	¼	teaspoon seasoned salt
½	medium onion, chopped	⅛	teaspoon ground cumin
½	cup chopped celery		Dash of cayenne pepper (optional)
½	teaspoon chopped garlic	½	cup cubed Munster cheese
½	cup sliced ripe olives	½	cup cubed Cheddar cheese
2	teaspoons beef bouillon crystals	¾	cup elbow macaroni, cooked al dente
1	(10-ounce) can tomatoes with green chilies		

Brown turkey, onion, celery and garlic. Add olives, bouillon, tomato, seasoned salt, cumin and cayenne. Mix well. Simmer 10 minutes. Stir in Munster cheese, Cheddar cheese and macaroni. Pour mixture into a 13 x 9 x 2-inch baking dish. Cover and bake at 350 degrees 20 minutes.

Yield: 8 servings

May cook mixture in a crockpot on high 1 hour and on low for travel.

Margorie L. Mullin • Long Bay Power Squadron • South Carolina

Crusted Honey Mustard Chicken

⅔	cup lite honey mustard dressing	1	green onion, finely sliced
⅛	teaspoon salt	1	cup cornflake crumbs
⅛	teaspoon pepper	1	pound boneless skinless chicken breast halves
2	teaspoons finely chopped dill		

Blend dressing, salt, pepper, dill and green onion. Remove ⅓ cup dressing mixture and set aside. Place crumbs in a shallow dish. Dip chicken in dressing mixture then dredge in crumbs. Place in a greased shallow baking dish. Bake at 425 degrees 15 minutes until chicken is golden. Drizzle reserved dressing mixture over hot chicken and serve.

Yield: 4 servings

Denise Fonk • Mt. Clemens Power Squadron • Michigan

Party Chicken & Spinach Casserole

1   (10-ounce) package
    frozen spinach, thawed
    and squeezed dry
1   (8-ounce) package cream
    cheese, softened
1   cup milk
1   cup shredded Monterey
    Jack cheese

½   teaspoon salt
¼   teaspoon garlic salt
½   cup grated Parmesan
    cheese, divided
2   cups cooked cubed
    chicken
½   cup cornflake crumbs

Spread spinach in the bottom of a 9 x 9 x 2-inch baking dish. Combine cream cheese, milk, cheese, salt, garlic salt and ¼ cup Parmesan cheese in a saucepan. Cook and stir sauce over low heat until smooth. Pour one-half sauce over spinach. Spread chicken over sauce. Pour remaining sauce over chicken. Sprinkle with remaining ¼ cup Parmesan cheese. Top with cornflake crumbs. Bake at 350 degrees 15 minutes until bubbly.

Yield: 6 servings

Misha Dunlap   •   Port St Lucie Power Squadron   •   Florida

Pecan Chicken

1   egg
¼   cup milk
2   boneless skinless chicken
    breast halves, cut into
    1-inch wide strips
¼   cup bread crumbs

¼   cup plus 3 tablespoons
    butter, divided
¼   cup packed brown sugar
1   (2¼-ounce) package
    chopped pecans

Beat egg and add milk. Dip chicken strips into egg mixture and coat in bread crumbs. Cook chicken in 3 tablespoons butter until golden browned. Melt ¼ cup butter in a saucepan. Stir in brown sugar until smooth and add pecans. Arrange chicken strips on a serving platter. Pour pecan sauce over chicken and serve immediately.

Yield: 2 servings

The sauce separates if not served immediately and crystallizes when it gets cold, so timing is very important.

Carol Philport-Jensen   •   Banana River Power Squadron   •   Florida

Baked Chicken with
Oranges, Apricots and Dried Cranberries

6	boneless skinless chicken breast halves	1	(11-ounce) can Mandarin oranges, drained
¼	cup minced onion	2	tablespoons all-purpose flour
¼	cup paprika		
½	teaspoon salt	2	cups orange juice, divided
¼	teaspoon dried rosemary	1	teaspoon dried orange zest
¼	teaspoon pepper	2	tablespoons Grand Marnier
½	cup minced dried apricots		
½	cup dried cranberries		Hot cooked rice or angel hair pasta

Arrange chicken in a single layer in a large roasting pan. Top with onion, paprika, rosemary, pepper, apricots, cranberries and orange. Whisk together flour with ½ cup juice. Add zest, Grand Marnier and remaining juice. Pour juice over chicken. Bake, uncovered, at 350 degrees 45 minutes, basting every 15 minutes with juice. Remove chicken from pan and cut into strips. Place strips on a bed of rice or angel hair pasta. Pour sauce over top.

Yield: 6 servings

Charlotte Ward • Hilton Head Sail & Power Squadron
South Carolina

Chinese Chicken

1	cup long grain rice		Juice of one lemon
1	chicken fryer, cut into serving size pieces	¼	cup honey
		1	teaspoon ground ginger
½	cup soy sauce	2	cups water

Spread uncooked rice in a greased 13 x 9 x 2-inch baking dish. Arrange chicken over rice. Blend soy sauce, juice, honey, ginger and water. Pour sauce over chicken. Cover with foil and bake at 350 degrees 1 hour. Uncover during the last 10 minutes of baking to brown chicken.

Yield: 4 servings

Marjorie S. Peterson • Bremerton Power Squadron
Washington State

Cherry Chicken

4	boneless skinless chicken breast halves	3	tablespoons packed brown sugar
¼	cup all-purpose flour	¼	teaspoon dried tarragon
¼	teaspoon salt	¼	cup dried cherries
1	tablespoon butter	1	tablespoon balsamic vinegar
½	cup cranberry juice	1	tablespoon cornstarch
½	cup port, Marsala or other sweet wine	2	tablespoons water
			Hot cooked rice

Dredge chicken in flour and season with salt. Cook chicken in butter 7 minutes each side. Transfer to a platter and keep warm. Combine juice, wine, brown sugar, tarragon, cherries and vinegar in skillet. Bring to boil. Reduce heat, cover and simmer 5 minutes. Whisk together cornstarch and water. Slowly add to juice mixture. Bring to boil. Cook and stir 1 minute until sauce thickens. Pour sauce over chicken. Serve over rice.

Yield: 4 servings

Chicken may be cooked ahead and reheated. The sauce may be prepared ahead and add cornstarch just before serving. Dried cranberries (craisins) can be substituted for dried cherries.

Donna Leone • Absecon Island Sail & Power Squadron • New Jersey

Alexander's Chicken Piccata

1½	cups all-purpose flour	3	tablespoons fresh lemon juice
1½	pounds chicken breast tenderloins, skinned	½	cup dry white wine
3	tablespoons vegetable oil	2	lemons, thinly sliced
3	tablespoons butter		Hot cooked rice

Place flour in a shallow pan. Coat chicken on all sides with flour. Heat oil and butter in a skillet. Brown chicken and place in an 11 x 7 x 2-inch baking dish. Blend juice and wine. Pour over chicken. Place lemon slices over chicken. Bake at 350 degrees 15 minutes or until fully cooked. Serve over white rice. Prepare Knorr lemon herb sauce made with half & half.

Yield: 6 servings

Pamela White • Pennsway Power Squadron • Pennsylvania

MAMA STAMBERG'S CRANBERRY RELISH

2 cups fresh cranberries
1 small onion
½ cup sugar
¾ cup sour cream
2 tablespoons horseradish

Grind cranberries and onion in a food processor. Transfer to a bowl. Stir in sugar, sour cream and horseradish. Spoon mixture into a plastic container and freeze. One hour before serving, thaw relish.

Yield: 3 cups

Leslie H. McCarthy
Brooklyn Power Squadron
New York

Chicken Breast with Ham and Asparagus

½	pound prosciutto ham	2	tablespoons butter
16-20	asparagus tips	2	tablespoons vegetable oil
4	boneless skinless chicken breasts, split and pounded thin	½	cup brandy
	All-purpose flour and paprika	½	cup chicken broth

Layer ham and 2 to 3 asparagus tips on each chicken breast. Roll up and secure with a toothpick. Sprinkle with flour and paprika. Heat butter and oil in a skillet. Cook chicken until lightly browned. Remove chicken and pour out pan drippings. Heat brandy and broth over high heat 1 minute. Return chicken to pan. Cover and simmer 10 minutes. If cooking in batches, keep cooked chicken warm in a 200 degree oven.

Yield: 8 servings

Barbara Schantz • Rockville Sail & Power Squadron • Maryland

Polynesian Chicken

1	(16-ounce) can whole cranberry sauce	½	cup water
1	(1¼-ounce) envelope onion soup mix	8	chicken thighs or 4 chicken breast halves
1	(8-ounce) bottle French dressing		Hot cooked rice

Combine cranberry sauce, onion mix, dressing and water. Place chicken in a 13 x 9 x 2-inch baking dish. Pour sauce over chicken. Bake at 350 degrees 45 minutes or until done. Serve over rice with salad and crusty bread.

Yield: 3 to 4 servings

J. M. Chapman • San Francisco Power Squadron • California

Chicken & Spaghetti

1	whole chicken
1	(16-ounce) can tomatoes
2	(8-ounce) cans tomato sauce
2	cups chopped celery
2	bell pepper, chopped
2	large onion, chopped
1	teaspoon garlic powder
3	bay leaves
1	(8-ounce) can sliced mushrooms
½	teaspoon ground thyme
1	teaspoon ground turmeric
¼	teaspoon crushed red pepper
½	teaspoon pepper
	Salt to taste
¼	cup all-purpose flour
1	cup warm water
1	pound spaghetti, cooked al dente

Boil chicken until tender. Cool and remove meat from bones. To broth add tomato, tomato sauce, celery, bell pepper, onion, garlic powder and bay leaves. Simmer 1 hour, 30 minutes. Add mushroom, thyme, turmeric, red pepper, pepper, salt and chicken pieces. Simmer 15 minutes. Blend flour with warm water. Slowly stir into sauce. Cook until thickened. Remove bay leaves. Serve over spaghetti.

Yield: 8 servings

Charlotte Ramsey • Ouachita Sail & Power Squadron • Texas

Chicken and Wild Rice

1	(6-ounce) package long grain and wild rice mix
2	chicken bouillon cubes
2	cups water
1	(8-ounce) can mushrooms, drained
3	cups cooked cubed chicken
⅓	cup bottled Italian dressing
1	cup sour cream

Cook rice according to package directions using bouillon cubes and water. Stir in mushroom, chicken, dressing and sour cream. Spoon into a lightly greased 2-quart casserole dish. Bake, uncovered, at 325 degrees 50 minutes or until bubbly. Cool 10 minutes before serving.

Yield: 4 servings

Sandy Ransom • Kinzua Power Squadron • Pennsylvania

PINEAPPLE MARINADE

2 cups pineapple
chunks, prefer fresh
1 (3-inch) piece ginger,
peeled and grated
1 garlic clove
Few dashes
Tabasco sauce
1 handful
cilantro leaves
½ cup soy sauce

Combine pineapple,
ginger, garlic, Tabasco,
cilantro and soy sauce
in a blender. Purée until
smooth. Pour over pork,
chicken or fish. Marinate
1 to 4 hours. Remove
meat from marinade and
grill to desired degree
of doneness. Serve with
grilled fresh pineapple,
lime wedges and
sweet potatoes.

Yield: 4 to 6 servings

Susan and Larry Bjork

Alamitos Sail & Power
Squadron

California

Chicken in Orange Sauce

1 (3-pound) chicken fryer,
cut into serving size
pieces
1 stick butter
¼ cup all-purpose flour
1 tablespoon packed brown
sugar
½ teaspoon ground ginger
1 teaspoon salt
⅛ teaspoon pepper
1½ cups orange juice
½ cup water
2 oranges, peeled and
sectioned or 1 (11-ounce)
can Mandarin oranges,
drained

Hot cooked rice and
chopped parsley

Brown chicken in butter in skillet. Transfer chicken to a plate. Blend
flour, brown sugar, ginger, salt and pepper into pan drippings. Cook,
stirring constantly, until mixture is bubbly. Slowly stir in orange juice
and water. Cook and stir until mixture boils 1 minute. Remove from
heat. Return chicken to pan. Arrange orange slices around chicken.
Simmer 15 minutes more or until chicken is tender. Serve over rice
and sprinkle with parsley.

Yield: 4 servings

Doris E. Shulze • Long Beach Power Squadron • California

Chicken Savoy

6 medium potatoes, peeled
and sliced
1 teaspoon dried oregano
1 teaspoon paprika
½ teaspoon garlic salt
1 bell pepper, chopped
1 medium onion, sliced
3 pounds boneless skinless
chicken breast halves,
cut up
1 pound turkey sausage
⅓ cup olive oil

Arrange potatoes in a roasting pan. Combine oregano, paprika and
garlic salt. Sprinkle ⅓ seasoning mixture over potatoes. Layer with
pepper and onion. Top with chicken and sausage. Pour oil evenly
over all. Sprinkle with remaining seasoning mixture. Cover with foil
and bake at 375 degrees 1 hour.

Yield: 4 servings

Lynn Stull • Rochester Power Squadron • New York

Chicken Captain

3   large fryer chickens, cut up
4   sticks plus 3-4 tablespoons butter, divided
2   bell peppers, chopped
2   medium onions, chopped
1   teaspoon curry powder
4   (28-ounce) cans tomatoes
     All-purpose flour and water
1½   cups blanched almonds
1   cup raisins
     Hot cooked rice

Season chicken with salt and pepper. Dust with flour. Melt 4 sticks butter in a large skillet. Cook chicken until golden browned. Transfer to a roasting pan. Melt 3 to 4 tablespoons butter in skillet. Sauté bell pepper, onion and curry about 15 minutes. Pour mixture over chicken and add tomato. Simmer, covered, at TEMP degrees 45 minutes or until chicken is tender. Combine flour and water. Add to sauce and stir until thickened. Add almonds and raisins. Arrange chicken around the edge of a large platter of rice. Pour some sauce over rice and remaining in a serving dish.

Yield: 10 servings

Gretchen A. Clark   •   Harris Chain Power Squadron   •   Florida

★ Fried Chicken with White Rice

¼   cup all-purpose flour
2   teaspoons salt
¼   teaspoon pepper
3   (2-pound) chickens, halved
5⅓   tablespoons butter
½   (6-ounce) can small mushrooms or 1 (8-ounce) package fresh
1   (10¾-ounce) can cream of mushroom soup
¼   cup dry white wine
¼   cup water
     Hot cooked rice

Combine flour, salt and pepper. Dredge chicken in flour mixture. Melt butter in heavy skillet. Brown chicken on all sides. Arrange chicken in a buttered casserole dish. Sauté mushroom in skillet. Blend soup, wine and water and pour over chicken. Scatter mushroom on top. Bake at 350 degrees 1 hour to 1 hour, 30 minutes. Serve over rice.

Yield: 8 to 10 servings

Jack Lucey   •   Evanston Power Squadron   •   Illinois

Chicken à la Pizziaol

1½ pounds chicken	3 tablespoons dried oregano
5-6 medium potatoes, sliced	
2 large onion, sliced	Salt and pepper to taste
1 (16-ounce) can crushed tomatoes	

Arrange chicken in a greased 13 x 9 x 2-inch baking dish. Top with potato and onion. Pour tomato on top. Sprinkle with oregano, salt and pepper. Bake at 375 degrees 1 hour or until chicken and potatoes are cooked. Stir mixture four times while baking.

Yield: 6 to 8 servings

Rosemarie Radomsky • Redondo Beach Power Squadron • California

Chicken Marbella

2 garlic cloves, minced	1 (4-ounce) jar capers and juice
¼ cup dried oregano	
½-1 teaspoon sea salt	6 bay leaves
Pepper to taste	10-12 boneless skinless chicken breast halves
¼ cup red wine vinegar	
½ cup olive oil	1 cup packed brown sugar
1 cup pitted prunes, halved	
	1 cup white wine
½ cup Spanish green olives	¼ cup flat leaf parsley or cilantro

Combine garlic, oregano, salt, pepper, vinegar, oil, prunes, olives, capers and bay leaves. Arrange chicken in a large roasting pan. Pour marinade over chicken. Cover with foil and refrigerate overnight.

Sprinkle chicken with brown sugar and pour wine around chicken. Bake at 350 degrees 50 to 60 minutes, basting with pan juices. Remove bay leaves. Sprinkle with parsley.

Yield: 10 to 12 servings

Una Ronne • Fort Worth Sail & Power Squadron • Texas

Spinach-Stuffed Chicken

6	cups spinach, torn	½	cup dry bread crumbs
½	cup chopped onion	3	tablespoons grated Parmesan cheese
½	cup chopped mushrooms	½	teaspoon paprika
1	garlic clove, minced	¼	cup cholesterol-free egg product
1	tablespoon olive oil or vegetable oil	1	tablespoon water
½	teaspoon dried oregano	2	tablespoons butter, melted
½	teaspoon salt		
6	boneless skinless chicken breasts halves		

Cook spinach in ½-inch water in a large non-stick skillet 2 minutes or just until wilted. Drain and set aside. In same skillet, sauté onion, mushroom and garlic in oil until tender. Stir in oregano and salt. Return spinach and mix well. Set mixture aside.

Pound chicken to ¼-inch thickness. Spread spinach mixture down the center in chicken. Fold one side over and roll up tightly. Secure with a toothpick. Combine bread crumbs, Parmesan cheese and paprika. In a separate bowl, blend egg product with water. Dip each stuffed chicken in egg mixture and roll in crumb mixture. Place chicken seam side down in a greased 13 x 9 x 2-inch baking dish. Drizzle with butter.

Bake, uncovered, at 350 degrees 20 to 25 minutes or until juices run clear. Discard toothpicks prior to serving.

Yield: 6 servings

Estelle Rutkowski • Palm Beach Sail & Power Squadron • Florida

Chicken Barbecued in Foil

3	tablespoons butter	¼	cup lemon juice
1	tablespoon packed brown sugar	½	cup ketchup
¾	cup chopped onion	2	tablespoons Worcestershire sauce
1	teaspoon vinegar	1½-3	pounds fryer chicken, cut up
1	teaspoon prepared mustard		Salt to taste

Combine butter, brown sugar, onion, vinegar, mustard, juice, ketchup and Worcestershire sauce in a saucepan. Bring to boil. Reduce heat and simmer 15 minutes. Season each chicken piece with salt. Place on a square of foil. Foil should be large enough to wrap chicken completely. Spoon a generous amount of sauce on each chicken piece. Close foil and wrap securely. Place on a baking sheet. Bake at 350 degrees 1 hour. Carefully open foil packets and broil until browned.

Yield: 6 to 8 servings

Arthura Ellen Holliday • Goldsboro Power Squadron
North Carolina

Chicken Marinade

½	cup mochiko (Japanese rice flour)	4	large eggs, beaten
½	cup cornstarch	4	garlic cloves, minced
½	cup sugar	1	teaspoon salt
½	cup chopped green onion	1	whole chicken, cut into pieces
½	cup soy sauce		

Combine mochiko, cornstarch, sugar, green onion, soy sauce, eggs, garlic and salt. Mix well. Pour marinade over chicken and refrigerate overnight. Drain marinade from chicken. Grill, broil or deep fry chicken until done.

Yield: 4 servings

Ellen Breymann • Alamitos Power Squadron • California

Chicken Vegetable Quiche

2 (9-inch) deep dish pie crusts, unbaked
3 cups cooked chicken, cubed or shredded
1 cup shredded Cheddar cheese
1 cup shredded Swiss cheese
1 (10-ounce) package frozen broccoli florets or spinach, thawed and well drained
1 small onion, chopped
1 sweet bell pepper, finely chopped
1 (12-ounce) can evaporated milk
1 cup mayonnaise
5 eggs, slightly beaten
½ teaspoon ground nutmeg
1 teaspoon Worcestershire sauce
   Tabasco sauce, salt and pepper to taste
   All-purpose flour for topping

Fill two pie crusts evenly with chicken, cheese, broccoli, onion and red pepper. Blend milk, mayonnaise, eggs, nutmeg, Worcestershire sauce, Tabasco, salt and pepper. Pour egg mixture over filling. Sprinkle with a little flour. Bake at 350 degrees 40 minutes or until tester comes out clean.

Yield: 10 to 12 servings

Chris Puckett • Greensboro Power Squadron • North Carolina

Italian Chicken with Rice

4	boneless skinless chicken breast halves	1	cup long grain rice
½	teaspoon salt	½	cup water
2	tablespoons butter	¼	cup grated Parmesan cheese
½	cup chopped onion	½	teaspoon Italian seasoning
1	(14½-ounce) can Italian stewed tomatoes	¼	teaspoon garlic powder
1	(14½-ounce) can chicken broth	4	ounces mozzarella cheese, cut into ½-inch slices

Sprinkle chicken with salt. Melt butter in a large skillet. Brown chicken 2 minutes each side. Transfer to a plate. Sauté onion 5 minutes until tender. Add tomato, broth, rice, water, Parmesan cheese, seasoning and garlic powder. Bring to boil. Reduce heat and simmer 5 minutes. Return chicken to skillet. Cover and simmer 15 minutes until rice is tender. Remove skillet from heat. Top chicken with mozzarella cheese slices. Cover 1 minute until cheese melts.

Yield: 4 servings

Judy and Tom Moore   •   Virginia Beach Sail & Power Squadron
Virginia

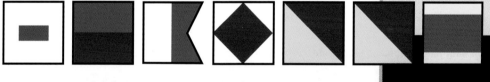

seafood

boating activities

where did you go last weekend?

USPS members boating activities encompass just about every kind of fun, sport and challenge one could imagine. Do you like to cruise, fish, race, sail, help the environment, explore or even study marine life. All of these activities are possible as part of boating with the Power Squadrons.

Members boating activities are designed to encompass all those activities mentioned above and even be helpful to the community. How? Well, local members work with the US Coast Guard, the US Army Corps of Engineers and the National Ocean Service chart division in providing corrections and verification data related to navigational aids, depths, clearances, currents, weather and other information for critical coastal and river marine and aeronautical charts.

These activities are usually wrapped around a social event where members have the opportunity to enjoy their sport of boating in whatever manner and be useful contributors to their communities. Squadron rendezvous encompass all the pleasures of the sport and occasionally the opportunity to serve. Group activities where numerous boats cruise together, play, swim hold a raft-up provide fun outings for all ages.

Why not join us?

For more information call 1-888-367-8777. Thanks for listening!

Shrimp & Scallop Fettuccine

1	pound medium size shrimp, peeled and deveined	1	(16-ounce) package fettuccine, cooked al dente
1	pound bay scallops, halved	1	tablespoon lemon juice
2	tablespoons olive oil	2	teaspoons dried dill
1	teaspoon chopped garlic	¼	cup grated Parmesan cheese
¾	cup white cooking wine	¼	teaspoon crushed red pepper
¼	cup clam juice		Salt and white pepper to taste
½	cup heavy cream		

Sauté shrimp and scallops in oil with garlic. Cook until shrimp are just turning pink. Add wine, clam juice. Simmer 3 to 5 minutes. Stir in cream and cook until thickened. Add sauce to fettuccine. Stir in lemon juice, dill, Parmesan cheese, red pepper, salt and pepper. Mix well. Serve with garlic bread and white wine.

Yield: 4 servings

Stephen M. Wheeler • Boulder Valley Sail & Power Squadron • Colorado

DID YOU KNOW?

A diesel oil, grease or gasoline fire should be extinguished with a class "B" fire extinguisher. Class B is dry chemical. Class A is water and C is Carbon Dioxide. The dry chemical will smother the fire. Know before you go, take a boating class.

Marinated Shrimp Kebabs

½	cup olive oil	16-20	large shrimp, peeled and deveined
1	cup white wine		Large basil leaves
	Juice of two lemons	16-20	slices Italian prosciutto
2	tablespoons Worcestershire sauce	1	sweet red pepper, cut into large chunks
½	cup balsamic vinegar	1	yellow pepper or vegetable of choice, cut into large chunks
	Salt and pepper to taste		
1	teaspoon dried oregano		
2	garlic cloves, minced		

Combine oil, wine, juice, Worcestershire sauce, vinegar, salt, pepper, oregano and garlic in a bowl. Add shrimp and toss to coat. Refrigerate 2 to 4 hours. Wrap each shrimp in a basil leaf. Wrap a slice of prosciutto around basil. Thread shrimp and peppers alternately onto skewers. Grill to desired degree of doneness.

Yield: 4 to 6 servings

Dan Moore • Tacoma Power Squadron • Washington State

Greek Style Prawns

20 ounces prawns, peeled and deveined	1½ cups white wine
All-purpose flour	½ cup feta cheese, crumbled
1 stick butter, clarified	1 cup Pernod (anisette)
Salt and white pepper to taste	10 small tomatoes, diced
1-2 white onions, thinly sliced	½ cup tomato sauce
1 cup sliced mushrooms	8 green onions, thinly sliced
2 garlic cloves, minced	Chopped parsley for garnish
Juice of one lemon	Hot cooked rice pilaf

Dust prawns with flour. Brown in clarified butter. Add salt, pepper, onion, mushroom, garlic and juice. Stir constantly to keep flour from burning. Cook until vegetables are browned. Add wine and feta cheese. Cook until cheese melts. Add Pernod, tomato and tomato sauce. Mix thoroughly. Just before serving, add green onion. Sprinkle with parsley and serve over rice.

Yield: 4 servings

Tish Cullen • Las Vegas Sail & Power Squadron • Nevada

Fettuccine with Shrimp and Tomatoes

3 (14½-ounce) cans diced tomatoes, undrained	⅓ cup olive oil
2 teaspoons dried basil	½ pound shrimp per person, peeled and deveined
4 garlic cloves, minced	
3 tablespoons minced shallot	1½ pounds fettuccine, cooked al dente
1 teaspoon pepper	Grated Romano cheese
½ teaspoon salt	

Sauté tomato, basil, garlic, shallot, pepper and salt in oil 5 to 7 minutes. Simmer 1 hour. Add shrimp and cook until shrimp turn pink. Pour mixture over pasta and top with Romano cheese. Serve immediately.

Yield: 6 to 8 servings

Sue Dorn • Beaufort Sail & Power Squadron • South Carolina

Shrimp Victoria

1 pound shrimp, peeled and deveined	1 tablespoon all-purpose flour
1 onion, finely chopped	¼ teaspoon salt
¼ cup chopped celery	Dash of cayenne pepper
4 tablespoons butter	1 cup sour cream
1 (6-ounce) can mushrooms	1½ cups cooked rice

Sauté shrimp, onion and celery in butter 5 to 6 minutes until shrimp turn pink. Add mushroom and cook 5 minutes. Sprinkle with flour, salt and cayenne. Stir in sour cream and simmer 5 minutes. Do not boil. Serve over cooked rice.

Yield: 4 to 6 servings

Marlene Sobkowich • Lake Pontchartrain Sail & Power Squadron
Louisiana

DID YOU KNOW?

The quickest and safest way to shut down a runaway diesel engine is to cut off the air supply. That may be accomplished by discharging a CO2 extinguisher into the air intake. These and other tips on the safe operation and maintenance of diesel engines is covered in the Power Squadron Engine Maintenance course.

Seafood Pasta with Basil Cream

3 tablespoons olive oil	1 pound favorite seafood, cooked (salmon or shrimp)
3 tablespoons butter	
1-2 garlic cloves, minced	Salt and white pepper to taste
3-4 tomatoes, seeded and chopped	
½ cup dry white wine	1 pound favorite pasta, cooked al dente
½ cup heavy cream	
½ cup basil leaves, finely chopped	Grated Parmesan cheese

Heat oil and butter in a saucepan. Gently sauté garlic 1 minute. Add tomato and simmer until softened. Pour in wine and cream. Simmer 5 to 10 minutes until sauce thickens. Stir in basil and seafood and simmer 2 to 3 minutes. Season with salt and pepper. Serve over pasta and top with cheese.

Yield: 6 servings

Susan Holmes • Peralta Power Squadron • California

Shrimp Creole

⅔	cup chopped onion	1	teaspoon salt
½	cup chopped bell pepper	½	teaspoon pepper
½	cup chopped celery	½	teaspoon dried oregano
2	garlic cloves, minced	½	teaspoon celery salt
2	tablespoons butter	2	tablespoons packed
2	(28-ounce) cans whole		brown sugar
	tomatoes, cut up and	1	pound shrimp, peeled
	reserve juice		and deveined
2	(8-ounce) cans tomato		Hot cooked rice or
	sauce		spaghetti
2	bay leaves		

Sauté onion, bell pepper, celery and garlic in butter. Add tomato, tomato sauce, bay leaves, salt, pepper, oregano, celery salt and brown sugar. Cover and simmer 40 minutes. Add tomato juice if mixture dries out. Add shrimp during last 5 minutes of cooking. Remove bay leaves. Serve over rice or spaghetti.

Yield: 6 to 8 servings

Delores Jorgensen • Manatee Sail & Power Squadron • Florida

Pasta with Shrimp

¼	cup extra virgin olive oil, divided	¼	cup chopped basil or 2 teaspoons dried, crushed
1	pound medium shrimp, peeled and deveined		Salt and pepper to taste
1	large garlic clove, finely chopped	1	pound farfalle pasta, cooked al dente
1	(28-ounce) can diced tomatoes, undrained		

Heat 2 tablespoons oil in a large saucepan. Sauté shrimp and garlic, stirring frequently, 3 to 4 minutes until shrimp turn pink. Remove from pan. Add remaining oil, tomato, basil, salt and pepper. Cook, stirring occasionally, 8 to 10 minutes. Add pasta and return shrimp to pan. Toss to coat and heat thoroughly.

Yield: 6 servings

Nancy Krupien • Patchogue Bay Power Squadron • New York

Shrimp Creole

⅔ cup vegetable oil
⅓ cup all-purpose flour
1 cup chopped onion
⅔ cup chopped bell pepper
⅔ cup chopped celery
½ cup chopped shallot
1 tablespoon minced garlic
3 cups canned tomatoes, chopped and drained
⅔ cup water
2 teaspoons lemon juice
1 teaspoon chopped parsley
2 bay leaves
½ teaspoon chili powder
½ teaspoon Creole seasoning
1 teaspoon ground allspice
½ teaspoon dried basil
½ teaspoon ground thyme
½ teaspoon cayenne pepper
1 tablespoon pepper
Salt to taste
2 pounds shrimp, peeled and deveined
Hot cooked rice

Heat oil in a heavy 8-quart stockpot. Whisk in flour to form a dark roux. Add onion, bell pepper, celery, shallot and garlic. Cook until vegetables are tender. Stir in tomato, water, juice, parsley, bay leaves, chili powder, Creole seasoning, allspice, basil, thyme, cayenne, pepper and salt. Simmer 45 minutes or until mixture is thick. Add shrimp and simmer 10 minutes until shrimp turn pink. Serve immediately over rice.

Yield: 8 to 10 servings

Beverlee Winslow • Peace River Power Squadron • Florida

Shrimp Rémoulade

¼ cup mayonnaise
1 bunch green onions, sliced
⅓ cup chopped parsley
2 tablespoons Dijon mustard
2 tablespoons Creole mustard
2-3 teaspoons horseradish
1 tablespoon lemon juice
2 pounds cooked shrimp

Blend mayonnaise, green onion, parsley, mustard, Creole mustard, horseradish and juice. Add shrimp, cover and refrigerate. Remove shrimp from sauce. Serve sauce for dipping.

Yield: 6 to 8 servings

Sheila Vaughan • Miles River Sail & Power Squadron • Maryland

RÉMOULADE SAUCE

½ cup ketchup
3 teaspoons lemon juice
¼ cup vinegar
1 teaspoon Worcestershire sauce
⅔ cup horseradish
⅔ cup hot Creole mustard
½ cup vegetable oil
1 onion, finely chopped

Blend together ketchup, juice, vinegar, Worcestershire sauce, horseradish, mustard, oil and onion. Mix well. Refrigerate until ready to use.

Yield: 2 cups

Carol Dickmann
New Orleans Power Squadron
Louisiana

Shrimp and Grits

Grits

4	cups water	1	stick butter
1	cup heavy cream	1	cup white corn grits
	Salt to taste		(regular not instant)

Combine water, cream, salt and butter in a saucepan. Bring to boil. Gradually add grits and return to boil. Reduce heat and simmer 45 minutes, stirring constantly. Keep warm.

Shrimp

36	shrimp, peeled and deveined with tail on	1	medium Vidalia onion, chopped
1	tablespoon butter	½	pound smoked sausage or andouille sausage, sliced
1	bell pepper, chopped		
1	sweet red pepper, chopped		Salt, pepper, garlic powder and hot chili pepper to taste
1	yellow pepper, chopped		

Sauté shrimp, bell pepper, red pepper, yellow pepper, onion and sausage in butter until shrimp turn pink and sausage is cooked. Serve over grits. Serve with brown gravy if desired.

Yield: 6 to 8 servings

Carol McVey • Swamp Fox Power Squadron • South Carolina

Seafood Casserole

1½	pounds crabmeat	1½	cups mayonnaise
½	pound small shrimp	2	(10-ounce) packages frozen peas, thawed
½	bell pepper, chopped		
⅓	cup chopped parsley		Salt and pepper to taste
2	cups cooked rice		

Combine crabmeat, shrimp, bell pepper, parsley, rice, mayonnaise, peas, salt and pepper. Pour into a greased 2-quart casserole dish. Cover and refrigerate. Bake, covered, at 350 degrees 1 hour.

Yield: 6 servings

Juanita S. Neumeister • Cape Fear Power Squadron • North Carolina

Shrimp Chow Mein

1 cup chopped onion	2 cups cooked shrimp
1 cup sliced celery	1 (3-ounce) can sliced
1 cup chopped bell pepper	mushrooms, drained
¼ cup hot vegetable oil	1 (5-ounce) can sliced
1 (10¾-ounce) can cream	water chestnuts,
of mushroom soup	drained
2 teaspoons cornstarch	1 (15-ounce) can bean
¾ cup cold water	sprouts or fresh
¼ cup soy sauce	4 cups hot chow mein
	noodles

Sauté onion, celery and bell pepper in oil 2 minutes. Stir in soup. Blend cornstarch with water and soy sauce. Gradually stir into soup mixture. Cook and stir until thickened. Add shrimp, mushroom, water chestnuts and bean sprouts. Heat thoroughly. Serve over chow mein noodles. Serve with soy sauce.

Yield: 6 to 8 servings

Lois W. Neef • Anclote Key Sail & Power Squadron • Florida

Seafood Newburg

1 stick butter	3 eggs, beaten
¼ cup cornstarch	1 pound shrimp, cooked,
1 teaspoon salt	peeled and deveined
1 teaspoon paprika	1 (6-ounce) can lobster
2 cups heavy cream	meat
2 cups milk	1 (6-ounce) can crabmeat
½ cup dry sherry	Hot cooked rice or pasta

Melt butter in a large stockpot. Whisk in cornstarch, salt and paprika. Remove from heat and slowly whisk in cream and milk until smooth. Return to medium heat, stirring constantly, until mixture boils 1 minute. Reduce heat and add sherry. Remove from heat. Stir 1 cup cream mixture into eggs. Add eggs back into creamed mixture. Stir in shrimp, lobster and crabmeat. Heat thoroughly. Serve over rice or pasta.

Yield: 12 servings

Joanne F. Van Ameyden • Sable Point Sail & Power Squadron • Michigan

DID YOU KNOW?

When thick fog develops, it is a good practice that all crew members and passengers don lifejackets, and have all safety equipment ready for use in an emergency. Safety is the first responsibility of the skipper. Know before you go, take a boating class.

Kickin' Finger Shrimp

4	tablespoons butter	2	tablespoons red Tabasco sauce
¼	cup olive oil		
¼	cup Worcestershire sauce	1	tablespoon green Tabasco sauce
1	tablespoon lemon juice		
1	tablespoon lime juice	½	teaspoon dried tarragon
6	garlic cloves, minced	1	pound shrimp, deveined with tails on
2	tablespoons crushed red pepper		Crusty bread
1	teaspoon dried oregano		

Heat butter, oil, Worcestershire sauce, lemon juice, lime juice, garlic, red pepper, oregano, red Tabasco, green Tabasco and tarragon in a saucepan. Cool and pour into a zip-top plastic bag. Add shrimp and toss to coat. Refrigerate at least 8 hours or overnight.

Pour marinade and shrimp into a skillet. Cook and stir 10 minutes or until shrimp turn pink. Serve shrimp with sauce in bowls with crusty bread for dipping.

Yield: 4 servings

Joanne Larsell • Portland Power Squadron • Oregon

Crab and Avocado Linguine

2	teaspoons grated fresh ginger	⅓	cup vegetable oil
		1	teaspoon salt, divided
2	teaspoons lemon juice	½	teaspoon lemon zest
1½	tablespoons wine vinegar	1	avocado, cut into ½-inch cubes
2	green onions, white and green parts chopped, dark green top sliced	¾	pound linguine, cooked al dente
1	teaspoon soy sauce	½	pound lump crabmeat

Combine ginger, juice, vinegar, green onion, soy sauce, oil and ½ teaspoon salt in a blender. Process until smooth. Add zest and avocado to dressing. Toss pasta with crabmeat. Add dressing and remaining ½ teaspoon salt. Toss to coat.

Yield: 4 servings

Judy Hauck • Susquehannock Power Squadron • Pennsylvania

Crab Stuffed Shrimp Lowell

½ pound large shrimp, peeled and deveined

Pizza or spaghetti sauce

⅓ cup crushed bread stuffing plus more for topping

3 tablespoons olive oil

½ cup mozzarella cheese

½ teaspoon Italian seasoning

½ teaspoon garlic powder

¼ teaspoon dehydrated minced onion

1 teaspoon lemon juice

1 teaspoon white wine

1 egg, beaten

¼ pound crabmeat, chopped into small pieces

1 stick butter, melted

Paprika to taste

Grated Parmigiano-Reggiano cheese

Butterfly cut the entire length of each shrimp. Set aside. Pour a layer of sauce in the bottom of an 11 x 7 x 2-inch baking pan. Arrange shrimp over sauce. Combine ⅓ cup bread crumbs, oil, cheese, seasoning, garlic powder, onion, juice, wine, egg and crabmeat. Mix well. Roll 1 rounded teaspoon crabmeat mixture into a compact ball. Place 1 ball on each shrimp and spoon 1 tablespoon of spaghetti sauce over shrimp. Sprinkle with bread crumbs and drizzle with butter. Top with paprika.

Bake at 300 degrees 25 minutes. Broil 1 minute. Remove from oven and sprinkle with Reggiano cheese.

Yield: 2 servings

Charlotte Ward • Hilton Head Sail & Power Squadron
South Carolina

Crabcakes

1 pint crabmeat

1 egg, beaten

¾ tablespoon all-purpose flour

Salt and pepper to taste

Canola oil

Combine crabmeat, egg, flour and season with salt and pepper. Shape 1 tablespoon mixture into a ball and drop into hot canola oil. Cook until done.

Yield: 4 servings

Lollie Holland • Greensboro Power Squadron • North Carolina

DID YOU KNOW?

After being underway for a few hours, your engine starts to run very hot. You know the problem is not the thermostat stuck shut. How do you know. If you have taken the Power Squadron Engine Maintenance course it would have helped with the diagnosis of the problem.

Frank's Garlic Crabs

Peanut oil	6	soft shell crabs, cleaned
2-3 tablespoons dark cream sherry or white wine		Dried oregano and crushed red pepper to taste
Old Bay spice to taste		
4 garlic cloves, minced		

Pour oil into a skillet to ¼ to ½-inch depth. Heat oil. Add sherry, Old Bay spice, garlic and crabs. Sprinkle with oregano, and red pepper. Partially cover to allow steam to escape. Cook until claws turn red. Turn and cook until joints turn red. Do not overcook.

Yield: 6 servings

Frank A. Leone • Absecon Island Power Squadron • New Jersey

Crabby Crab Lovers Casserole

1	(14-ounce) can artichoke hearts, drained	Paprika and pepper to taste
1	pound crabmeat	1 teaspoon Worcestershire sauce
1	(8-ounce) package sliced mushrooms, sautéed	1 cup heavy cream
4	tablespoons butter	Cayenne pepper to taste
1½	teaspoons all-purpose flour	½ cup grated Parmesan cheese
½	teaspoon salt	

Arrange artichokes in the bottom of a greased 2-quart casserole dish. Spread a layer of crabmeat and then a layer of mushroom. Melt butter in a saucepan. Whisk in flour until smooth. Add salt, paprika, pepper, Worcestershire sauce, cream and cayenne, stirring well after each addition until sauce is smooth. Pour sauce over casserole layers. Sprinkle with Parmesan cheese. Bake at 325 degrees 30 minutes.

Yield: 4 to 6 servings

Nita Neumeister • Cape Fear Power Squadron • North Carolina

Crab Benedict

Hollandaise Sauce

6   egg yolks
¼   cup fresh lemon juice
2   sticks unsalted butter,
      melted

Dash of cayenne pepper
Salt and pepper to taste

Heat water in the bottom of a double boiler until hot but not boiling. Combine egg yolks and juice in the top of a double boiler. Whisk until smooth. Gradually add butter in a steady stream. Stir in cayenne, salt and pepper. Whisk sauce until thickened. Keep warm.

Crab

8   English muffins, split and
      toasted
16   eggs
1   pound crabmeat, drained
      and flaked
½   cup chopped bell pepper

½   cup chopped celery
2   tablespoons mayonnaise
1   tablespoon
      Worcestershire sauce
1   tablespoon butter, melted

Place 2 muffin halves on 8 individual plates and keep warm in a 200 degree oven. Poach the eggs. Place one egg on each muffin half and return to oven. Combine crabmeat, bell pepper, celery, mayonnaise and Worcestershire sauce. Sauté mixture in butter until thoroughly heated. Divide mixture among remaining muffin halves. Ladle warm sauce over each muffin.

8 servings

Charlotte Ward • Hilton Head Sail & Power Squadron
South Carolina

Crabmeat Quiche

1	(10-inch) pie crust, unbaked	1	teaspoon lemon juice
8	ounces crabmeat	½	cup mayonnaise
½	cup bread crumbs	1	teaspoon Worcestershire sauce
1	teaspoon dry mustard	1	(8-ounce) package shredded Swiss cheese
½	cup evaporated milk		Salt and pepper to taste
2-3	eggs, slightly beaten		Paprika for garnish
2	teaspoons chopped parsley		

Pierce the bottom of the pie crust with a fork. Bake at 450 degrees 8 minutes. Remove from oven and cool. Reduce heat to 350 degrees. Combine crabmeat, bread crumbs, mustard, milk, eggs, parsley, juice, mayonnaise, Worcestershire sauce, cheese, salt and pepper. Mix well. Pour mixture into pie crust. Sprinkle with paprika. Bake at 350 degrees 35 to 45 minutes or until firm in the center and tester comes out clean.

Yield: 6 to 8 servings

Cynthia Vansil • Akron Power Squadron • Ohio

Barbecued Alaskan Salmon

2	tablespoons butter	1	tablespoon lemon juice
2	tablespoons packed brown sugar	2	teaspoons soy sauce
1-2	garlic cloves, minced	½	teaspoon pepper
		4	salmon steaks, 1-inch thick

Combine butter, brown sugar, garlic, juice, soy sauce and pepper in a saucepan. Cook and stir until sugar melts. Grill salmon, covered, over medium-high heat 5 minutes. Turn salmon, baste with sauce and grill 7 to 9 minutes longer. Turn, baste and cook until salmon flakes easily.

Yield: 4 servings

Billie J. Raynolds • Las Vegas Sail & Power Squadron • Nevada

Kate's Grilled Salmon

¼ cup mayonnaise
1½ teaspoons Dijon mustard
Dash of sherry wine
Dash of lemon juice

Dash of garlic powder
4 salmon steaks with skin on
Garlic pepper to taste

Blend mayonnaise, mustard, wine, juice and garlic powder. Sprinkle both sides of steak with garlic pepper. Place salmon skin-side down and grill 15 minutes. Turn and grill an additional 5 minutes. Transfer to a broiler pan. Spread sauce over salmon and broil 5 minutes or until bubbly and browned. Serve immediately.

Yield: 4 servings

William F. Mullin • Long Bay Power Squadron • South Carolina

Orange-Merlot Salmon

2 tablespoons olive oil
2 garlic cloves, minced
2 salmon fillets
½ cup Merlot wine
Juice of one-half orange

Juice of one-half lemon
¼-⅓ cup maple syrup
Cooked garlic mashed potatoes

Heat oil in a skillet. Sauté garlic 5 minutes. Place salmon in skillet skin-side up. Cover and cook 3 minutes. Turn salmon, cover and cook an additional 3 minutes. Transfer salmon to a plate and keep warm. Add wine, orange juice, lemon juice and syrup to skillet. Heat thoroughly. Return salmon skin-side up and heat 3 minutes. Remove salmon and reduce sauce, stirring constantly, 3 minutes. Pour sauce over salmon. Serve with garlic mashed potato.

Yield: 2 servings

For garlic mashed potatoes, cook red-skinned potato in salted water with garlic cloves until tender. Drain and mash. Add fresh minced garlic, butter and your choice of milk, sour cream or plain yogurt.

This is a wonderful, romantic meal for two but can be doubled for four.

Dan Moore • Tacoma Power Squadron • Washington State

DID YOU KNOW?

In a head-on, crossing or overtaking situation the vessel making the change should make its intentions known in an obvious and early fashion. Delay or subtle fashion will not alert the vessel staying its course and thus may cause an accident. The USPS Boat Smart course helps students understand their responsibilities.

Salmon Bake

2	(1-pound) cans salmon, drained and flaked, reserving juice	2	tablespoons pickle relish
¾	cup milk	1	tablespoon lemon juice
½	cup bread crumbs	1	egg, beaten
		3	tablespoons unsalted butter, melted

Blend enough salmon juice with the milk to equal 1 cup. Combine salmon, milk, bread crumbs, relish, juice, egg and butter. Mix well. Pour mixture into a microwave safe ring mold or pie plate. Cover with wax paper or plastic wrap. Microwave on high 9 to 11 minutes. Cool 5 minutes before serving.

Yield: 4 servings

Judy James • Anchor Bay Power Squadron • Michigan

Poached Salmon

Salmon

1	whole salmon, rinsed, dried and wrapped in cheesecloth	1	onion, sliced
			Celery leaves
2	teaspoons salt	3	tablespoons white wine vinegar
1	teaspoon pepper		

Pour water into a poaching pan to a 3-inch depth. Add salt, pepper, onion, celery leaves and vinegar. Bring to boil. Place fish in bouillon and simmer 6 minutes per pound or until is opaque and flesh is juicy. Cool fish and remove skin. Arrange fish on a serving platter with lettuce leaves. Refrigerate.

Sauce

1	(8-ounce) package cream cheese, softened	1	cup mayonnaise
			Juice of one lemon
¼	cup bouillon from poaching	4-6	teaspoons chopped dill

Combine cream cheese, bouillon, mayonnaise, juice and dill in a saucepan. Cook and stir until cheese melts and sauce is smooth. Spread sauce over cold fish.

Yield: 6 to 8 servings

Jean Ruckdeschel • New York Power Squadron • New York

Barbara's Salmon Wellington

1	cup crabmeat		Salt, pepper, dried dill or dried tarragon to taste
1	egg, beaten	1	whole salmon
1	cup bread crumbs	1	(17-ounce) package frozen puff pastry, thawed
2	tablespoons mayonnaise		
2	tablespoons heavy cream	1	egg white

Combine crabmeat, egg, bread crumbs, mayonnaise, cream, salt, pepper and dill. Spread on one side of salmon. Roll up salmon in jelly-roll fashion. Wrap both puff pastry sheets around salmon. Use excess pastry to seal edges by brushing with egg white. Brush top and sides with egg white. Bake at 475 degrees 45 to 50 minutes until pastry puffs and is well browned. Slice roll and serve hot.

Yield: 6 servings

Barbara Johnson • Pasadena Sail & Power Squadron • California

Sweet and Sour Salmon

5	tablespoons peanut oil	3	tablespoons sherry
3	tablespoons soy sauce	¼	cup red wine vinegar
1	garlic clove, minced	2-3	pounds fish (cod, salmon, halibut, tuna), rinsed with lemon juice
½	teaspoon salt		
⅛	teaspoon pepper		
2	teaspoons sugar		

Blend oil, soy sauce, garlic, salt and pepper in a sealable bowl. Stir in sugar and sherry. Pour in vinegar and mix well. Add fish and toss to coat. Refrigerate at least 2 days, turning fish several times.

Remove fish from marinade. Broil or grill fish, basting with marinade, about 6 to 8 minutes per side depending on thickness. Fish is done when it flakes easily.

Yield: 4 to 6 servings

Beverly Sams • Vermillion Sail & Power Squadron • Ohio

★ Hangtown Fry

8	large oysters	¼	cup grated Parmesan cheese
	All-purpose flour	¼	cup chopped parsley
1	stick butter		Salt and pepper to taste
6	eggs	6	thick slices bacon, cooked
3	tablespoons heavy cream		

Dredge oysters in flour. Sauté lightly in butter in a cast iron skillet. Blend eggs, cream, cheese, parsley, salt and pepper. Pour over oysters and cook until eggs are set. Place skillet under the broiler until mixture is slightly browned. Cut into wedges and place a slice of bacon over each wedge.

Yield: 4 to 6 servings

James H. "Pou" Bailey • Raleigh Sail & Power Squadron
North Carolina

Fish Skillet Meal

½	cup olive or vegetable oil	2	cups sliced mushrooms
4	medium red potatoes, cubed with skin on	1	carrot, sliced
		1	stalk celery, minced
1-1½	pounds catch of the day, cut into ¾-inch cubes	1	medium onion, minced
		3	garlic cloves, minced
½	cup all-purpose flour	5	teaspoons lemon juice

Heat oil in a large skillet. Sauté potato 8 to 10 minutes until lightly browned. Dredge fish in flour. Add to skillet and cook 3 minutes, stirring occasionally. Stir in mushroom, carrot, celery, onion and garlic. Cover and cook 5 to 6 minutes. Remove from heat and stir in juice. Serve immediately.

Yield: 4 servings

Elmer Bakalla • Titusville Sail & Power Squadron • Florida

Mahi-Mahi with a Ginger Glaze

1¼	pounds mahi-mahi fillets, 1-inch thick, rinsed and patted dry	2	teaspoons grated ginger
2	tablespoons molasses	½	teaspoon minced garlic
2	teaspoons soy sauce	¼	teaspoon toasted sesame oil

Cut fish into 4 portions. Blend molasses, soy sauce, ginger, garlic and oil. Grill fish on a greased rack about 5 minutes. Turn fish and generously brush with molasses sauce. Grill 5 minutes longer or until fish flakes.

Yield: 4 servings

Ted Wallace • Watchung Power Squadron • New Jersey

Elegant Fish Roll-Ups

White Sauce

3	tablespoons butter	¾	cup chicken broth
3	tablespoons all-purpose flour	¾	cup milk

Melt butter in a saucepan. Whisk in flour until bubbly. Pour in broth and milk. Whisk over low heat until thickened. Keep warm.

Fish

2	pounds frozen or fresh flounder fillets	1	(7¾-ounce) can red salmon, drained and flaked
	Salt to taste	2	tablespoons dried parsley
¼	cup chopped onion		Pepper to taste
1	tablespoon butter	1	cup shredded Swiss cheese
		½	teaspoon paprika

Sprinkle fillets with salt. Sauté onion in butter. Stir in salmon, parsley and pepper. Spread 3 tablespoons mixture over each fillet. Roll up fillet and place seam side down in an 11 x 7 x 2-inch baking dish. Pour sauce over roll-ups. Microwave, uncovered, on high 8 to 9 minutes, turning once until fish flakes. Sprinkle with Swiss cheese and paprika. Microwave 1 minute or until cheese melts.

Yield: 8 servings

Anita L. Fontes • Banana River Power Squadron • Florida

Did you know?

A cylindrical buoy, tapered at the top and typically red in color is called a "nun" buoy. One that is cylindrical, flat on the top and green or black is called a "can" buoy. Markings identify the direction of sail and mark the channel boundaries. The ability to read and understand channel markings is extremely valuable for safety. Know before you go, take a boating class.

Oven Fried Snapper

2	pounds red snapper fillet
½	cup vegetable oil
1	teaspoon salt
1	garlic clove, minced

Parmesan cheese and bread crumbs for coating

Cut fillet into 6 equal portions. Blend oil, salt and garlic in a glass baking dish. Add fish and toss to coat. Marinate 10 minutes. Turn once and marinate an additional 10 minutes. Remove fish and roll in cheese and then in bread crumbs. Place on a greased baking sheet. Bake at 500 degrees 12 to 15 minutes or until fish flakes easily.

Yield: 6 servings

Sandy and Ken Boyd • Costa de Oro Power Squadron • California

Psari Plaki (Baked Fish with Vegetables)

2½-3	pounds haddock or scrod, cut into serving size pieces	2	garlic cloves, sliced
	Salt and pepper to taste	½	cup chopped parsley
		2	stalks celery, chopped
½	cup vegetable or olive oil	2	carrots, sliced ⅛-inch thick
2	tablespoons butter	1	large potato, cubed
2	medium onions, chopped	1	(8-ounce) can tomato sauce
2	tomatoes, chopped	⅓	cup water
			Dash of dried oregano

Arrange fish in a greased 13 x 9 x 2-inch baking dish. Season with salt and pepper. Set aside. Combine oil, butter, onion, tomato, garlic, parsley, celery, carrot and potato in a large skillet. Sauté until vegetables are tender but not browned. Pour in tomato sauce and water and cook 5 minutes longer. Season with salt, pepper and oregano. Cool sauce. Pour sauce over fish. Bake at 350 degrees 35 minutes.

Yield: 8 servings

Mary and Theo Kuliopulos • Beverly Power Squadron • Massachusetts

Decock Baked Halibut

1 (15-ounce) package
    frozen spinach, thawed
    and squeezed dry
3 tablespoons lemon juice,
    divided
1 (4-ounce) can sliced
    mushrooms
1 egg, beaten
½ cup bread crumbs

Grated Parmesan cheese,
    pepper and garlic salt to
    taste
2 pounds halibut
½ cup sour cream
½ cup mayonnaise
1½ cups shredded Cheddar
    cheese
4 green onions, chopped

Combine spinach, 1 tablespoon juice and mushroom. Spread mixture in the bottom of a 13 x 9 x 2-inch baking dish. Blend egg with 1 tablespoon lemon juice. Combine bread crumbs, Parmesan cheese, pepper and garlic salt. Dip fish in egg and coat in bread crumb mixture. Lay over spinach. Combine sour cream, mayonnaise, Cheddar cheese, and remaining 1 tablespoon juice. Spread mixture over fish. Bake at 350 degrees 30 minutes or until fish flakes easily.

Yield: 6 servings

Simone Decock • Bellevue Power Squadron • Washington State

Fish Casserole

1 (12-ounce) package
    frozen spinach soufflé,
    thawed
1½ pounds fish fillet

⅓ cup sour cream
⅔ cup mayonnaise
Grated Parmesan cheese

Layer spinach in the bottom of a 13 x 9 x 2-inch baking dish. Place fish over spinach. Blend sour cream and mayonnaise. Spread over fish. Sprinkle with Parmesan cheese. Bake at 350 degrees 40 minutes.

Yield: 4 servings

George Koentje • Hempstead Bay Power Squadron • New York

DID YOU KNOW?

When preparing for winter lay-up, it is important to use fuel stabilizer before hauling on the last cruise. If added at this time, all components of the engine and fuel system will be protected. The Power Squadron Engine Maintenance course helps students prepare for proper fuel system maintenance.

Tilapia with Tomato and Herbs

1½ pounds tilapia fillets	¼ teaspoon salt
2 medium tomatoes, diced	⅛ teaspoon pepper
1 medium onion, chopped	Juice of one lemon
¼ cup chopped parsley	¼ cup olive oil
1 teaspoon dried oregano	½ cup shredded mozzarella
1 teaspoon dried basil	cheese
1 teaspoon dried tarragon	

Fold each tilapia fillet in half and place in a row in an 11 x 7 x 2-inch baking dish. Combine tomato, onion, parsley, oregano, basil, tarragon, salt, pepper, juice and oil. Mix well. Pour mixture over rolled fish. Sprinkle with cheese. Bake at 375 degrees 20 to 30 minutes.

Yield: 4 servings

Tim Hanlon • Miles River Sail & Power Squadron • Maryland

Fish and Chips

1¾ cups all-purpose flour	2 pounds whitefish
1 teaspoon baking soda	(haddock, cod or
¼ teaspoon salt	flounder)
1 cup water	Salt to taste
Vegetable oil for cooking	2 pounds potatoes, peeled
	and sliced into strips

Combine flour, baking soda and salt in a bowl. Make a well in the center. Slowly add the water and stir until smooth. If too thick, add more water. Let batter stand 1 hour.

Heat oil in a skillet. Dry fish with a paper towel and lightly sprinkle with salt and flour. Dip fish in batter and fry 5 minutes until golden browned. Drain on a paper towel and keep warm in the oven. Cook potato in oil until golden browned. Sprinkle with salt. Serve fish and chips with malt vinegar.

Yield: 6 servings

Kathy Somogyl • Sacandaga Power Squadron • Connecticut

Sautéed Sole Fillets with Herbs

2 tablespoons unsalted butter
1 shallot, finely chopped
1 teaspoon chopped chives
1 tablespoon chopped parsley
1 teaspoon chopped tarragon or ¼ teaspoon dried

1 teaspoon chopped chervil
1 teaspoon lemon juice
White pepper to taste
Herb or vegetable salt to taste
Sole fillets, sautéed

Melt butter in a skillet. Sauté shallot, stirring constantly, 3 minutes until tender. Reduce heat to low, add chives and cook, stirring constantly, 2 minutes. Add parley, tarragon and chervil and cook 1 minute. Stir in juice, pepper and salt. Serve over sautéed sole fillets or fish of your choice.

Yield: 2 servings

"Pepper" Wardle • Diablo Sail & Power Squadron • California

Grilled Sea Scallops Brochettes, Greek Style

12-16 large sea scallops
3 tablespoons extra virgin olive oil
1 garlic clove, crushed
1 tablespoon oregano leaves, stripped from stems and chopped

Salt and pepper to taste
1 lemon, halved and cut into ¼-inch slices
4 California bay leaves, broken in half crosswise

Soak wooden skewers in water 1 hour. Combine scallops, oil, garlic, oregano, salt and pepper in a bowl. Toss to coat. Thread each skewer with 3 to 4 scallops alternating with 3 to 4 lemon slices and 2 pieces of bay leaves. Grill on a greased grill 5 to 10 minutes until scallops are opaque. Serve hot.

Yield: 4 servings

Roberta L. Dougherty • Absecon Island Power Squadron • New Jersey

★ Scallops and Mushrooms in Wine Sauce

1	pound bay scallops	12	shrimp, cut up
1	cup dry white wine	2	shallots, chopped
¼	cup snipped parsley	3	tablespoons all-purpose flour
½	teaspoon salt		
7	tablespoons butter, divided	½	cup half & half
		½	cup shredded Swiss cheese, divided
1	(4-ounce) can sliced mushrooms, drained		
		1	cup soft bread crumbs

Place scallops, wine, parsley and salt in a 3-quart saucepan. Add just enough water to cover scallops. Bring to boil. Reduce heat and simmer, uncovered, 8 minutes until scallops are tender. Remove scallops with a slotted spoon. Boil liquid until reduced to 1 cup. Strain and reserve liquid.

Melt 5 tablespoons butter in same saucepan. Sauté mushrooms, shrimp and shallot 5 to 6 minutes until tender. Remove mixture from pan. Whisk in flour until smooth and bubbly. Remove from heat and stir in reserved liquid. Cook and stir 1 minute. Pour in half & half and return scallops, mushrooms, shrimp and shallot mixture. Stir in ¼ cup Swiss cheese. Heat until cheese melts.

Combine bread crumbs and 2 tablespoons melted butter. Divide scallop mixture among 4 to 5 buttered ramekin cups. Top with bread crumbs and remaining cheese. Broil 5-inches from heat source about 3 to 5 minutes until crumbs are toasted.

Yield: 4 servings

Dick Miner • Birmingham Power Squadron • Michigan

Fettuccine Alfredo with Fresh Seafood

½ pound medium shrimp, peeled and deveined
½ pound bay scallops
1 stick plus 2 tablespoons unsalted butter
½ cup white wine or dry sherry
 Kosher salt and pepper to taste

1 (12-ounce) package fettuccine or similar pasta
1 tablespoon vegetable oil
1 pint heavy cream
1 cup grated Parmesan cheese
 Chopped flat-leaf parsley

Sauté shrimp and scallops in 2 tablespoons butter and wine about 3 minutes. Season with salt and pepper while cooking. Remove seafood with slotted spoon and keep warm. Cook and stir sauce until reduced by half. Set aside.

Cook pasta in boiling water with oil and salt. Drain well.

Heat cream until hot. Add 1 stick butter and stir until butter melts. Stir in cheese until it melts. Add ¼ cup reserved sauce and stir until smooth. Season with salt and pepper. Add pasta and seafood. Heat thoroughly. Spoon into four individual dishes and sprinkle with parsley.

Yield: 4 servings

Lance J. Jensen • Bellevue Power Squadron • Washington State

Roasted Oysters

1 dozen oysters in shell
 Kosher salt
1 small shallot, finely chopped

4 tablespoons butter
¼ cup dry white wine
 Grated Parmesan cheese
 Plain bread crumbs

Shuck oysters. Place raw oysters on half shell. Place on a baking sheet on a bed of kosher salt. Sauté shallot in butter 5 minutes until soft. Pour in wine and cook 3 to 4 minutes. Remove from heat and cool slightly. Spoon small amount of shallot over each oyster, reserving some shallot mixture. Sprinkle with cheese and bread crumbs. Dot with remaining shallot mixture. Bake 8 to 10 minutes or until slightly browned.

Yield: 2 to 4 servings

Joseph Gottfried • Neptune Power Squadron • New York

Clam Spaghetti Sauce

1 stick butter
¼ cup olive oil
6 garlic cloves, minced
12 clams minced with liquor
¼ cup chopped parsley
1 tablespoon dried basil

3 tablespoons grated Parmesan cheese
1 (8-ounce) can tomato sauce
Hot cooked vermicelli

Melt butter and oil in a saucepan. Add garlic, clams, parsley, basil, cheese and tomato sauce. Mix well and heat thoroughly. Serve over vermicelli.

Yield: 4 servings

Lollie Holland   •   Greensboro Power Squadron   •   North Carolina

Linguine with Sea Scallops and Sun-Dried Tomatoes

6 tablespoons butter
½ cup chopped basil
1 pound sea scallops
    Salt and white pepper to taste
1 tablespoon chopped garlic
1 cup tomato sauce
1½ cups heavy cream or half & half

⅓ cup sun-dried tomatoes packed in oil, sliced or more to taste
1 (16-ounce) can diced tomatoes
1 pound linguine
    Grated Parmesan cheese and chopped parsley for garnish

Heat butter with basil. Sauté scallops 1 minute. Season with salt and pepper. Add garlic, tomato sauce, cream, sun-dried tomato and tomato. Cook 3 minutes until scallops are firm. Do not overcook. Spoon a thin layer of sauce onto heated plates. Place pasta on plate and spoon more sauce over pasta. Arrange scallops around edge and garnish with cheese and parsley.

Yield: 6 servings

Rosemary Stevenson   •   Lake Hartwell Sail & Power Squadron
South Carolina

White Clam Sauce

1 pint shucked clams or 2 (6½-ounce) cans chopped clams	¼ cup dry white wine
	⅛ teaspoon white pepper
¼ cup thinly sliced green onion	2 tablespoons snipped parsley
1 garlic clove, minced	5 ounces linguine, cooked al dente
1 tablespoon olive oil	Lemon wedges for garnish

Drain clams and reserve liquid. Cut up whole clams. Set aside. Sauté green onion and garlic in oil until tender. Stir in reserved clam liquid, wine and pepper. Bring to boil. Reduce heat and simmer 8 minutes or until liquid is reduced by half. Add clams and parsley. Cook and stir 2 minutes until clams are heated thoroughly. Toss clam mixture with pasta until well coated. Serve immediately. Serve with lemon wedges.

Yield: 4 servings

Joyce Ann Newman • Palm Beach Sail & Power Squadron • Florida

Foil-Baked Mahi-Mahi with Vegetables

8 (8-ounce) mahi-mahi steaks, rinsed and patted dry	1½ tablespoons chopped oregano
	⅓ cup olive oil
1 small eggplant, julienned	1 tablespoon balsamic vinegar
2 sweet red peppers, julienned	Salt and pepper to taste
½ cup marinated artichoke hearts	

Cut 8 foil rectangles large enough to wrap fish. Coat foil pieces with oil. Place a steak on each foil piece. Combine eggplant, red pepper, artichokes, oregano, oil and vinegar. Spoon mixture over steaks. Season with salt and pepper. Seal foil packets and bake at 400 degrees 12 minutes. Place foil packets on individual serving plates. Cut open packets.

Yield: 8 servings

Rose Closter • Manhasset Bay Power Squadron • New York

SAUCE FOR FISH

2 tablespoons butter
1 tablespoon vinegar
1 teaspoon lemon juice
1 tablespoon chopped parsley
½ teaspoon salt
¼ teaspoon pepper

Heat butter in a skillet until browned. Add vinegar, juice, parsley, salt and pepper. Bring to boil. Remove from heat and serve over fried or broiled fish.

Yield: 2 servings

Tish Cullen

Las Vegas Power Squadron

Nevada

Bouillabaisse

4	medium red potatoes	2	garlic cloves, minced
1½	cups thinly sliced onion	2	lemon slices
½	cup dry white wine	1	(14½-ounce) can no sodium whole tomatoes, drained
¼	cup chopped parsley		
1½	tablespoons tomato paste	1	bay leaf
1	tablespoon olive oil	¾	pound medium shrimp, peeled
½	teaspoon dried thyme		
¼	teaspoon salt	¾	pound cod or other lean whitefish fillets, cut into 1-inch pieces
¼	teaspoon saffron threads		
¼	teaspoon pepper		
⅛	teaspoon fennel seeds		
2	(8-ounce) bottles clam juice		

Pierce potato with a fork. Arrange potato in a circle on a paper towel in the bottom of a microwave. Cook on high 10 minutes, rearranging potato after 5 minutes. Wrap in a towel and let stand 5 minutes. Peel and cube potato. Set aside.

Combine onion, wine, parsley, tomato paste, oil, thyme, salt, saffron, pepper, fennel seeds, clam juice, garlic, lemon slices, tomato and bay leaf in a 3-quart casserole. Mix well. Cover and microwave on high 10 minutes, stirring after 5 minutes. Add potato, shrimp and fish. Cover and microwave on high 3 minutes or until fish flakes easily. Discard bay leaf before serving.

Yield: 8 servings

Bill Payne • Cape Fear Power Squadron • North Carolina

SeaVester

desserts

youth and community outreach programs

young people at work

USPS is an organization with 90 years of history educating experienced and novice boaters. This rich heritage is being shared with many young boater organizations across the country. One of the first and most successful has been the Sea Scout-BSA Venturing project. USPS and the Boy Scouts of America, Sea Scout organization, are sharing educational materials as USPS is working to aid in developing the boating safety leadership of the future.

WaterSmart From the Start[SM]*, a computerized learning tool, has been completed and is generating broad interest among young America in mastering the skill of skippering a vessel on a course past hazards and over waterways that give the young person a learning experience in a gaming atmosphere. Phase two of the game has been completed with multiple levels and stages. This computer game is available on the usps4kids website.*

*Speaking of the website, **www.usps4kids.org** site has games and programs developed for young people. Eventually this site will host numerous programs for young people ages five through teen-age, kindergarten through high school. Why not join us and help with this worthwhile project?*

For more information call 1-888-367-8777.

Lemon Cheesecake

Crust

2¼ cups graham cracker   ¼   cup sugar
      crumbs   6   tablespoons butter, melted

Combine crumbs, sugar and butter. Press into the bottom and up sides of a 9-inch springform pan. Bake at 350 degrees 5 minutes. Cool completely.

Filling

3	(8-ounce) packages cream cheese, softened	3 tablespoons lemon juice
3	eggs	2 teaspoons vanilla extract, divided
1⅓	cups plus 3 tablespoons sugar, divided	1 pint sour cream

Beat cream cheese with an electric mixer at high speed until smooth. Add eggs, one at a time, beating well after each addition. Gradually add 1⅓ cups sugar, beating well after addition. Add lemon juice and 1 teaspoon vanilla. Pour filling into cooled crust. Bake at 350 degrees 40 minutes. Blend sour cream, remaining teaspoon vanilla and 3 tablespoons sugar. Set aside in a warm place. Remove cheesecake from oven and gently spread sour cream mixture over top. Return to oven and bake an additional 12 minutes. Cool on a rack 30 minutes. Refrigerate until top is cool but not completely chilled.

Glaze

½	cup sugar	2 tablespoons lemon juice
1	tablespoon plus 2 teaspoons cornstarch	3 drops yellow food coloring
½	cup water	

Combine sugar and cornstarch in a saucepan. Blend in water, juice and food coloring until smooth. Bring to boil, stirring constantly until thickened. Cook 3 minutes. Refrigerate until cool but not set. Spread glaze over cheesecake. Refrigerate for several hours or overnight.

Yield: 10 to 12 servings

Vinnie Gordy • Greensboro Power Squadron • North Carolina

Swedish Nut Cake

Cake

2	cups sugar	1	teaspoon vanilla
2	cups all-purpose flour	1	(20-ounce) can crushed pineapple, undrained
2	teaspoons baking soda	½	cup nuts
2	eggs		

Combine sugar, flour, baking soda, eggs, vanilla, pineapple and nuts. Mix well by hand. Pour batter into a 13 x 9 x 2-inch baking dish. Bake at 350 degrees 40 minutes.

Frosting

1	stick butter, softened	1¾	cups powdered sugar
4	ounces cream cheese, softened	1	teaspoon vanilla
		½	cup nuts

Cream butter and cream cheese. Slowly mix in powdered sugar until smooth. Add vanilla and nuts. Frost cake while it is warm.

Yield: 10 to 12 servings

Doris Smith Hollister • Des Moines Power Squadron • Iowa

Butterscotch Pound Cake

2½	sticks butter, softened	3	cups all-purpose flour
1	(8-ounce) package cream cheese, softened	1	(12-ounce) package butterscotch chips
2¾	cups sugar	1½	cups chopped pecans
6	eggs		

Cream butter and cream cheese. Gradually add sugar. Stir in eggs and flour and mix well. Fold in butterscotch chips and pecans. Pour batter into a greased and floured 10-inch tube or Bundt pan. Bake at 350 degrees 1 hour, 15 minutes or until tester comes out clean.

Yield: 12 servings

Sandy Johnson • Norman Sail & Power Squadron • Oklahoma

Heavenly Coconut Cake

Cake

1	(18-ounce) package yellow cake mix	½	cup vegetable oil
1	(3½-ounce) package instant vanilla pudding mix	½	cup water
		½	cup coconut milk
		½	cup chopped pecans
4	eggs	⅓	cup coconut

Beat cake mix, pudding mix, eggs, oil, water and milk with an electric mixer about 2 minutes. Sprinkle pecans and coconut in the bottom of a greased Bundt pan. Pour batter into pan. Bake at 325 degrees 55 minutes to 1 hour.

Glaze

4	tablespoons butter	3	tablespoons coconut milk
2	tablespoons water		Coconut for garnish
½	cup sugar		

Combine butter, water and sugar in a saucepan. Bring to boil and cook, stirring constantly, 2 minutes. Remove from heat and stir in milk. When done baking, leave cake in pan and pierce bottom of cake with a toothpick. Pour half of glaze over cake. Let stand 10 minutes. Turn out cake from pan. Pierce top with a toothpick. Pour remaining glaze over cake. Sprinkle with coconut.

Yield: 15 servings

Bettie Black • Clearwater Power Squadron • Florida

DID YOU KNOW?

The reef or square knot is not recommended for lengthening lines and should be used sparingly. Knots, bends and hitches are covered in the Power Squadron learning guide of the same name. This marlinspike knowledge is extremely valuable to the seaman.

Yogurt Cake

2¼	cups all-purpose flour		1	(8-ounce) container yogurt, any flavor but prefer blueberry
2	cups sugar			
½	teaspoon salt		3	extra large eggs
½	teaspoon baking soda			Milk and powdered sugar for a glaze (optional)
1	teaspoon vanilla			
2	sticks butter, softened			

Combine flour, sugar, salt, baking soda, vanilla, butter, yogurt and eggs. Beat at medium speed 3 minutes until well blended. Pour batter into a 10-inch tube pan. Bake at 350 degrees 1 hour to 1 hour, 10 minutes. Cool 15 minutes in pan before removing. Blend milk and powdered sugar. Drizzle over cake.

Yield: 15 to 20 servings

Betty Parks • Patapsco River Power Squadron • Maryland

Martine's Angel Cake

1	(12-ounce) package semi-sweet chocolate chips		1	pint heavy cream, divided and whipped
2	tablespoons water		½	cup chopped nuts
4	eggs, separated		1	prepared angel food cake, torn into walnut-size pieces
2	tablespoons powdered sugar			
			10-12	maraschino cherries

Melt chocolate chips in water. Cool. Beat egg whites until stiff. Beat egg yolks until pale yellow. Stir egg whites and egg yolks into chocolate mixture. Add powdered sugar, half the whipped cream and nuts. Combine cake pieces and chocolate mixture and mix well. Pour mixture into a 13 x 9 x 2-inch baking pan. Refrigerate until set. Cut into desired serving size. Top each slice with whipped cream and a cherry.

Yield: 10 to 13 servings

Jane W. Malatak • Mid-Potomac Power Squadron • Virginia

Coca-Cola Cake and Icing

Cake

2	cups all-purpose flour	½	cup buttermilk
2	cups sugar	2	eggs, beaten
2	sticks butter	1	teaspoon vanilla
1	cup cola-flavored carbonated beverage	2	cups miniature marshmallows
3	tablespoons cocoa		

Combine flour and sugar. Melt butter in a saucepan. Add carbonated beverage and cocoa. Bring to boil. Pour into dry ingredients. Add buttermilk, eggs and vanilla. Stir in marshmallows. Pour batter into a greased 13 x 9 x 2-inch baking pan. Bake at 350 degrees 35 minutes.

Icing

1	stick butter, softened	1	(16-ounce) package powdered sugar
6	tablespoons cola-flavored carbonated beverage	1	teaspoon vanilla
1	cup chopped nuts	3	tablespoons cocoa

Cream butter until smooth. Add carbonated beverage, nuts, powdered sugar, vanilla and cocoa. Mix well. Pour icing over warm cake while still in pan.

Yield: 8 to 10 servings

Charlotte Ramsey • Ouachita Power Squadron • Louisiana

Easy, But Good, Dump Cake

1	(20-ounce) can crushed pineapple, undrained	1	(18-ounce) package yellow cake mix
1	(21-ounce) can cherry pie filling	2	sticks butter, melted
1	(3½-ounce) can flaked coconut	1	cup pecans, chopped

Pour pineapple with juice into the bottom of a 13 x 9 x 2-inch baking dish. Top with pie filling and coconut. Sprinkle with cake mix. Evenly pour butter over cake mix. Top with pecans. Bake at 325 degrees 1 hour.

Yield: 12 to 16 servings

Karen Moore • Honolulu Sail & Power Squadron • Hawaii

Hummingbird Cake

Cake

3 cups all-purpose flour
2 cups sugar
1 teaspoon baking soda
1 teaspoon salt
1 teaspoon cinnamon
3 eggs, beaten

1½ cups vegetable oil
1½ teaspoons vanilla
1 cup chopped pecans
1 (8-ounce) can crushed
   pineapple, with juice
1 cup chopped bananas

Combine flour, sugar, baking soda, salt and cinnamon. Add eggs and oil and stir just until moistened. Do not over mix. Add vanilla, pecans, pineapple and bananas. Mix gently. Divide batter among three greased 9-inch round cake pans. Bake at 350 degrees 25 to 30 minutes. Cool completely.

Frosting

2 sticks butter, softened
2 (8-ounce) packages
   cream cheese, softened

2 (16-ounce) packages
   powdered sugar
1 teaspoon vanilla
1 cup chopped pecans

Cream butter and cream cheese. Slowly mix in powdered sugar until smooth. Add vanilla and pecans. To assemble, turn one cake onto a cake platter. Spread a layer of frosting over cake. Repeat with two other layers, stacking on top of each other. Frost top and sides of cake.

Yield: 8 to 10 servings

Cindy Tauscher • Johnson City Power Squadron • Tennessee

Norwegian Pound Cake (Formkake)

2	sticks butter, softened	½	teaspoon baking powder
½	cup vegetable shortening	1	cup milk
2¾	cups sugar	2	teaspoons vanilla
5	eggs	1	teaspoon lemon extract
3	cups all-purpose flour	1	teaspoon almond extract
½	teaspoon salt		

Cream butter, shortening and sugar. Add eggs, one at a time, beating well after each addition. Combine flour, salt and baking powder. Add to creamed mixture. Stir in milk, vanilla, lemon extract and almond extract until well blended. Pour batter into a greased and floured 10-inch tube pan or two 9 x 5-inch loaf pans. Bake at 300 degrees 1 hour, 20 minutes.

Yield: 12 servings

Kris and Michael Cranford • Winston-Salem Sail & Power Squadron
North Carolina

Mexican Fruit Cake

Cake

2	cups all-purpose flour	1	(20-ounce) can crushed pineapple, undrained
2	cups sugar	1	cup chopped pecans
2	teaspoons baking soda	2	eggs

Combine flour, sugar, baking soda, pineapple with juice, pecans and eggs. Mix well. Pour batter into a 13 x 9 x 2-inch baking dish. Bake at 350 degrees 45 minutes.

Icing

1	(8-ounce) package cream cheese, softened	2	cups powdered sugar
1	stick butter, melted	2	teaspoons vanilla

Blend cream cheese and butter. Slowly stir in powdered sugar until smooth. Add vanilla. Spread icing over the cake just out of the oven.

Yield: 10 to 12 servings

Janell F. Boyd • Cape Fear Power Squadron • North Carolina

Pumpkin Cake

Cake

2	cups canned pumpkin	1	teaspoon baking powder
4	eggs	1	heaping teaspoon cinnamon
1	cup vegetable oil	¼	teaspoon ground nutmeg
2	cups sugar	1	teaspoon salt
2	cups all-purpose flour		
2	teaspoons baking soda		

Blend pumpkin, eggs, oil and sugar. Add flour, baking soda, baking powder, cinnamon, nutmeg and salt. Mix well. Pour batter into a greased and floured 13 x 9 x 2-inch baking dish. Bake at 350 degrees 1 hour. Cool completely.

Icing

1	stick butter, softened	1	(16-ounce) package powdered sugar
1	(8-ounce) package cream cheese, softened	1	teaspoon vanilla

Cream butter and cream cheese. Slowly add powdered sugar until smooth. Stir in vanilla. Spread frosting over cake.

Yield: 10 to 12 servings

Joanne Hancock • Stark County Power Squadron • Ohio

Texas Wine Cake

1	(18-ounce) package yellow cake mix	4	eggs
1	(3½-ounce) package instant vanilla pudding mix	¾	cup vegetable oil
		¾	cup crème sherry
		1	teaspoon ground nutmeg

Combine cake mix, pudding mix, eggs, oil, sherry and nutmeg. Beat 5 minutes with an electric mixer at medium speed. Pour batter into a greased 10-inch tube pan. Bake at 350 degrees 45 minutes to 1 hour or until cake tester comes out clean. Cool in pan 10 minutes. Remove to a serving platter.

Yield: 10 to 12 servings

Annette Slater • San Antonio Sail & Power Squadron • Texas

Ravani (Greek Sponge Cake)

Cake

6	eggs	1	teaspoon orange juice
1	cup farina (cream of wheat)		Zest of one orange
1	cup all-purpose flour	2	teaspoons baking powder
1	cup sugar	2	sticks butter, melted

Beat eggs until frothy. Add farina, flour, sugar, juice, zest and baking powder. Beat until blended. Slowly beat in butter. Pour batter into a 13 x 9 x 2-inch baking pan. Bake at 350 degrees 25 to 30 minutes or until cake springs back when touched.

Syrup

2½	cups sugar		Cherries, halved or finely chopped nuts for garnish
3	cups water		
1	cinnamon stick		
¼	teaspoon lemon juice		

Combine sugar, water and cinnamon stick in a saucepan. Bring to boil. Add juice. Reduce heat and simmer until cake is done. Remove cinnamon stick. Ladle syrup over cake. Slice cake into four lengthwise sections. Ladle with syrup. Slice each section into 1½-inch diamonds or squares. Pour remaining syrup over cake. Garnish each with a cherry half or sprinkle with nuts. Cover and refrigerate overnight.

Yield: 12 to 15 servings

Charlotte G. Ward • Hilton Head Power Squadron • South Carolina

DID YOU KNOW?

*When anchoring for
the night when a storm
in forecast, the total of the
anchor rode should be about
10 times the combined
depth of water, the height
of tide and the distance
from the bow to the
waterline. Thus if the
depth is 15 feet, the tide
is 3 feet and the bow to
waterline is 4 feet the scope
should be 220 feet. Know
before you go, take a
boating course.*

Chocolate Sheet Cake

Cake

2	cups all-purpose flour	½	cup buttermilk
2	cups sugar	2	eggs, slightly beaten
2	stick butter	1	teaspoon baking soda
¼	cup cocoa	1	teaspoon cinnamon
1	cup water	1	teaspoon vanilla

Sift together flour and sugar. Set aside. Combine butter, cocoa and
water in a saucepan. Bring to a rapid boil ad pour over flour mixture.
Mix well. Add buttermilk, eggs, baking soda, cinnamon and vanilla.
Pour into a greased 15 x 10 x 1-inch jelly-roll pan. Bake at 400 degrees
20 minutes.

Icing

1	stick butter	1	(16-ounce) package
¼	cup cocoa		powdered sugar
6	tablespoons milk	1	teaspoon vanilla
		1	cup chopped pecans

Prepare icing 5 minutes before cake is done. Heat butter, cocoa and
milk in a saucepan. Bring to boil. Remove from heat. Slowly stir in
powdered sugar, vanilla and pecans. Mix well. Spread hot icing onto
hot cake.

Yield: 18 servings

Mary Mazoch • Orange Power Squadron • Texas

Apple Coconut Cake

Cake

3	cups all-purpose flour	2	teaspoons vanilla
1	teaspoon baking soda	2	cups chopped pecans
1	teaspoon salt	3	cups peeled chopped cooking apples
1	cup vegetable oil	½	cup flaked coconut
3	eggs		
2¼	cups sugar		

Combine flour, baking soda and salt. Set aside. Combine oil, eggs, sugar and vanilla. Beat with an electric mixer at medium speed 2 minutes. Add dry ingredients and mix at low speed until blended. Fold in pecans, apples and coconut. Batter will be stiff. Spoon batter into a greased and floured 10-inch tube pan. Bake at 350 degrees 1 hour, 10 minutes.

Glaze

½	cup packed light brown sugar	¼	cup milk
		1	stick butter

Combine brown sugar, milk and butter in a saucepan. Bring to boil and cook, stirring constantly, 2 minutes. Cool to lukewarm. Remove cake from pan and immediately drizzle with glaze.

Yield: 10 to 12 servings

Susie Orren • Johnson City Power Squadron • Tennessee

Grandma Pearl's Hot Milk Sponge Cake

1	cup milk	2	cups all-purpose flour
3	tablespoons butter	2	teaspoons baking powder
4	eggs	¼	teaspoon salt
2	cups sugar		

Heat milk and butter. In a bowl, beat together eggs and sugar. Sift flour, baking powder and salt. Stir flour mixture into egg mixture. Pour in hot milk and mix well. Pour batter into two greased and floured 9-inch round cake pans. Bake at 350 degrees 30 minutes. Glaze with powdered sugar icing if desired.

Yield: 10 to 12 servings

This recipe is very old, handed down from one generation to the next. Its original form was given to Mom in the late fifties. The butter was measured as a lump as big as an egg, the salt was a dash and Grandma used a coffee cup to measure the flour. For Dad's birthday party, each of us three girls made this, his favorite cake, for the occasion. Each turned our different!

Roberta J. McCormick • Youngstown Power Squadron • Ohio

Pauline's Black Russian Cake

1	(18-ounce) package yellow cake mix	4	eggs
1	(3½-ounce) package instant chocolate pudding mix	¼	cup vodka
		½	cup Kahlúa
		¾	cup water
1	cup vegetable oil	½	cup powdered sugar
			Few drops of Kahlúa

Combine cake mix, pudding mix, oil, eggs, vodka, Kahlúa and water. Beat 4 minutes until smooth. Pour batter into a greased and floured Bundt pan. Bake at 350 degrees 50 minutes. Cool 30 minutes and remove from pan. Blend powdered sugar and Kahlúa. Spread glaze over cake.

Yield: 8 to 10 servings

Elaine Keller • Balboa Power Squadron • California

Swedish Cake

Cake

2	cups sugar	2	cups all-purpose flour
2	eggs	1	teaspoon vanilla
1	(20-ounce) can crushed pineapple, undrained	½	cup chopped walnuts or pecans
2	teaspoons baking soda		

Combine sugar, eggs, pineapple with juice, baking soda, flour, vanilla and walnuts. Mix well. Pour batter into a greased and floured 13 x 9 x 2-inch baking dish. Bake at 350 degrees 35 to 40 minutes.

Frosting

1	stick butter, softened	1¾	cups powdered sugar, sifted
1	(3-ounce) package cream cheese, softened	1	teaspoon vanilla
		½	cup chopped nuts

Cream butter and cream cheese. Add powdered sugar, vanilla and nuts. Mix until smooth. Frost cake while still warm.

Yield: 10 to 12 servings

Helen Meyer • Cape Coral Power Squadron • Florida

Yummy Boaters Tiramisu

1	cup part-skim milk ricotta cheese	24	ladyfingers (two 3-ounce packages)
2	(3-ounce) packages Neufchâtel cream cheese, softened	½	cup Kahlúa, divided
½	cup sugar	1	tablespoon unsweetened cocoa

Combine ricotta cheese, cream cheese and sugar in a food processor. Process until smooth. Split ladyfingers in half lengthwise. Arrange 24 halves in a single layer in an 11 x 7 x 2-inch baking dish. Drizzle ¼ cup Kahlúa. Let stand 5 minutes. Spread half of cheese mixture over ladyfingers. Repeat layers of ladyfingers, Kahlúa and cheese mixture. Sprinkle with cocoa.

Yield: 10 servings

Laura Erstad • Tampa Power Squadron • Florida

Buckeye Pie

1	(3-ounce) package Neufchâtel cream cheese, softened	2	(9-inch) reduced fat graham cracker pie crusts
1	cup powdered sugar	2	(3½-ounce) packages instant chocolate pudding mix
¾	cup peanut butter		
2	(8-ounce) containers fat-free whipped topping, divided	3	cups cold skim milk

Blend cream cheese, powdered sugar, peanut butter and 1 container whipped topping. Divide mixture between two crusts. Whisk pudding mix and milk until smooth. Divide between two crusts. Top each with remaining container whipped topping.

Yield: 2 (9-inch) pies

Marilyn Kerr • Fostoria Sail & Power Squadron • Ohio

Easy Pie Crust

3	cups all-purpose flour	1	egg
1½	cups vegetable shortening	1	teaspoon vinegar
1	teaspoon salt	5	tablespoons water

Combine flour, shortening and salt until crumbly. In a separate bowl, beat egg, vinegar and water. Add to flour mixture. Roll out dough into three pie crusts.

Yield: 3 pie crusts

Roberta L Dougherty • Absecon Island Power Squadron • New Jersey

Southern Pecan Pie

1 cup light corn syrup
1 cup packed dark brown sugar
⅓ teaspoon salt
5⅓ tablespoons butter, melted

1 teaspoon vanilla
3 eggs, slightly beaten
1½ cups pecan halves
1 (9-inch) pie crust, unbaked

Combine syrup, brown sugar, salt, butter and vanilla. Add eggs and pecans. Pour filling into pie crust. Bake at 350 degrees 45 to 55 minutes.

Yield: 6 servings

L. D. Brown • Bellevue Power Squadron • Washington State

Red Hot Apple Pie

1 (15-ounce) package refrigerated pie crusts
¾ cup sugar
½ cup water
½ cup cinnamon red hots candy

6 medium apples, peeled and sliced
1 tablespoon all-purpose flour
1 teaspoon lemon juice
1 tablespoon butter

Prepare pie pastry for a double crust pie using a 9-inch pie pan. Combine sugar, water and cinnamon candies in a saucepan. Cook until candies dissolve. Add apples and simmer until red in color. Drain apples, reserving syrup. Arrange apples in pie crust. Blend flour with half the cooled syrup. Stir in juice. Pour syrup over apples. Dot with butter. Top with second pie pastry. Bake at 450 degrees 10 minutes. Reduce heat to 350 degrees and bake an additional 30 minutes.

Yield: 8 servings

Iris Reddy • Perdido Bay Power Squadron • Alabama

⚓ Great Boating Dessert

2	(8-ounce) packages cream cheese, softened	1	(9-inch) graham cracker crust
¼	cup milk	1	(21-ounce) can cherry or blueberry pie filling
½	cup sugar		
1	teaspoon almond extract		

Blend cream cheese, milk, sugar and almond extract. Spread mixture into pie crust. Top with pie filling. Refrigerate until ready to serve.

Yield: 8 servings

Anita Wedge • Knoxville Power Squadron • Tennessee

Mystery Pecan Pie

Filling

1	(8-ounce) package cream cheese, softened	1	teaspoon vanilla
1	egg	1	(9-inch) pie crust, unbaked
⅓	cup sugar	1¼	cups chopped pecans

Beat cream cheese, egg, sugar and vanilla until fluffy. Spread mixture in the bottom of pie crust. Sprinkle with pecans.

Topping

3	eggs	1	teaspoon vanilla
1	cup light corn syrup	¼	teaspoon salt
¼	cup sugar		

Beat eggs until well blended but not foamy. Add corn syrup, sugar, vanilla and salt. Mix well. Pour over pecans. Bake at 350 degrees 40 minutes or until nuts are lightly browned. Topping will rise like a soufflé and sink as it cools. Serve warm or cold.

Yield: 8 servings

Carol Lochner • Boca Ciega Sail & Power Squadron • Florida

French Caramel Apple Pie

6-7 cups peeled diced apples	1 (9-inch) pie crust, unbaked
2 teaspoon cinnamon, divided	1 stick butter, softened
1¼ cups packed brown sugar, divided	1 cup all-purpose flour

Combine apples, 1 teaspoon cinnamon and ¾ cup brown sugar. Pour mixture into pie crust. Blend butter, ½ cup brown sugar, 1 teaspoon cinnamon and flour. Sprinkle topping over filling. Bake at 425 degrees 50 to 60 minutes.

Yield: 8 servings

Sue Farrell • Duluth Power Squadron • Minnesota

Brown Derby Pie

1 stick butter, melted	1 cup English walnuts
1 cup sugar	1 cup light corn syrup
4 eggs, slightly beaten	1 (9-inch) pie crust, unbaked
1 cup semi-sweet chocolate chips	Whipped topping for garnish (optional)
1 tablespoon vanilla	

Combine butter, sugar, eggs, chocolate chips, vanilla, walnuts and syrup. Mix well. Pour filling into pie crust. Bake at 350 degrees 45 minutes. Serve with whipped topping.

Yield: 8 servings

June Carey • Vulcan Power Squadron • Alabama

Honey-Pecan Tart

1	cup sugar	2½	cups pecan halves, coarsely chopped
¼	cup water	1	(15-ounce) package refrigerated pie crusts
1	cup heavy cream		
4	tablespoons unsalted butter, sliced	2	teaspoons sugar, divided
¼	cup honey	2	ounces bittersweet chocolate, chopped
½	teaspoon salt		

Heat sugar and water to boil, stirring until sugar is dissolved. Cover and cook over medium heat without stirring 8 minutes. Swirl pan occasionally. Remove from heat and stir in cream. Add butter, honey and salt, stirring until smooth. Stir in pecans and simmer 5 minutes. Remove from heat and cool completely.

Unfold one pie pastry on a lightly floured surface. Roll into an 11-inch circle. Press into a 9-inch tart pan with a removable bottom. Trim edges and freeze crust 30 minutes. Spread pecan mixture into crust. Roll second pie pastry into a 10-inch circle. Place over pecan mixture, pressing into bottom crust to seal. Trim edges. Sprinkle with 1 teaspoon sugar. Freeze 30 minutes. Bake at 400 degrees 30 minutes. Cool on a rack.

Place chocolate in a small heavy-duty zip-top plastic bag and seal. Submerge bag in hot water until chocolate melts. Snip a tiny hole in corner of bag. Drizzle chocolate over tart. Sprinkle with remaining sugar.

Yield: 12 to 15 servings

Cindy Tauscher • Johnson City Power Squadron • Tennessee

Glazed Apple Cream Pie

Filling

1 (15-ounce) package refrigerated pie crusts	4 tablespoons butter
½ cup sugar	2 tablespoons cornstarch
½ cup milk	2 tablespoons milk
½ cup heavy cream	1 teaspoon vanilla

Prepare pie pastry for a double crust pie using a 9-inch pie pan. Combine sugar, milk, cream and butter in a saucepan. Cook, stirring occasionally, until hot and butter is melted. Blend cornstarch and milk. Add to cream mixture. Cook and stir 7 minutes until thickened or coats back of spoon. Remove from heat and stir in vanilla. Cool and pour into crust.

Apple Layer

4 medium apples, peeled and thinly sliced	1 tablespoon all-purpose flour
	½ teaspoon cinnamon

Combine apples, flour and cinnamon. Mix well. Arrange apples over filling. Top with second pie pastry. Seal and flute edges. Cut slits in top crust. Bake at 400 degrees 30 to 40 minutes or until golden browned. Cool 30 minutes.

Glaze

½ cup powdered sugar	¼ teaspoon vanilla
1 tablespoon milk	1 tablespoon butter, softened

Blend powdered sugar, milk, vanilla and butter until smooth. Spread glaze over warm pie. Refrigerate 1 hour, 30 minutes before serving. Store in the refrigerator.

Yield: 8 servings

Lyann Provast • Flint Power Squadron • Michigan

DID YOU KNOW?

If you approach a vessel at night and she is showing a white light over a red light on the mast she is a pilot boat. The saying is "white over red, pilot ahead". These and other lighting configurations on boats are important for the navigator for safety reasons. The Power Squadron boating courses explain the various lighting systems.

Canadian Butter Tarts

Pastry

5½	cups all-purpose flour	1	tablespoon vinegar
2	teaspoons salt	1	egg, slightly beaten
4	sticks butter, chilled		Chilled water

Combine flour and salt. Cut in butter with a pastry blender until mixture resembles large peas. In a one cup measuring cup, combine vinegar and egg. Add enough water to equal 1 cup. Slowly stir into flour mixture until just moistened. Shape dough into a ball, wrap in plastic wrap and refrigerate. Dust rolling pin and surface with flour. Divide dough into 6 equal portions. Roll dough to ⅛-inch thickness. Cut twelve 5-inch diameter circles. Press pastry into 12 muffin cups.

Filling

½	cup raisins	1	egg, slightly beaten
4	tablespoons butter	½	teaspoon vanilla
½	cup packed brown sugar	½	teaspoon lemon juice
¼	teaspoon salt	½	cup chopped pecans
½	cup corn syrup		

Pour boiling water over raisins. Set aside to soak. Cream butter and brown sugar. Add salt, syrup, egg, vanilla and juice. Mix well. Drain water from raisins. Fold in raisins and pecans. Spoon mixture into tart pastry, filling about ⅔ full. Bake at 350 degrees 15 to 18 minutes. Cool 20 minutes. Remove tarts from pan.

Yield: 12 servings

May substitute pastry mix or frozen tart shells for homemade pastry.

Louise Rea • Kalamazoo Power Squadron • Michigan

Danish Puff

Puff

2 cups sifted all-purpose flour, divided

2 sticks butter, divided and softened

1 cup plus 2 tablespoons water

1 teaspoon almond extract

3 eggs

Combine 1 cup flour and 1 stick butter. Cut in with a pastry blender. Add 2 tablespoons water and mix with a fork. Shape dough into a ball. Divide into two equal pieces. Place each piece on a baking sheet at least 3-inches apart. Cover with wax paper and roll into two 10 x 3-inch long strips.

Combine remaining stick of butter and 1 cup water in a saucepan. Bring to boil. Add almond extract. Remove from heat. Gradually stir in remaining 1 cup of flour until smooth and thickened. Try to prevent lumping. Add eggs, one at a time, mixing well after each addition until smooth. Divide and spread mixture evenly over pastry. Bake at 350 degrees 1 hour or until top is crispy and browned. Cool.

Frosting

3 tablespoons butter, softened

3 cups powdered sugar

1 tablespoon milk

1 tablespoon cherry juice

Almonds or maraschino cherries for garnish

Cream butter. Gradually add sugar until well blended. Stir in milk and juice until mixture reaches a spreading consistency. Drizzle frosting over puff. Garnish with almonds or cherries.

Yield: 12 to 15 servings

AnneMarie Muskulinski • Buffalo Power Squadron • New York

Apple Dumplings

1½ cups sugar	2 teaspoons baking powder
1½ cups water	1 teaspoon salt
¼ teaspoon cinnamon	⅔ cup vegetable shortening
¼ teaspoon ground nutmeg	½ cup milk
6 drops red food coloring	6 medium apples, peeled and cored
3 tablespoons butter	
2 cups all-purpose flour	Sugar for garnish

Combine sugar, water, cinnamon, nutmeg and food coloring. Bring to boil. Add butter. Remove from heat and set syrup aside. Sift together flour, baking powder and salt. Cut in shortening. Stir in milk until just moistened. Divide dough into six pieces.

Roll each piece on a lightly floured surface into a circle large enough to wrap an apple. Place an apple on each dough round. Drizzle each apple with some syrup. Wrap dough around apples and place 1-inch apart in a 13 x 9 x 2-inch baking dish. Pour syrup around dumplings. Sprinkle with sugar. Bake at 375 degrees 35 minutes or until apple is cooked. Serve warm.

Yield: 6 servings

Francine Hall • Cape Fear Power Squadron • North Carolina

Grandma Johnson's Apple Crisp

1 cup sugar	1 stick butter, softened
2 teaspoons cinnamon	1½ cups packed brown sugar
Dash of salt	1 cup all-purpose flour
3 pounds McIntosh apples, peeled and sliced	

Mix sugar, cinnamon and salt. Add apples and toss to coat. Place apples in a 13 x 9 x 2-inch baking dish. Blend butter, brown sugar and flour until resembles cornmeal. Sprinkle evenly over apples. Bake at 350 degrees 45 minutes. Serve hot or cold with ice cream.

Yield: 10 to 12 servings

Jim Stewart • Skokie Valley Power Squadron • Illinois

Date Torte Cookies

2 eggs
1 cup sifted powdered
     sugar plus more for
     dusting
2 tablespoons all-purpose
     flour

½ teaspoon salt
1 teaspoon baking powder
1 cup pitted dates,
     chopped
1 cup broken walnuts

Beat eggs until light and fluffy. Gradually beat in powdered sugar until thickened. Sift together flour, salt and baking powder. Add date and walnuts to dry ingredients. Fold into egg mixture. Spread mixture into a greased 9 x 9 x 2-inch baking dish. Bake at 350 degrees 30 to 35 minutes. Cool and cut into 16 squares. Dust with powdered sugar.

Yield: 16 servings

Doris Pfenniger • Hollywood Power Squadron • Florida

Serendipity's Poppy Seed Cookies

1¼ cups sugar, divided
2   sticks butter, softened
3   eggs
3   cups all-purpose flour
2   teaspoons baking powder

½ cup poppy seeds
¼ cup boiling water
1 teaspoon cinnamon
1 cup chopped nuts

Cream ¾ cup sugar, butter and eggs. Add flour and baking powder and mix thoroughly. Place poppy seeds in boiling water. Add to creamed mixture and mix well. Refrigerate 30 minutes.

Roll dough out on a floured surface. Cut into shapes with cookie cutter. Combine cinnamon, ½ cup sugar and nuts. Sprinkle over cookies. Place on an ungreased baking sheet. Bake at 350 degrees until edges are browned.

Yield: 4 dozen

Howard Bernbaum • Coco Beach Power Squadron • Florida

Alaskan Cowboy Cookies

2	sticks butter, softened	2	cups old-fashioned rolled oats
1	cup sugar		
1	cup packed brown sugar	1	(12-ounce) package semi-sweet chocolate chips
2	eggs		
1	teaspoon vanilla	1	(10-ounce) package coconut
2	cups all-purpose flour		
¼	teaspoon baking powder	1	(12-ounce) package raisins
½	teaspoon baking soda		
½	teaspoon salt	1	(12-ounce) package chopped nuts
			Dried apricots pieces

Cream butter, sugar and brown sugar. Add eggs, one at a time, beating well after each addition. Stir in vanilla. Sift together flour, baking powder, baking soda and salt. Mix creamed mixture into dry ingredients. Add oats and mix well. Add your choice of any or all of chocolate chips, coconut, raisins, nuts or apricots. Mix well. Drop dough by teaspoonfuls onto an ungreased baking sheet. Bake at 275 degrees 12 minutes until lightly browned.

Yield: 4 dozen

Dorie Backus • Toledo Power Squadron • Ohio

Thimble Cookies

2	sticks butter, softened	¼	teaspoon salt
½	cup powdered sugar	¼	teaspoon baking powder
2	cups all-purpose flour	1	cup favorite jam

Cream butter and powdered sugar. Sift together flour, salt and baking powder. Gradually add to creamed mixture. Roll dough into balls ¾-inch diameter. Press a hole with thumb in the center. Fill with jam. Bake at 350 degrees 20 minutes.

Yield: 2 dozen

Fred Tobey • Agate Pass Sail & Power Squadron • Washington State

Kourabiedes (Greek Cookies)

4	sticks unsalted butter, softened	2	tablespoons brandy or rum
½	cup powdered sugar	¾	cup walnuts or pecans, finely chopped
3	egg yolks	4½	cups sifted all-purpose flour
1	tablespoon orange zest		
	Juice of one-half orange, strained	2	teaspoons baking powder
1	tablespoon vanilla		Powdered sugar for coating

Cream butter and powdered sugar. Add egg yolks, zest, juice, vanilla, brandy and walnuts. Mix well. Sift together flour and baking powder. Gradually add to creamed mixture. Refrigerate 2 hours. Roll dough into small balls. Bake at 350 degrees 15 to 30 minutes, depending on size of ball. When cool, cover generously with powdered sugar. Store in a tightly sealed container in a cool place. May store for weeks.

Yield: 4 dozen

Kitty St. Romain • Northern Virginia Power Squadron • Virginia

★ Cowboy Cookies

2	sticks butter, softened	½	teaspoon baking powder
1	(16-ounce) package brown sugar	2	cups old-fashioned rolled oats
2	eggs	1	cup chopped nuts
2	cups whole wheat flour	1	(12-ounce) package semi-sweet chocolate chips
1	teaspoon baking soda		
1	teaspoon salt	1	teaspoon vanilla

Cream butter, brown sugar and eggs. Add flour, baking soda, salt, baking powder, oats, nuts, chocolate chips and vanilla. Mix well. Drop by teaspoonfuls on a greased baking sheet. Bake at 350 degrees 9 minutes. Cool slightly. Remove from sheet and cool completely.

Yield: about 3 dozen

Hal Spoelstra • Portland Power Squadron • Oregon

Did you know?

When winterizing your engine (diesel or gasoline) it is a good practice to run the engine without a coolant water source until no water comes out of the exhaust. This prevents freezing of water in the engine and cooling water lines. Even better, run some antifreeze through at the pick-up.

Hawley's Almond Roca Chocolate Chip Cookies

6   cups all-purpose flour
2   teaspoons baking soda
2   teaspoons salt
2   cups butter flavored
    shortening
1½ cups sugar
1½ cups packed brown sugar
2   teaspoons vanilla

5   eggs
2   cups semi-sweet
    chocolate chips
2   cups chopped walnuts
2   cups Almond Roca bits
    or a crushed chocolate
    almond caramel candy
    bar

Combine flour, baking soda and salt in a bowl. Beat shortening, sugar, brown sugar, vanilla and eggs until creamy. Add dry ingredients, 1 cup at a time. Stir in chocolate chips, nuts and almond roca bits. Drop by rounded ice cream scoops, 2 tablespoons size, onto an ungreased baking sheet. Bake at 375 degrees 9 to 11 minutes or until lightly browned. Cool 2 minutes on sheet. Remove to racks to cool completely.

Yield: 100 cookies

Richard K. Hawley • Poverty Bay Power Squadron • Washington State

 # Frosted Caramel Squares

1   cup sugar
½   cup vegetable shortening
2   eggs, saving one egg
    white
1½ cups all-purpose flour

1   teaspoon baking powder
⅛   teaspoon salt
1   teaspoon lemon extract,
    divided
1   cup packed brown sugar

Cream sugar and shortening. Set aside one egg white and beat balance of eggs. Add to creamed mixture. Sift together flour, baking powder and salt. Add to creamed mixture. Stir in ½ teaspoon lemon extract and mix well. Spread batter into a 9 x 9 x 2-inch baking dish. Beat egg white until stiff. Add brown sugar and ½ teaspoon lemon extract. Spread frosting over creamed mixture. Bake at 350 degrees 30 minutes.

Yield: 8 to 10 servings

Bud Gordon • Diablo Sail & Power Squadron • California

Chocolate Pecan Caramel Shortbread

Shortbread Crust

1½ cups sifted all-purpose flour	6 tablespoons unsalted butter, softened
¼ teaspoon salt	3 tablespoons sugar
¼ teaspoon baking powder	1 large egg
	¼ teaspoon vanilla

Sift together flour, salt and baking powder. In a separate bowl, beat butter and sugar until light and fluffy. Add egg and vanilla. Mix at low speed and add flour mixture in three batches. Press dough into the bottom and up sides of a 9-inch fluted tart pan with a removable bottom. Set aside.

Pecan Filling

1 stick unsalted butter, sliced into tablespoons	½ cup packed light brown sugar
2 tablespoons honey	1 cup pecan halves
2 tablespoons sugar	2 tablespoons heavy cream

Combine butter, honey, sugar and brown sugar in a saucepan. Bring to boil, stirring constantly. Boil 3 minutes. Remove from heat and add pecans. Stir in cream. Pour pecan mixture into prepared crust. Bake at 350 degrees 30 minutes. Cool on a rack 1 hour.

Chocolate Topping

½ cup heavy cream	⅔ cup semi-sweet chocolate chips
1 tablespoon sugar	

Combine cream and sugar in a saucepan. Bring to boil, stirring constantly. Remove from heat and add chocolate chips. Whisk until smooth. Set aside ⅓ cup topping in the refrigerator for garnish. Pour remaining warm topping over pecan filling. Spread our evenly with a spatula. Refrigerate 15 minutes to set chocolate.

Garnish

1 ounce white chocolate, coarsely chopped	8 pecan halves

Melt white chocolate. Pipe chocolate in fine lines across the top of tart in a crisscross pattern. Fill pastry bag fitted with a medium star tip with reserved chocolate topping. Pipe 8 rosettes around edge of tart. Top each rosette with a pecan half.

Yield: 8 servings

Karen Mesenburg • Columbus Power Squadron • Ohio

DID YOU KNOW?

*Dead reckoning or
"DR" positions are
determined by calculating
the vessel's position using
course steered and distance
made. The term "dead"
evolved from "ded"
the abbreviated form
of deduced.*

Cake

2	cups sugar	4	ounces unsweetened chocolate
4	eggs, beaten		
1	cup all-purpose flour	2	sticks butter

Slowly add sugar to eggs. Stir in flour. Melt chocolate and butter. Pour chocolate sauce into creamed mixture. Mix well. Spread dough on a foil-lined 16 x 11 x 1-inch jelly-roll pan. Bake on lower rack at 350 degrees 15 minutes. Move to top rack and bake an additional 5 minutes. Cool completely.

Filling

3	cups powdered sugar	1-2	teaspoons peppermint extract
6	tablespoons butter, softened		
¼	teaspoon vanilla	2-3	drops green food coloring Milk

Cream powdered sugar, butter, vanilla, peppermint extract and food coloring. Add enough milk to reach spreading consistency. Spread filling over cake. Refrigerate.

Topping

3	tablespoons butter	½	cup semi-sweet chocolate chips

Heat butter and sauce until butter melts. Spread over filling. Refrigerate. Cut into 32 bars.

Yield: 32 bars

Doris Schrader • Peace River Power Squadron • Florida

 # Hello Dollys

1   cup graham cracker crumbs
1   stick butter, melted
1   cup shredded coconut
1   cup semi-sweet chocolate chips

1   cup chopped nuts
½   cup butterscotch chips
1   (14-ounce) can sweetened condensed milk

Combine crumbs and butter. Press mixture into the bottom of an 8 x 8 x 2-inch baking dish. Mix together coconut, chocolate chips, nuts and butterscotch chips. Spoon over crust. Pour milk over top. Bake at 350 degrees 30 minutes. Cut into 12 squares.

Yield: 12 pieces

A sinfully delicious way to welcome spring, summer, fall or whatever.

Pam Miner   •   Birmingham Power Squadron   •   Michigan

Lemon Squares

Crust

2½ cups all-purpose flour
½   cup sifted powdered sugar

2   sticks butter

Combine flour and powdered sugar. Cut in butter. Press mixture into the bottom of an ungreased 15 x 10 x 1-inch jelly-roll pan. Bake at 350 degrees 20 minutes.

Topping

4   eggs, beaten
1½ cups sugar
6   tablespoons lemon juice
¼   cup all-purpose flour

1   teaspoon baking soda
    Powdered sugar for garnish

Blend eggs, sugar and juice. Add flour and baking soda. Pour over crust. Bake at 350 degrees 25 minutes. Remove from oven and immediately sprinkle with powdered sugar. Cool, cut into squares and refrigerate.

Yield: 15 servings

Barbara Sargent   •   Chattanooga Power Squadron   •   Georgia

Mid-Illini Bars

1 (18-ounce) package
   German Sweet
   Chocolate cake mix
⅔ cup evaporated milk,
   divided
1 cup chopped nuts

1¼ sticks butter, melted
1 (14-ounce) package
   caramels, about 50
2 cups semi-sweet
   chocolate chips

Combine cake mix, ⅓ cup evaporated milk, nuts and butter. Mix well. Divide batter between two greased 13 x 9 x 2-inch baking dishes. Bake at 350 degrees 6 minutes. Heat caramel and ⅓ cup evaporated milk until caramel melts. Divide and pour over each cake. Sprinkle each pan with 1 cup chocolate chips. Bake an additional 15 minutes Cool in refrigerator. Cut into squares.

Yield: 16 to 20 servings

Judy Ann Magnuson • Mid-Illini Power Squadron • Illinois

Almond Bars

2 sticks butter
2 cups all-purpose flour
½ cup cold water
1 (8-ounce) can almond paste

1 cup sugar
2 eggs
½ teaspoon vanilla

Cut butter into flour until crumbly. Add water and mix well. Divide dough in two. Wrap in wax paper and refrigerate several hours or overnight.

Let dough stand at room temperature until soft enough to handle. Roll out each dough piece on a lightly floured surface to a 14 x 10-inch rectangle. Press first dough into the bottom of a 13 x 9 x 2-inch baking dish. Crumble almond paste into a bowl. Add sugar, eggs and vanilla. Mix well. Spread filling over dough. Roll out remaining dough and place over filling. Seal edges with bottom dough. Bake at 400 degrees 30 to 35 minutes. Cool before cutting into squares.

Yield: 12 to 15 servings

Pat Johnston • Dearborn Power Squadron • Michigan

Cherry Chocolate Bars

1 (18-ounce) package
   chocolate cake mix
1 (21-ounce) can cherry pie
   filling
1 teaspoon almond extract
2 eggs, beaten

1 cup sugar
5 tablespoons butter
⅓ cup milk
1 (6-ounce) package semi-
   sweet chocolate chips

Combine cake mix, pie filling, almond extract and eggs. Mix well.
Pour batter into a greased and floured 13 x 9 x 2-inch baking dish.
Bake at 350 degrees 25 to 30 minutes or until tester comes out clean.
Combine sugar, butter and milk in a saucepan. Bring to boil, stirring
constantly, 1 minute. Remove from heat and stir in chocolate chips
until smooth. Pour frosting over partially cooled bars.

Yield: 3 dozen bars

Jo Gene Hurley • Phoenix Sail & Power Squadron • Arizona

Honey Squares

5 eggs
2 cups sugar
3 tablespoons honey
3 cups all-purpose flour
3 teaspoons baking powder
1 teaspoon cinnamon
1 teaspoon ground cloves

1 teaspoon ground allspice
1 cup ground chocolate
1 cup walnuts, chopped
½ cup citron or raisins
1 cup powdered sugar
   Milk

Combine eggs, sugar and honey. Add flour, baking powder, cinnamon,
cloves, allspice, chocolate, walnuts and raisins. Mix well. Spread mixture
into a 14 x 10 x 2-inch baking dish. Bake at 350 degrees 20 minutes.
Blend powdered sugar and enough milk to reach a spreading consistency.
Spread icing over warm cake. Cool before cutting into squares.

Yield: 10 to 14 servings

David V. Beyer • Diablo Sail & Power Squadron • California

Oatmeal Fudge Bars

Crust

2	sticks butter, softened	1½	cups all-purpose flour
2	cups packed brown sugar	1	teaspoon baking soda
2	eggs	1	teaspoon salt
1	teaspoon vanilla	4	cup old-fashioned rolled oats

Cream butter and sugar. Add eggs and vanilla. Stir in flour, baking soda and salt. Mix well. Add oats and mix thoroughly. Reserve 2 cups mixture. Press remaining mixture onto a greased baking sheet.

Filling

2	cups semi-sweet chocolate chips	2	teaspoons vanilla
		2	tablespoons butter
1	(14-ounce) can sweetened condensed milk	½	teaspoon salt

Combine chips, milk, vanilla, butter and salt in a saucepan. Cook and stir over low heat until smooth. Spread over crust. Top with reserved oatmeal mixture. Bake at 350 degrees 15 minutes. Cool in pan. Cut into bars.

Yield: 12 to 15 servings

Susan Bjork • Alamitos Power Squadron • California

Butterscotch Bars

1	(12-ounce) package butterscotch chips	1	(8-ounce) package cream cheese, softened
5⅓	tablespoons butter	1	(14-ounce) can sweetened condensed milk
2	cups graham cracker crumbs	1	teaspoon vanilla
1	cup chopped walnuts	1	egg

Combine butterscotch chips and butter in a saucepan. Heat until melted. Stir in crumbs and walnuts. Press half crumb mixture into the bottom of a greased 13 x 9 x 2-inch baking dish. Beat cream cheese until fluffy. Add milk, vanilla and egg. Mix until smooth. Spread cheese mixture over crust. Top with remaining crumb mixture. Bake at 350 degrees 25 to 30 minutes.

Yield: 12 to 15 servings

Katie Young • Susquenango Power Squadron • New York

Oregon Brownies

Brownies

2	cups all-purpose flour	¼	cup dark unsweetened cocoa
2	cups sugar	½	cup buttermilk
1	stick butter	2	eggs
½	cup vegetable shortening	1	teaspoon baking soda
1	cup strong brewed coffee	1	teaspoon vanilla

Combine flour and sugar. In a saucepan, combine butter, shortening, coffee and cocoa. Bring to boil, stirring constantly. Pour over flour and sugar. Mix well. Add buttermilk, eggs, baking soda and vanilla. Mix with a spoon or electric mixer. Pour batter into a buttered 15 x 11 x 1-inch jelly-roll pan. Bake at 400 degree 20 minutes.

Frosting

1	stick butter	3½	cups powdered sugar
1	tablespoon dark cocoa	1	teaspoon vanilla
¼	cup milk		

Combine butter, cocoa and milk in a saucepan. Bring to boil, stirring constantly. Stir in powdered sugar and vanilla until smooth. Pour warm frosting over brownies as soon as dish comes out of the oven. Cool. Cut into 48 bars.

Yield: 48 bars

Andrea VanderHorst • Portland Power Squadron • Oregon

Double Chocolate Mint Dessert

Cake

1	stick butter	1	cup sugar
1	(16-ounce) bottle chocolate sauce	1	cup all-purpose flour
4	large eggs	1	cup chopped walnuts

Beat butter, chocolate sauce, eggs and sugar until creamy. Stir in flour. Fold in walnuts. Pour batter into a greased 13 x 9 x 2-inch baking dish. Bake at 350 degrees 30 to 40 minutes or until top springs back when touched. Cool completely in pan.

Mint Cream

2½	cups powdered sugar	2	tablespoons water
4	tablespoons butter, softened	½	teaspoon mint extract
		3	drops green food coloring

Blend powdered sugar, butter, water, mint extract and food coloring until smooth. Spread over cake. Refrigerate until set.

Chocolate Topping

7	tablespoons butter	⅓	cup sliced almonds
1¼	cups semi-sweet chocolate chips		

Combine butter and chocolate chips in a microwave safe bowl. Heat on high 1 minute to 1 minute, 30 seconds. Stir until chocolate melts. Pour topping over mint layer. Sprinkle with almonds. Cover and refrigerate at least 1 hour before cutting.

Yield: 12 to 15 servings

Phyllis Swope • Pensacola Sail & Power Squadron • Florida

Bread Pudding with Bourbon Sauce

Bread Pudding

1 **cup sugar**	1 **tablespoon vanilla**
1 **stick butter, softened**	¼ **cup raisins**
5 **eggs, beaten**	12 **slices French bread, 1-inch thick**
1 **pint heavy cream**	
Dash of cinnamon	

Cream sugar and butter. Add eggs, cream, cinnamon, vanilla and raisins. Mix well. Pour batter into a 9 x 9 x 2-inch baking dish. Arrange bread slices over egg mixture, pressing down into egg. Soak 5 minutes. Turn bread and allow to soak 10 minutes more. Set dish in a larger baking dish. Fill outer dish with water to reach ½-inch from top. Cover with foil. Bake at 350 degrees 45 to 50 minutes. Uncover during last 10 minutes to brown the top. Custard will be soft not firm.

Bourbon Sauce

1 **cup sugar**	½ **teaspoon cornstarch**
1 **cup heavy cream**	¼ **cup water**
Dash of cinnamon	1 **tablespoon bourbon**
1 **tablespoon unsalted butter**	

Combine sugar, cream, cinnamon and butter in a saucepan. Bring to boil. Blend cornstarch with water. Stir into sauce until clear. Remove from heat. Add bourbon. Pour sauce over each slice of bread pudding.

Yield: 8 to 10 servings

Josie Metzler • New Orleans Power Squadron • Louisiana

Capirotada
(Bread Pudding from Jalisco)

Custard

7	cups whole milk	1½	tablespoons cornstarch
1	cinnamon stick	2	egg yolks
½	cup sugar	½	teaspoon vanilla

Heat milk with cinnamon and sugar. Blend in cornstarch. Break open egg yolks into a bowl. Add a small amount of warm milk to egg yolks and quickly mix until smooth. Stir in more milk then return egg mixture to saucepan. Cook and stir until sauce thickens. Add vanilla and set aside.

Bread Pudding

2	tablespoons vegetable oil	½	cup heaped chopped pecans
6	(5-inch) corn tortillas	½	cup raisins
1	ripe Plantain banana		Crème fraîche or whipped cream for garnish
16	stale bread slices, ½-inch thick		
1	(10-ounce) can dried prunes, pitted		

Heat oil in a skillet. Fry tortillas on both sides until leathery not crisp. Blot dry and line an 8 x 3-inch tube pan. Cook plantain until golden browned. Set aside. Place layer of bread over tortillas. Top with prunes, pecans, raisins and one-third of plantain. Very slowly pour 1½ cups custard over layers. Allow bread to absorb custard. Bake at 350 degrees 40 minutes or until most of the liquid is absorbed. Cool 20 minutes. Serve lukewarm with crème fra°che or whipped cream.

Yield: 6 to 8 servings

Karl McNulty • Greenwich Bay Power Squadron • Rhode Island

Sticky Toffee Pudding

1   (6-ounce) package dates, pitted and chopped
1¼ cups water
1   teaspoon baking soda
4   tablespoons unsalted butter, softened
¾   cup sugar

2   eggs
¾   cup self-rising flour
1   teaspoon vanilla
1¼ cups heavy cream
2   tablespoons packed dark brown sugar
2   teaspoons molasses

Boil dates in water about 5 minutes until soft. Add baking soda, being careful as mixture will foam up. Cream butter and sugar until light and fluffy. Add eggs and beat well. Add dates, flour and vanilla. Pour mixture into a greased 11 x 7 x 2-inch baking dish. Bake at 350 degrees 30 to 40 minutes or until just firm to touch. Combine cream, brown sugar and molasses in a saucepan. Bring to boil, stirring constantly. Remove from heat. Pour half of sauce over hot pudding. Allow sauce to soak in. Serve remaining sauce with each serving.

Yield: 6 to 8 servings

Peter Mitchelson • Vero Beach Power Squadron • Florida

Creamy Double Decker Fudge

1   cup peanut butter chips
1   (14-ounce) can sweetened condensed milk, divided

1   teaspoon vanilla, divided
1   cup semi-sweet chocolate chips

Line an 8 x 8 x 2-inch baking dish with foil. Place peanut butter chips and ⅔ cup milk in a microwave bowl. Microwave on high 1 minute to 1 minute, 30 seconds, stirring after 1 minute or until chips are melted. Stir mixture until smooth. Add ½ teaspoon vanilla. Spread evenly into prepared pan.

Place remaining milk and chocolate chips in another microwave bowl. Repeat procedure. Stir in ½ teaspoon vanilla. Spread evenly over peanut butter layer. Cover and refrigerate until firm. Remove from pan and peel of foil. Cut into squares. Store in an airtight container. Do not double recipe.

Yield: 4 dozen pieces

Jane Michaels • Montgomery Power Squadron • Alabama

 PRETZELS

1 package active
dry yeast
¾ cup warm water
(110-115 degrees)
1 cup whole wheat flour
1 cup unbleached
all-purpose flour
1 tablespoon sugar
Dash of kosher salt
1 egg
Kosher salt

Mix yeast and water. Let stand 5 minutes. Combine wheat and white flour, mixing with hands. Stir in sugar. Add salt and mix well. Stir in yeast until mixture forms a ball. Roll dough on a floured surface about 5 minutes. Shape dough into strands to form pretzels or create your own shape. Sprinkle with salt. Bake at 425 degrees 12 to 15 minutes or until golden browned.

Yield: 6 to 8 servings

Dorie Backus
Toledo Power Squadron
Ohio

Peanut Butter Peanut Brittle

2	cups peanut butter	2	cups peanuts
1½	cups sugar	1	teaspoon baking soda
1½	cups light corn syrup	1	teaspoon vanilla
¼	cup water	6	(7-ounce) chocolate
2	tablespoons butter		candy bars (optional)

Butter two large baking sheets. Heat peanut butter over low heat in the top of a double boiler. Keep warm. Butter sides of a large saucepan. Combine sugar, syrup and water in a saucepan. Cook and stir until syrup reaches the hard crack stage in cold water or a candy thermometer reaches 300 to 310 degrees Fahrenheit. Stir in butter. Add peanuts and stir until candy begins to brown. Remove from heat. Quickly sprinkle baking soda over mixture, stirring constantly. Add vanilla.

Gently stir in warm peanut butter until well blended. Immediately pour candy onto prepared sheets. Quickly spread as thin as possible with a spatula. Melt candy bars in the top of a double boiler. Spread evenly over candy. Cool and cut into pieces.

Yield: 20 to 25 servings

Sue Comstock • Covina Power Squadron • California

Old-Fashioned Sponge Candy

1	cup sugar	1	tablespoon baking soda
1	cup dark corn syrup		Dipping chocolate
1	tablespoon white vinegar		

Lightly butter a large baking sheet with sides. Combine sugar, syrup and vinegar in a large saucepan. Cook and stir over medium heat until sugar dissolves. Continue cooking until candy thermometer reaches 300 degrees Fahrenheit or syrup separates into brittle threads when dropped in cold water. Remove from heat. Stir in baking soda being careful as mixture will foam up. Quickly pour onto prepared sheet. Cool completely. Break into pieces. Coat pieces in chocolate if desired.

Yield: ½ pound candy

Andrea Davis • St Paul Sail & Power Squadron • Minnesota

Dad's Famous Maple Peanut Butter Fudge

1   **cup peanut butter**
1   **(14-ounce) can sweetened condensed milk**

⅛   **teaspoon salt**
3   **cups real maple syrup**
     Vegetable cooking spray

Spray all the following with cooking spray: 3-quart saucepan, wooden spoon, beaters of electric mixer, rubber spatula, large glass bowl and foil-lined baking sheet. Set mixer near bowl with rubber spatula and kitchen mitt. Place peanut butter in glass bowl.

Combine milk, salt and syrup in saucepan. Cook over low-medium heat, stirring constantly with wooden spoon, 10 minutes or until mixture begins to boil or reaches 218 degrees Fahrenheit. Continue to cook and stir until water boils off. The temperature will rise while cooking over the next 10 to 15 minutes. Keep on low heat as to not burn candy.

When mixture reaches 234 degrees Fahrenheit, remove from heat. Pour hot syrup over peanut butter. Beat at low speed until mixer slows down. Using mitt, pick up bowl and scrape out hot mixture with rubber spatula onto baking sheet. Cool completely. Cut into squares.

Yield: 1 pound fudge

Allan W. Lakin • Valley Ho Power Squadron • California

 ANTS
ON A LOG

Celery stalks
Peanut butter
Raisins

Cut celery into 3-inch pieces. Fill center with peanut butter. Place 3 to 4 raisins in a row on peanut butter.

Yield: 1 to numerous servings

Robert Peters
Swiftwater Power Squadron
New York

Buttermilk Pralines

2   **cups sugar**
1   **cup buttermilk**
1   **teaspoon baking soda**
     Dash of salt

4   **tablespoons butter**
1   **tablespoon vanilla**
2   **cups pecans**

Combine sugar, buttermilk, baking soda and salt in a saucepan. Cook and stir over medium heat until the firm ball stage or 245 degrees Fahrenheit on a candy thermometer. Remove from heat. Add butter, vanilla and pecans. Mix well and cool slightly. Stir mixture until begins to harden. Quickly drop 20 spoonfuls onto a foil-lined baking sheet.

Yield: 20 pralines

Kim Viator • Acadiana Power Squadron • Louisiana

 PLAYDOUGH

1 cup all-purpose flour
1 cup water
½ cup salt
**1 tablespoon
vegetable oil**
**1 teaspoon
cream of tartar**
**Food coloring
and sweetened flavored
drink mix powder of
your choice**

Combine flour, water, salt, oil and tartar in a saucepan. Cook over medium heat until mixture forms a ball. Cool slightly. Knead until smooth. Add food coloring for different colors. Add drink mix to make dough smell good. Store in a zip-top plastic bag when cool.

Yield: 1½ cups

Dorie Backus

Toledo Power Squadron

Ohio

Homemade Reese's Cups

1   (12-ounce) jar crunchy
    peanut butter
1   (16-ounce) package
    powdered sugar

1½ sticks butter, melted
1   (8-ounce) chocolate
    candy bar, melted

Cream peanut butter and powdered sugar. Stir in butter. Press mixture evenly into an 8 x 8 x 2-inch baking dish. Spread chocolate over mixture. Cool to set chocolate. Cut into small squares.

Yield: 15 to 20 servings

Mary Cele Bain • Charlotte Power Squadron • North Carolina

 Chocolate Clusters

1   (12-ounce) package semi-
    sweet chocolate chips

⅓ cup peanut butter
2   cups finely chopped nuts

Combine chocolate chips and peanut butter in a saucepan. Cook and stir until chocolate melts. Add nuts. Drop by spoonfuls onto a wax paper-lined baking sheet. Cool to set.

Yield: 15 to 20 servings

Ted Smith • Grosse Pointe Power Squadron • Michigan

Tumbleweeds

1   (12-ounce) can salted
    peanuts
1   (7-ounce) can potato
    sticks

3   cups butterscotch chips
3   tablespoons peanut
    butter

Combine peanuts and potato sticks in a bowl. Cook butterscotch chips and peanut butter in the top of a double boiler until butterscotch melts. Stir sauce until smooth. Pour sauce over peanuts and stir until well coated. Drop by tablespoonfuls onto a wax paper-lined baking sheet. Refrigerate 5 minutes until set. Store in an airtight container.

Yield: 4½ dozen

Anita L. Fontes • Banana River Power Squadron • Florida

Frozen Fruit Cup

1 cup sugar
2 cups water
1 (12-ounce) can frozen orange juice concentrate, thawed and undiluted
2 (8-ounce) cans crushed pineapple, drained
1 (16-ounce) can apricots, drained and chopped
1 (10-ounce) package frozen sliced strawberries, partially thawed
5-7 bananas, mashed
2 tablespoons lemon juice
Maraschino cherries for garnish

Boil sugar and water. Add orange juice and cool. Stir in pineapple, apricots, strawberries, bananas and lemon juice. Pour mixture into 5-ounce paper cups, plastic cups or paper-lined muffin cups. Freeze. Garnish with a cherry.

Yield: 18 to 20 (5-ounce) cups

Edith Little • Kennebec River Power Squadron • Maine

 Fishbowl Jell-O

Red and green grapes
2 **(3-ounce) packages blue gelatin**

Gummy fish

Place grapes in the bottom of a new 1-quart fishbowl to symbolize rocks. Prepare gelatin according to package directions. Pour in enough gelatin to cover grapes (rocks). Refrigerate until partially set. Refrigerate remaining gelatin until almost set. Spoon gelatin over "rocky bottom", placing gummy fish into gelatin (water) as you go. Refrigerate completely.

Yield: 6 servings

Sue Shontz • Sandusky Power Squadron • Ohio

 SILLY PUTTY

2 cups white liquid glue
1½ cups water
3 teaspoons Borax, divided
Food coloring or glitter

Mix together glue and water. In three separate containers combine ⅓ cup water and 1 teaspoon Borax. Stir to dissolve Borax. Add food coloring or glitter to Borax mixture. Add borax mixture to glue until it forms into a solid. May not need all three containers of water and Borax.

Yield: 3 cups

Bobby Shaw
Beaverton Power Squadron
Oregon

FACE PAINT

2 tablespoons
vegetable shortening
2½ teaspoons cornstarch
1 teaspoon
all-purpose flour
3-4 drops glycerin
Food coloring,
cold cream and
cotton swabs

Combine shortening,
cornstarch and flour until
a paste forms. Stir in
glycerin until mixture
becomes smooth. Add
food coloring a drop at
a time to desired color.
For ease of paint removal,
smooth a dab of cold
cream on child's face
before painting. Use cotton
swabs to create simple
designs. Paint washes off
with soap and water.

Yield: about ¼ cup paint

Dorie Backus
Toledo Power Squadron
Ohio

Chocolate Chip Delight

1	(3-ounce) package lime flavored gelatin
1	cup boiling water
1	pint vanilla ice cream
½	teaspoon peppermint extract
¼	cup semi-sweet chocolate chips
	Whipped topping and chocolate chips for garnish

Dissolve gelatin in water. Add ice cream by spoonfuls and stir until melted. Stir in extract and chocolate chips. Spoon into a serving bowl. Refrigerate 30 minutes to 1 hour until set. Garnish with whipped topping and chocolate chips.

Yield: 6 servings

Marjorie Ross • Captree Power Squadron • New York

Piña Colada Flan

2	cups sugar, divided
1	cup unsweetened pineapple juice
1½	cups unsweetened coconut milk
¼	teaspoon salt
⅓	cup rum
8	large eggs, slightly beaten
	Whipped topping for garnish (optional)

Heat 1 cup sugar in a metal saucepan over low-medium heat. Stir constantly with a wooden spoon until sugar melts. Continue cooking until clear syrup becomes a golden brown color. Pour caramel into a 7 x 3-inch flan mold or metal or heat resistant mold. Tilt mold around to coat bottom and sides. Set aside to cool.

Pour water into a 13 x 9 x 2-inch baking dish to reach ⅔ the height of mold. Combine pineapple juice, coconut milk and 1 cup sugar. Stir until sugar dissolves. Add rum and eggs. Mix well without foamy. Strain mixture into the prepared mold. Allow foam to subside. Set mold in water bath. Bake at 325 degrees 1 hour, 30 minutes or until tester comes out clean. Cool 2 hours. Cover and refrigerate. Invert mold onto a rimmed platter. Garnish with whipped topping.

Yield: 6 to 8 servings

Dorothy Ojeda • Ponce Power Squadron • Puerto Rico

Pots de Crème

4	ounces semi-sweet chocolate		2	egg yolks, slightly beaten
2	tablespoons sugar		½	teaspoon vanilla
¾	cup condensed milk		2	egg whites (optional)
2	teaspoons instant coffee		1	cup sugar (optional)

Heat chocolate, sugar and milk, stirring constantly until smooth. Add coffee. Gradually stir chocolate mixture into egg yolks. Add vanilla. As an option, beat egg whites until stiff. Gradually beat in sugar. Fold into chocolate mixture. Divide mixture among 6 individual serving dishes. Refrigerate at least 8 hours.

Yield: 4 to 6 servings

May substitute 1 (14-ounce) can sweetened condensed milk for sugar and milk.

Wilbur Hugli • Fort Walton Sail & Power Squadron • Florida

Amaretto Sandwich

1	(42-ounce) package ice cream sandwiches		1	(12-ounce) package frozen whipped topping, thawed
1-1½	cups amaretto			Toasted sliced almonds
1	(10-ounce) package almond toffee bits			

Cover bottom of a 13 x 9 x 2-inch baking dish with ice cream sandwiches. Pierce sandwiches with a fork. Pour ½ to 1 cup amaretto over sandwiches. Sprinkle with half of toffee bits. Blend ½ to ¾ cup amaretto with whipped topping. Spread topping over toffee. Top with remaining toffee bits. Sprinkle with almonds. Freeze until ready to serve.

Yield: 16 servings

Khaki Simank • Shreveport Power Squadron • Louisiana

 EGGS
IN A FRAME

12 bread slices
Butter for spreading
12 eggs
Salt to taste

Remove center of bread slice or cut out with a biscuit cutter. Butter bread generously on both sides. Brown bread "frames" on one side in a buttered skillet. Turn over and break an egg into the center of bread. Cover and cook slowly until egg white is set. Season with salt. Remove with a spatula.

Yield: 7 to 12 servings

Alexander Baker
Swiftwater Power Squadron
New York

 SALT PAINT

2 teaspoons salt
1 teaspoon liquid starch
Several drops
of tempera paints

Combine salt, starch
and paint. Apply with a
brush. Dry completely.
Add an icy touch to
winter pictures.

Yield: about
1 tablespoon paint

Dorie Backus

Toledo Power Squadron

Ohio

"Twist"ed Tidbits

1	(8-ounce) package cream cheese, softened	¾	cup sugar substitute
1	cup sugar free Twist Chocolate Spread or peanut butter	1	tablespoon vanilla
		1	(8-ounce) container frozen whipped topping, thawed

Beat cream cheese, chocolate spread, sugar substitute and vanilla with an electric mixer until well blended. Gently stir in whipping topping. Spread mixture in an 8 x 8 x 2-inch baking dish. Freeze 4 hours or until firm. Let stand a few minutes before cutting. Cut into 16 squares and serve immediately.

Yield: 16 servings

Rita Wise • Daytona Beach Power Squadron • Florida

Oven Caramel Popcorn

1	cup packed brown sugar	½	teaspoon baking soda
1	stick butter	3	quarts popped corn
¼	cup corn syrup		Nuts (optional)
½	teaspoon salt		

Combine sugar, butter, syrup and salt in a saucepan. Bring to boil. Cook 5 minutes or microwave 2 minutes. Remove from heat and stir in baking soda. Mix well. Pour over popped corn and nuts, tossing to coat. Spread in a 13 x 9 x 2-inch baking dish. Bake at 200 degrees 1 hour, stirring every 15 minutes. For microwave, cook 8 to 9 minutes, stirring every 2 minutes. Remove from oven and spread on wax paper to cool. Store in an airtight container.

Yield: 8 to 10 servings

Linda Grotjan • Chattanooga Power Squadron • Georgia

INDEX

by land or by sea
UNITED STATES POWER SQUADRONS
P.O. BOX 30423
RALEIGH, NC 27622
1-888-367-8777

Please send me:

_____ copies of **by land or by sea**   at $25.00 each _____

          Postage and handling   at $ 6.95 each _____

          North Carolina residents add 7% sales tax   at $ 1.88 each _____

                                                           TOTAL _____

Name _____

Address _____

City _____ State _____ Zip _____

❏ Check Enclosed *(Payable to United States Power Squadrons)*

Please charge to: ❏ Visa ❏ MasterCard ❏ American Express ❏ Discover Card

Card Number _____ Expiration Date _____

Signature _____

----

by land or by sea
UNITED STATES POWER SQUADRONS
P.O. BOX 30423
RALEIGH, NC 27622
1-888-367-8777

Please send me:

_____ copies of **by land or by sea**   at $25.00 each _____

          Postage and handling   at $ 6.95 each _____

          North Carolina residents add 7% sales tax   at $ 1.88 each _____

                                                           TOTAL _____

Name _____

Address _____

City _____ State _____ Zip _____

❏ Check Enclosed *(Payable to United States Power Squadrons)*

Please charge to: ❏ Visa ❏ MasterCard ❏ American Express ❏ Discover Card

Card Number _____ Expiration Date _____

Signature _____